prime

Also by Dr. Pepper Schwartz

American Couples: Money, Work, Sex (with Philip Blumstein)

Finding Your Perfect Match

The Lifetime Love and Sex Quiz Book

Everything You Know About Love and Sex Is Wrong

201 Questions to Ask Your Kids/Parents

Ten Talks Parents Must Have with Their Children About Sex and Character
(with Dominic Cappello)

The Love Test (with Virginia Rutter)

What I've Learned About Sex (with Debra Haffner)

The Gender of Sexuality: Exploring Sexual Possibilities (with Virginia Rutter)

The Great Sex Weekend (with Janet Lever)

Love Between Equals: How Peer Marriage Really Works

prime

ADVENTURES AND ADVICE ON
Sex, Love,
AND THE *Sensual* YEARS

DR. PEPPER SCHWARTZ

Collins
An Imprint of HarperCollinsPublishers

I have tried to tell the truth to the best of my ability to recall
it. There may be errors of memory in this book or things I see
differently from the way someone else might. There are some
omissions and I have changed names and some descriptions of
people to protect them and their present relationships. In the
interest of those protections, I have changed some order of events,
times, and places. To protect the identity of the woman who
shares her tale of marrying a Balinese Kuta cowboy, I have created
a composite character from a number of women I met and heard
about who married Kuta cowboys. Other than the changes noted, my
adventure is presented as it was lived.

HarperCollins books may be purchased for educational, business, or
sales promotional use. For information, please write:
Special Markets Department, HarperCollins Publishers,
10 East 53rd Street, New York, NY 10022.

FIRST EDITION

Designed by Nicola Ferguson

Library of Congress Cataloging-in-Publication Data is available
upon request.
978-0-06-117358-5
ISBN-10: 0-06-117358-4

07 08 09 10 11 ❖/RRD 10 9 8 7 6 5 4 3 2 1

To my fabulous children, Ryder and Cooper—

My endless appreciation for your support, your good humor, your

love, and all the fun we have had, and will have, together. And to

the men in my life—and the man in my life—you know who you

were—you know who you are.

contents

one

HOW DID I GET HERE?

Asking Questions

Dear Dr. Pepper:

I am a single woman, divorced after 23 years of marriage, with my kids off to college. Ideally, I would like to have a serious relationship, but if that isn't around the corner, I still want sex and companionship. I find myself in a world of chat-room hookups, cybermatchmaking, and coconut-flavored glow-in-the-dark condoms. I feel as sexually alive as I did when I was 25, but the number and availability of men for me has changed. How do I look for a life partner and enjoy sexual adventures along the way? Oh, yes, and did I mention that I really enjoy sex?

Advice, please.

Sincerely,

A Single Sexologist in Seattle

After three decades of answering people's questions about their emotional, sexual, and romantic lives, after writing numerous books on sex and relationships, after thirty-five years as a professor of sociology at the University of Washington, you would think I could come up with an easy answer to my own question. The situation was at least humorous and in no small part ironic.

I had plenty of good advice for women in my situation based on solid scientific research. But I had not always followed what I knew to be the best course since my own divorce. Still, I am five years older than when I left my husband, and I think a wiser person than the woman who reentered the singles scene after almost a quarter of a century as a married woman.

A Special Time, Place, and Situation

Here I am on a teak lounge chair, west of Kuta Beach on Bali, which is one of the most romantic islands on earth. I am thinking about what I want out of my life and from men. Bali is my muse for this reverie and she never ceases to inspire me. This is an island that celebrates the senses. Hospitality and massage are honed to fine arts. Perhaps most important, the island is enduringly attractive and easy to live on, at least in part because it's a place where a single woman can feel safe strolling the beaches and villages. I can even banter and flirt with local men of all ages and not worry that anything unwanted is going to happen.

On this island, if my last two trips here were any indication, I will soon find myself in a place I rarely get to spend much my time—the reflective, contemplative present. I'm usually speeding through life, juggling appointments, putting out fires, and scheduling for the near and far future. The prospect of trimming away all of that for a while is exciting.

My friend interrupts my soul-searching.

"Enjoying the guide book?" asks the tall, trim man with salt-and-pepper hair.

Dom has returned from his postlunch stroll down the beach. He is a welcome break from my *what am I doing with my life?* train of thought. Dominic is in the top tier of my favorite traveling companions. When I told him I needed support for the book I was writing, he suggested that he was the man for the job. I agreed and he signed up to accompany me to Bali for two weeks while I finished it. My first thought as I look at him striding toward me is that he has come to get me to take a walk with him. That's usually fun since we are quite the sight together:

He is about six-foot-four and I don't quite reach five feet. But Dom is worried that I have been rushing around too much and he is on a program to slow me down.

"It's so good to finally be here at the same time," Dom says. He looks rested and tan, and I can see that his week on Bali prior to my arrival has been calming and rejuvenating.

"I'm going to get us some cold water. I'll be right back," Dom says. "I want you to enjoy this peaceful afternoon and just unwind after your long flight. By tomorrow you'll feel fantastic."

My friend the Zen Buddhist was always trying to get me to be more peaceful—which was usually a very hard thing for me to do. This time, however, I had signed up for the program. Bali was going to be different.

"Relaxing is going to be easy," I say. "I think counting waves would be a fine activity for today. I've had my head down, eyes on the finish line for this book for a little too long. It's got to be done by September, but I can see the end and I'm less nervous now."

"Well, it looks like you have the perfect afternoon. Just remember you have your appointment for the four-hand massage at Antique Spa at four thirty. And I want a full report on what those two men actually do."

I laugh at Dom's alternate mothering and voyeurism. "Hey, Dom, if I ever forget I have an appointment for two guys to work on my body, just shoot me right then! Anyhow, I promise to reveal all over our sunset drink."

Dom turns to me, sporting a mischievous grin. "And Pepper, please promise me you will tuck away your laptop, cell phone, and Blackberry and just unwind for a few hours, okay?"

I smile. Dom knows me well.

A Warning

My tall friend heads up to the vendor stands. The sun is high in the sky and I return to my Bali guidebook, shifting my chair a bit so I catch some shade. I turn to a page Dom has bookmarked for me about typical travelers' dos and don'ts. A special warning for women catches my eye. The guidebook cautions "female tourists in the beach town of Kuta (*Koo-tah*)" need to be on the alert for a special breed of gigolo called a "Kuta cowboy." I laugh. I find it humorous that the author is worried about female tourist morality. Most women, I think, will get the picture: There are a number of sleekly built, dark-haired, sweet-talking young men on the island whose job it is to seduce female travelers. It's a barter system: The women find a guide, a restaurant companion, or vacation lover, while the men enjoy being treated to meals, elegant hotels, and/or gifts in the form of clothes or cash. The women can decide if they are interested or not. I'm interested, but primarily as part of my professional work. As a sex researcher, I was aware of the gigolos on Bali, and on a previous trip to Bali had met a woman who actually ended up marrying one. Since then I've learned about several other women who made the same choice. So while it wasn't true that having a Balinese lover was a national fad, it was true that more than a few Western women had discovered that Bali offered something besides batik. As a champion of adventurous women, I was intrigued. As a single woman "of a certain age" I am thinking about *it*.

My eyes wander. To my left, the vast beach curves gently to the right. I can see a long line of beach chairs full of tourists, with local vendors strolling among their potential clients. A forty-minute walk west would bring me to the heart of Kuta. About six lounge chairs over, I spy a young Asian man with a smooth, well-defined chest flirting with two somewhat amused young blonde women. The women sound like they are from Australia and seem to know their sexy friend. The man speaks and I hear his Australian accent.

Oops. Not a real Kuta cowboy sighting.

To my right the beach heads to Seminyak and becomes less populated by tourists. I catch sight of another attractive twenty-something Asian man in orange shorts and a white tank top strolling near the water. He has long dark hair and a huge tattoo covering his left bicep. Mr. Bali is in an animated conversation with a woman who is forty-ish or possibly a well-kept fifty-ish. She is wearing a loose white blouse and bluish sarong that flows languidly in the breeze. I study them both carefully as they near me. I hear the smiling, relaxed blonde woman speak English with an accent and I peg her as either German or Dutch. The young man is listening attentively with his eyes fixed on her. I believe I am experiencing my first glimpse of a Kuta cowboy in his natural habitat. I try to imagine myself as this woman, a tourist in the company of a seductive, attentive, and charming local, but for some reason I can't quite see myself in her place. At least not yet.

What Next?

Here I am, a woman who has confidently experimented with romantic and sexual relationships over my lifetime. I am trying to think about what this stage of my life should be about. I have a blossoming relationship back home but it's not clear if it is going to be serious, and I don't want to exaggerate its importance. Maybe it's time for an erotic adventure—and a Kuta cowboy could be just the ticket. On the other hand, I am at a point in my life where some adventures are not as interesting as they once were. And I know that if I don't put some energy into this new relationship back home, it definitely won't have much of a chance of surviving, much less attaining significance. I have a lot to think about.

I look up from my reverie. There is a handsome Asian man slowly approaching me. He does not appear to be a vendor. I check him out: short hair, tan shorts, white t-shirt, taller than me, warm brown eyes, trim body, gentle, unthreatening demeanor, beautiful bronze smooth skin, and a kind smile with pure white, perfectly chiseled straight teeth. This last detail indicates he is most likely a local since the Balinese have their teeth filed during a ceremony in adolescence. He is most definitely about half my age. Is this a Kuta cowboy approaching me?

The man strolls slowly by me in the direction of Gado Gado, the beachfront bistro behind me. I meet his gaze and I experience a response that is pure Bali. He smiles broadly and sweetly. I feel a bit of internal warmth flow through me. I like being looked at by this attractive young man. When you are over fifty, it is a pleasure to not feel ignored. Another pleasure: He welcomes my gaze. Neither of us feels self-conscious. It's only a moment, but those are the moments that make you feel sensual and alive. I cast my eyes back to my guidebook. Much as I have enjoyed this quick interaction, I do not want to give the man—Kuta cowboy or not—any indication that I am in the market for company. He walks by.

I have more important things to do right now than initiate a vacation affair. I have come to this island to take stock of my life. For me, that means thinking about love and sexuality. I want to take control of my future. I feel that I am in the prime of my life, a special time when experience, self-knowledge, and sexual maturity have created an outer patina and an inner confidence that I want to use well. I want to make good decisions about my emotional and physical needs during this phase of my life. Time is precious and I am going to use it to figure out what my past has taught me and what I need for my future.

two

BEING SINGLE

Is Sex a Sandwich?

Thinking Back

My story has to start five years ago when I became single after almost two and half decades of marriage. I was in better shape than many women who face that transition. I had been a professor of sociology at the University of Washington since 1972 and that gave me a secure economic base. My kids were off to college. But my life was anything but normal.

Back in Class

I was doing what I love to do in the fall quarter, teaching my large lecture classes. My 1:30 class was Sociology 287, The Sociology of Sexuality, and while I didn't exactly have a close, personal relationship with the approximately 700 students who filled up the huge lecture hall, I was proud of the fact that most of them attended the class straight through the quarter and felt they got something out of it besides a few extra masturbatory fantasies.

It was showtime though—keeping the attention of 700 students is a challenge and when I snapped on that microphone I turned into a mixture of scholar, motivational speaker, stand-up comedian, thera- pist, coach, and doctor. "Dr. Schwartz. Dr. Schwartz," the young man yelled, his hand frantically waving about halfway down the main floor. I was midway into my "Who Does What to Whom" lecture.

"Hi—what's the emergency?" I responded. "Is this a question about the lecture? If so, can't it wait until I'm finished?"

The student was frantically waving.

"It's a question about the movie yesterday on religion and sexual- ity and I really need the answer. It's personally important to me," the student said.

"You know," I said, "I do a whole session the last day of class on 'Everything You Wanted to Know About Sex and Are Entitled to Ask.' We could wait until then. Then you could write it on a piece of paper and it would be anonymous."

"I really can't wait," bellowed the student.

"Tell you what: Why don't you just come to my office during office hours and we'll answer it." I looked down to resume my lecture.

"Dr. Schwartz, please, just one quick question," pleaded the student.

By this time half the class was giggling and half of them were rest- less and ticked off at this guy, so I figured I had better just let him ask his question and go on.

"All right, but be brief because I really have a lot of material to get through before the bell."

"Okay—the movie we saw in class said that the ancient Chinese felt that ejaculation wasted your Chi and reduced your life force, right?

"Right," I said.

"Well, this is very important to me, because I feel the same way," said the young man. "I think too much ejaculation is bad for you. But I have been having fights with my girlfriend over this. When I heard it was part of the Taoist tradition, it was the first time I had support. I need to hear if you think there is a scientific basis to this position."

People were bent over laughing. That will teach me to try to be nice and take a question from a frantically waving young man.

I took the class back into my control.

"Pay no mind to the laughing," I said. "Laughing happens when we are nervous about something deeply personal and when sharing anything that is about our own sex life." The students laughed briefly again but they got the message.

"Okay, an answer to your question—which is obviously the question of many others in the room," I offered. "Do not create a savings account for your semen. There is no scientific proof that holding onto it increases your virility or your life span. In fact, there is a great article in a recent *Journal of the American Medical Association* that indicates that the more emissions you have, the less likely it is that you will have prostate cancer. So you need to catch up on those emissions, buster." The class roared.

The class was a little under two hours and by the time it was over, I was spent. I needed a little quiet time in my office before escaping to my home and horse ranch—where more work projects waited for me on the weekend.

Coffee with Lana

It was a rainy Saturday morning and I was sharing coffee in my kitchen with Lana. Lana, an elegant woman of exotic appearance, was a guilty pleasure of mine. I adored her company. She was smart and caring, and had a wicked talent for character analysis. That was the pleasure part. The part I felt guilty about was that she was a much sought-after counselor, coach, and therapist and here I had her all to myself—gratis.

Lana, not one to do an end run around anything, immediately inquired about how I was adapting to being single. Then she asked me when I might be entering the dating world.

"Well, I don't think that's entirely in my hands," I said, meaning that I could try to date but I didn't know how long it would take me to find someone.

"B.S." said Lana with a grin. "You are in charge of your own life."

I laughed and said, "I know that. I am just feeling a little insecure about what my reception will be." She made a face signifying how wimpy and unattractive that sounded.

I smiled.

"Not to worry, Lana. I am gearing up. If I can, I want a partner. I want a romantic and sexual relationship with a special man. Or . . ."

I stopped for a moment and smiled widely. "If I can't find a deep relationship with a really special man, I will settle for shallow relationships with some guys that are just pretty good!"

"Bravo," said Lana. And we clicked coffee cups together.

"But seriously," I added, "I have to admit that the idea of dating feels fundamentally different in the second half of my life. When I told some people I knew that I was getting divorced, a few of them got this sorrowful look in their eyes, as if I were about to condemn myself to a nunnery."

"How did you feel about that?" Lana asked as she sipped her coffee.

"I refuse to take on that identity," I said, unsure whether it was adrenalin or my second latte that was making me feel so strongly about this point. "My good friends who know me know that that is *not going to happen*."

"Yes, Pepper, we fully expect you to rise like a phoenix from the ashes," Lana said with a grin.

"Still, confident as I am about my chances of meeting new and wonderful men, I wonder if some of the women with the sad look in their eyes know something about my marketability that I don't know."

The thoughts and fears rained down. Were there sobering issues about being single after fifty that I needed to face up to? Was it really that bad "out there" for older women? Was my age more of a damper on my libido and heart than I was prepared to acknowledge? Was the libido of men my age spoken for by younger women?

Arousals and Appetites

It was late on a Monday night and my university office was unusually quiet. I was dug into a nest of papers and books on my desk and surrounded by ten-foot bookcases holding hundreds of books related to sexology, sociology, and relationship research. I sat at my large, rather elegant wood desk that I had had for almost all of my adult life, whose good looks had not surfaced in as many years. It was totally covered with reports, articles, and dozens of papers I was supposed to be grading. I was having trouble concentrating: All I could think about was sex. Sex. How inconvenient! But there it was. If love wasn't going to drive me back to dating, sex was.

I have always had a strong sex drive. Since about age fifteen I have walked around with sex on my mind. Probably daily. I know not every woman or man has this sort of appetite but the truth about me is that I always had the kind of itch for sex that people only attribute to men.

Sex and the Sandwich

Perhaps some of my own comfort with sexual arousal comes from a set of more positive associations. Not only was my mother supportive of my budding sexual interest as a child but my earliest sexual relationships gave me a sense of power rather than vulnerability. As I got older, most of my sexual life happened in serious relationships with boyfriends, but I also found I could enjoy sex for the sake of sex. I remember defending my newly formed philosophy of sex with a roommate in graduate school who was slightly-to-greatly appalled by the turnover I had in my dating life.

We were staying up late talking about life and love. Abby was talking about how sacred and wonderful and special sex had to be and how she was going to wait until she was married to experience its "wonder." I might have leaned a little heavier on the secular aspects of sex just to shock her but I was gagging on the gooeyness of her vision.

"Listen, Abby," I said, "let's assume that sex can be just gorgeous—

and that sometimes it is the most beautiful thing that can happen between a man and a woman. But don't you also think that it can be just
practical? Like when you're hungry and want a sandwich. You don't
love the sandwich. You don't hate the sandwich. You just want to eat
the sandwich."

Abby looked nonplussed and said, "If sex is a sandwich, then why
not go for something better. Like a really great meal. Why have a sandwich when you can have fine food? Why not have dinner instead of fast
food?" I have to say this for her: She could run with a metaphor.

But so could I. "Okay, lets accept the fact that 'just sex' is a sandwich and 'love' is the real deal, a full-course meal. But do you want
a five-course meal every goddamn night? If you had to sit down to a
whole table of appetizer and salad and a little palate refresher and a
steak and dessert and cheese course and Port every night wouldn't you
long for a sandwich? I mean, isn't there room in this world for both a
sandwich and a five-course meal?"

A Philosophy of Sex

My mind returned to the present. Obviously, paper grading was going slowly. I pondered my feelings. I wanted intimacy, romance, and
a deep connection between myself and my partner. But truth be told,
I didn't need emotional intimacy at this moment.

I sat there thinking about how sex and dating at this age would
work. Given the way I had always approached sex prior to marriage,
with my "sex is a sandwich" philosophy, I assumed that being single
would not be a reason to restrict myself purely to the company of
vibrators. I won't have sex with someone I don't like, but, like many
other women, I can tolerate a lot of flaws. My mind flashed on Masters and Johnson, the famous sex researchers, who had concluded
that you *can* have sex, and can *want* sex, way into old age, *if* you never
stop doing it. I was very sure I never wanted to stop doing it. And
that would mean putting myself in the running and focusing, to
some degree, on my appearance and figuring out ways to meet worthy and available men.

Getting in Shape

I looked at myself differently now that I was single. While I had been trying to stay in shape while married, travel and a way-too-healthy appetite had not let me keep as physically fit as I wanted to be.

X-treme Fitness sounded like the right place for me. When I walked in the door of the gym I saw that it was filled with sculpted personal trainers working intently with clients. And I quickly learned that a trainer would push me to the limits of what I could do for thirty grueling minutes, three days a week.

"Can we talk about your goals here?" Joe asked as he looked at me head to toe as though evaluating a racehorse that had "slow" written all over it. He made marks on his clipboard with intake form in hand.

"I suppose I'd like to be as fit as possible," I offered.

How could a man whose whole life is organized around fitness possibly relate to my situation where just finding an extra few hours in a week to work out seemed near impossible.

"Fit," the earnest Joe said, "is a relative term."

I decided to be utterly candid with this body fat–free coach. I figured I was paying this guy to help me so I should just speak to him about my weight in the way I felt most comfortable.

"I have battled my weight all my life and have gone back and forth between a size six and a size ten. Every woman knows that is a huge continuum and I look very different even one dress size from another. I got down to a size six for a while but my weight continued to fluctuate. I'm happier when I'm a smaller size."

"That's very helpful, Pepper." Joe said as he made notes on his chart. I found myself looking at Joe's very ripped chest. His biceps were distracting. What I wanted to say but thought the better of was, "But my sex drive stays intact in any size body."

Joe wasn't interested in my sex drive, anyhow. It seemed he was more interested in giving me a heart attack. The intake exam included a stress test to see just what my body could do. Among other things, I was supposed to run on a treadmill for six or seven intervals at the highest speed and incline I could tolerate. It was excruciating after the second interval and only stubbornness and pride allowed me to finish the test. I really couldn't breathe at the end of it, but Joe was unimpressed with both my performance and the fact that I seemed to be dying. I begged for water, which got me a thirty-second respite, and then he had me go through a series of weightlifting, balancing, and lunges which were only slightly less painful than the stress test. I was dripping with sweat and bright red.

When the clock finally released me from what I had now defined as a near-death experience, I fled to the shower, yearning to collapse on the shower floor. This was just a fantasy, however, because it was a very public bathroom with a lot of gym members walking around who would not have enjoyed seeing me huddled on the tile. I did turn on the water as hot as I could stand, and stayed there for quite a while vacantly staring at the wall. Eventually, I gathered up some residual strength and managed to walk out of there without falling on my face.

I started seeing Joe three times a week, professionally speaking.

A Public Face

One Saturday, a few weeks into singlehood, I had worked up a sweat after a morning of cleaning some horse stalls when the guy who usually did it didn't show up at the ranch. I decided to drive into town to get some groceries for dinner that night.

There I was waiting in line in the supermarket when a tall, fiftyish man got in line behind me, his cart filled with a typical bachelor's purchases of premade dinners. He had rugged good looks, freshly pressed khaki pants, and a blue sports shirt. No wedding band was in sight. Here I was with a potentially serendipitous, meeting-cute-like-they-do-in-the-movies moment—with unwashed, uncombed hair, no makeup, chipped nails, and wearing ripped jeans that smelled of horses and an old t-shirt from a public education campaign with the large text "Can We Talk About Sex and AIDS?"

I don't think this guy met my eyes once. I didn't blame him, of course, but it was definitely a missed opportunity. From that moment on I started watching how I looked every time I showed my face outside of my house. I tried to feel good about how I looked all the time.

Shopping

I had set impossibly ambitious goals. Tuesday lunch break was with Donna the manicurist. Wednesday evening was with Lucy who did pedicures and expert leg massage. Thursday afternoon was with Ramon the colorist, followed by Dani the stylist. Personal training was three times a week between various work duties. Friday morning, before office hours, I'd stop downtown for an eyebrow cleanup. Saturday a few girlfriends who knew what they were doing took me to boutiques to update my wardrobe, especially my shoes.

Underwear was a particular problem. My teenage daughter had made a very pointed remark about my boring underwear and had actually doubled up with laughter over some of my more conservative panties and bras. She personally signed up to escort me to Victoria's Secret. Amid a sometimes-crazed life of almost constant travel, writing, research, teaching, and media work, I vowed to give attention to my appearance. I was definitely updated and ready for action.

Casting the Net

So there I was, trying to figure out how to meet the right kind of men. To make an understatement, dating in the information age is profoundly different from dating pre-Internet. Professionally, as someone researching how people met and coupled, I had been following the rise of online dating services for many years and had started working with perfectmatch.com, helping them design their compatibility matching system.

There are all kinds of options on the Net for people with different goals and agendas. Some people were there for affairs, some for hookups, others were just looking for dates and among them were some people looking for a serious relationship. Sites catered to every sexual orientation, race, religion and socioeconomic status. Even mail-order brides and grooms in developing countries could be found posting their availability. Potential spouses and lovers were everywhere on the planet with Internet access.

Prior to Entering Cyberspace

Before I entered the world of online dating I did what I always did when I was doing something new and consequential: call a friend to gather some objective advice.

"Hi, Dom, it's Pepper," I said cheerfully, buzzing on my second latte. "How are things in New York?"

"Just groovy," said Dom, using his trademark adjective with his warm laugh. Dom is a writer and a designer, and we had collaborated on a book series in the late 1990s and became great friends. Of course there were differences. He grew up as a California kid, which has given him a West Coast mellowness that I have sought to emulate but never truly acquired. He also has this Italian-American thing going, and I find that his passion for good food and romance dovetails well with my own. Now having migrated to Manhattan, he was single and always ready to talk about dating men.

"And to what do I owe the pleasure of this phone call?" asked Dom.

"Well, I am ready to post my profile but want to run my plan by you."

"So . . . my Pepper finally enters cyberspace as a customer instead of as Dr. Pepper! Welcome to my world." Dom was actively laughing now.

I had anticipated some joshing from Dom so I waited until he had unloaded a few more cracks. "Done yet, Dom?"

"Not quite," he said, "I am trying to imagine you cherry-picking the site by pirating all good-looking profiles."

"Look, I am not going to do that and I am trying to be discreet and ethical. So listen up, please. Here's my issue: I don't want to be public about being a relationship expert looking for love. There is just something awkward about that. So I don't want to post my picture on my profile."

"Perfectly understandable," said Dom, "but you do realize that not posting a picture on a profile is the kiss of death, the assumption being that a person without a pic is either unattractive, married, or has something to hide from the Feds."

"Yes, I know. But hear me out," I said. "I figure I would just go look at the pictures of the men on the site, see if anyone appealed to me, contact them with a hopefully irresistible e-mail, and then, if they are interested, send them a picture from a somewhat anonymous sounding e-mail address."

"Hmmm. Sounds possible. And really, what's the worst that can happen?" Dom offered. "Someone you go out with mentions it to someone else who mentions it to someone else and pretty soon some news station thinks its pretty funny that a national relationship expert—the voice of reason on sex and love—is cruising cyberspace for a date. The upshot is . . ."

Dom stopped for a minute in midsentence.

"Yes," I said, feeling slightly nervous.

"Well, I suppose you will be considered a normal human being who uses technology to her advantage—as she recommends to every woman she knows. I think it's a good practice-what-you-preach headline in the making."

I thought for a moment about Dom's armchair analysis of the situation.

"Thanks," I said. "I am going online this evening. Stand by for details as they develop."

I spent the evening scanning the profiles. I had narrowed my search to guys who were single, with at least a BA, the income of at least a public school teacher, height between five-foot-six and six-foot-two, build trim to average to twenty pounds extra, and everything else was negotiable. I looked for literate self-descriptions that indicated a sense of humor, a sense of adventure, and sensuality. I saw lots of red flags as I scanned profile after profile including spelling mistakes and a laundry list of what their ideal woman had to be. Some guys actually wrote about how women had to dress, while more than a few wrote about wanting women who liked to live on golf carts.

Choices

After two weekends of scanning the relationship site, I was ready to respond to some profiles. I had found a handful of compelling men that seemed like a potentially good match. All had crisp clear pictures showing face, eyes, and body type. I had nixed some interesting men wearing sunglasses. I needed to see their eyes, which for me would need to indicate warmth, kindness, and intelligence. I started to receive replies to my inquiries and this convinced me that cyberdating was going to be a very efficient way to meet men.

Far from the fears I had heard voiced by friends about meeting only the guys who just wanted a quickie, the majority of the men who were corresponding with me appeared to be seeking love and intimacy. I was pleased. I had decided that sex was only going to occur if a deeper emotional attraction existed along with old-fashioned lust. I had three e-mail correspondences to work on and I was enjoying the slow process of getting to know these guys through old-fashioned letter writing—even if it was in electronic form. I had sent my picture to three men. In a few days, happily, two out of the three were interested. The sting of the one rejection was very mild.

Going slow felt right. Gone were the 1960s when I didn't even ask for the depth of information a driver's license might provide before I found myself in some interesting erotic situation.

▣ Advice to Myself (And Others) ▣

Choosing To Be a Sensualist

Of all the advice I can give myself and other women, one of the most important is that in order for a woman to enjoy the prime of her life, she needs to preserve her physicality. We need to stay in touch with our bodies, keeping sexually alive and sensually lush. This doesn't mean we have to always have a sexual partner, but it does mean that we should use our body, relate to another human being in a sensual way, and have emotional connections with some regularity. We need body contact.

This isn't just my opinion. There are buckets of research showing that some kind of body touch is critical for our physical as well as emotional health. Touch connects us and calms us and even cures us. It is found in the enthusiastic hugs of family and friends, or the sensual caressing by lovers and spouses.

I think we all know how important touch is but sometimes after a particularly painful break up or brutal experience, it is tempting to forgo physical intimacy. The safer option seems to be alone, even if it means never again experiencing the embrace of a lover. I think it's possible to survive without that embrace but I think it's a much greater loss than we imagine. It takes energy, courage, resilience, and time to pursue a relationship, but I believe the rewards of touch, caring, company, and sexual pleasure far outweigh the costs to us.

Why This Is the Prime of Your Life

It may seem questionable to call this the prime of my life: divorces, losses, and a love affair that lasted for years and then didn't work out. A lot of women look at this much emotional yardage and feel like it's more reasonable to leave the field than stay in play. They see their sexual and sensual life behind them, and their children, family, and friends as their future.

I understand this but I don't agree. I feel that I have a capacity to love that is unequaled at any time of my life. I feel, as many of my women peers do, smarter, more generous, more evolved, more successful, and more open to innovation than I have ever been. It seems to me to be a time when the best of who you are—or can be—can come together in a package that will create a better person, and thus, potentially, a better lover. Furthermore, I feel less needy than I used to be. I can enjoy the present much more even if the present is all there is. How much more prime could any period be? I don't want to overexaggerate progress—but in relative terms I know I am the best me I've been and I know a lot of other women over fifty who feel that way, too.

This is a time to be one's strongest, happiest, most sensuous self. I admit my body is not as glorious as it used to be—but it didn't bring me more happiness when it was as perfect as it was ever going to be. I do believe emotionally, intellectually and spiritually, that what we own as mature women is significantly better than what we owned in our twenties and thirties—and maybe even our forties. It is the time when joy and pleasure can be embraced without inhibition—if we allow it.

This is the time to question those tired sex roles that dictate what a woman can or can't do in bed or anywhere else. Prime is a time to get over fears and set new goals for the next fifty years.

Sensuality—with Yourself or a Partner

It is quite possible to be a sensualist without a romantic relationship. It's a frame of mind. There are phases in life when a woman can't find a lover who meets her standards. But that doesn't mean you start to wither and dry up. Women can stay physically awake through all kinds of options: massage, Pilates, working out, sports, dance, hiking, yoga, etc. Experiencing bodily pleasures is hardly dependent on falling in love or lust. The key decision is to commit to keeping sensually vibrant.

Pleasing Yourself

One way of staying sexually alive is taking care of your own pleasure with your own hand or a number of really effective sex toys. Amazingly, we seem to find this the most threatening of sexual acts. Girlfriends will share sexual exploits in detail, but masturbation stories are conspicuously absent. I suppose its embarrassing to talk about touching yourself, although it's interesting how eager women were to discuss the *Sex and the City* episode that celebrated "The Rabbit"—an especially pleasing gizmo that will vibrate and turn internally while the little "rabbit ears" stimulate the clitoris.

Still, this may always be the frontier of sexual pleasure because it is about sex without a partner, never for procreation and always just for personal pleasure. My thought: Why not talk about it? Encourage it. Why not assume, as most men do, that masturbation will be a sexual mainstay of one's life. Partners may come and go, but we have a pretty good chance of our hands staying with us throughout our life cycle. We may want a partner for our heart's health and well-being, but we don't need a partner to stay sexually alive. I am not encouraging women to always choose a vibrator over a relationship. I merely want to be on record that there is a good reason to keep a vibrator in the drawer next to your bed. Thus far I haven't found one that says "I love you" when you squeeze it, so I don't think they endanger wanting or creating a relationship. What they do accomplish are efficient orgasms and, coupled with a good fantasy, enough stimulation to keep one's sensual and sexual responses intact. In my book, that's worth a lot.

Risk Taking

Looking for love, sex, or companionship isn't easy—it has all kinds of risks. You have to know how to take a rejection, because you will surely get some. The risk of being emotionally hurt in the search for love is not only likely, it's inevitable. If there is anyone who has had only pleasant and rewarding experiences dating, I haven't met her. I know, personally, that the loss of someone you love can set you back for a long time.

But the other choice—giving up romance and possibly love forever—is not an optimal alternative. I understand we can become strong, calm, contemplative women, living alone on a coast with a big dog, beachcombing for exercise, and a close friend for enlightenment and companionship. This is not a bad or sad scenario. I understand that if a woman has struggled to reach emotional independence after a significant romantic disappointment (or series of romantic disappointments), a rational choice might be to leave well enough alone. And yet—it's hard for me to accept that decision as the best one. Romantic love, sex, and sensuality enlarge the heart and soul in a way that is uniquely rich and life giving. I hate to see it put away.

Biological Impediments and Opportunities

The older we get, the more physical changes we have to contend with. Some of these changes are inevitable, and the main one that is discussed in conjunction with sexuality is when menstruation becomes inconsistent or disappears and ultimately estrogen levels plummet and menopause officially begins. For some women, menopause is a really difficult transition and it can take a long time. My transition was almost nonexistent. In fact it was so mild and so sudden that when I missed a period in my early fifties I panicked, thinking I was pregnant! But how menopause affects an individual, or her relationship, seems to be highly individualized, although some research indicates there might be some inherited patterns.

Menopause has symbolic as well as biological impact. It is the end of fertility and therefore it signals the closing of certain options. It is the official announcement of middle age. Even if you look thirty, it is an undeniable marker of the aging process.

This period of a woman's life is often pointed to as the villain in the diminution of female sex drive. And that may be true for many women. Still, I think it's fair to say it's not clear how much loss of interest is due to biology and how much is due to being bored or not having a suitable partner. Sex is a habit like other things we do. If people put it aside, it often becomes less compelling.

I do know that a significant percentage of our sex drive is psychologically controlled. In one study, women who thought they were taking a drug to enhance sexual desire had an increase in sexual appetite even when the drug was a placebo. People who actually had the drug, but thought they did not, had no change in sexual desire. I also think that some women who do not have much erotic energy do not have a biological problem—they have a problem finding their partner attractive, or a problem of a flagging relationship or a sex life that's lost its oomph.

That doesn't mean a medical problem (like a hormone imbalance) couldn't be implicated—and a visit to a doctor to find out more information is a good idea. Sometimes an impediment to sexual enjoyment turns out to be superficial and easily solved. The most common example of this I see is when mature women have ceased to enjoy intercourse because it's painful. Pain during intercourse can happen at any time during the life cycle, but it is especially likely when estrogen levels are down and vaginal tissues are thinner and can be torn or hurt more easily. Just applying a topical estrogen or at least a really good lubricant (long lasting and smooth) can make a huge difference. The bottom line here is that postmenopausal women are not necessarily doomed to the loss of sexual desire. There is a lot that can be done to regenerate sexual interest and enjoyment—if a woman is motivated to look for an answer.

Setting Your Criteria for Men

On the positive side, as we get older, we have better instincts, we trust them more, and we have learned a lot from past relationships. We know a lot more about which men to choose. On the negative side, we get into problems when we get too choosy. Laundry lists of everything a man has to be before we will deign to look at him are a surefire recipe for being lonely. I think a better plan is to take your list of the twenty

things you want most in a man and then just look for the top three or
four. My own priorities:

   a. Character (values, ethics, trustworthiness)
   b. Similarity of lifestyle and long-term goals
   c. Desire to communicate and ability to do so
   d. Mental and physical attraction (I sometimes joke
      that I really need a man to do only two things for
      me—make me laugh and make me moan.)

Of course, there are personal issues like health that are increasingly important especially for women dating older men. Most women
think carefully about the age of the man they will commit to. A lot of
women are worried about turning into caretakers in their best years
when they finally have some time for themselves. This isn't selfish.
Caution about someone else's health is a realistic thing to take into
account.

I suppose that's why women and men both tend to want someone
their own age or maybe even a little younger. Men tend to marry wom-
en about their own age the first time they get married and a woman
five years or more younger the second time around. Women have not
had the same pattern historically, but it seems that is changing. Why? I
think it's because women are taking better physical care of themselves,
believing in their sexuality and acting more seductive than they used
to during their fifties and sixties and older. They want someone who
is capable of responding to them.

Younger men see some of the benefits in older women that younger women have seen in older men. Older women are often richer,
more successful and more self-confident than younger ones. They
don't usually want children and may be available for a more carefree
lifestyle. And older women can see the advantages of having a younger
partner: his energy, sexual appetite, enthusiasm, optimism, and his
general health. He may be more liberal about women's roles in a relationship and therefore less likely to be looking for a caretaker and
more interested in a partner. Of course, there is always beauty. Youth

almost always has the advantage of good looks, and women, like men, are not averse to staring in wonderment at someone gorgeous in their bed. It's not the be-all and end-all, but it's not bad, either.

Creating Your Philosophy About Sex

I believe that all adults are entitled to sexual pleasure, and think people who know ecstasy are the better for it. Unless someone is caught up in a compulsive-obsessive sexuality that doesn't respect the right of a partner to have a less active appetite, I think the bigger the sexual appetite, the better. Many women believe that all sexual contact should be in the context of relationships, touching the soul and evoking the sacred. I know that can happen, but for most people, that is about as common as winning the grand prize in the lottery. I think that sex can be transformative—but it can also be play. For myself, I have always felt that mutual respect, creativity, generosity of spirit, and non-trivial feeling for one another were enough, and those criteria alone could create a sexual relationship that could deepen physically and emotionally.

I pledged to myself that if I did not violate my own philosophical guidelines, guilt about sex was a useless emotion and one to be avoided.

Part of my credo is that sex should be intentional—if I make a decision to have sex with someone, it's a decision I make consciously. I don't, as I did when I was much younger, wait until I've had two drinks before I am brave enough to decide what to do. I don't do something sexual because someone has a great need and I feel the pressure to be a generous person. I don't have sex to be a people-pleaser.

I take responsibility for my acts and for possible consequences. I try to forecast risk as much as I can, and then if I act, I accept my fate, intended or unintended. I might decide not to do it again for various reasons but I am very seldom sorry for the choice I made.

Once I am involved with someone, it is highly unusual for me to have any conflicting emotions. I try to focus and stay in the moment, and if I do have conflicting feelings I get out of the situation until I know what I am doing and why I am doing it.

I believe in giving sex your all, exploring the intensity and passion of the moment, and not editing your feelings or responses. If I am "in the moment" I am really there. Tell me there is someone next door starting a fire and I will try to get my orgasm and my partner's orgasm accomplished before running for safety.

I am as body conscious as the next person but I refuse to let my figure flaws restrict my sexuality. If I am involved, I forget about my butt, thighs, tummy, whatever imperfections I might have that would disqualify me from wearing a thong—I just want to make love with this person and give and receive pleasure. I want to avoid what researchers Masters and Johnson called "spectatoring," watching yourself and your partner rather than being in the moment.

Great sex can only happen when someone is having as much pleasure as you are. I believe I should be conscious of my partner's needs and talk to him about what he wants and needs. And vice versa. I think communication of any kind cannot rest upon assumptions—you need knowledge. And to get real information, I need to ask questions and be involved with someone who will enjoy giving me answers. I love the man who looks for ways to tell me what he needs, and when I am with a man who genuinely tries to find out what works for me then I consider myself sexually well matched. I believe no sexual act, mutually desired and practiced, is out of bounds. If I feel respected and give respect, then any way we can give pleasure to each other is great.

I admire other people who have a well-worked out philosophy of sex. It doesn't have to be anything like mine. It helps me know who I am dealing with, in what ways we do or do not see the world in the same way, and if we share enough in common to be compatible. Being different doesn't necessarily say we are wrong for one another—but it does give us things to talk about and work on. If we do have incompatible ethics, values, and practices, we can see that right away and spare both of us some frustration and rejection.

three

DISCOVERING SEX AND SEXOLOGY

Reflecting on the Past

My Twenties

Early in my twenties, first at Washington University in St. Louis and later at Yale, I became very sexually adventurous. I had had a boyfriend throughout undergraduate school—a beautiful blonde-haired man with Paul Newman blue eyes. My boyfriend was all I could ask for most of my undergraduate years but the relationship ran its course by my master's year and crashed and burned when I had a brief affair with a movie star who was making a film in East St. Louis, Illinois.

When I hit Yale, I was emotionally unencumbered and eager to take advantage of the sex ratio of what was then an all-male under-graduate body. It felt like it was about two hundred women in a sea of ten thousand men. It was the Promised Land for me. I had weekly af-fairs, and numerous adventures with both undergraduate and gradu-ate men. This level of sexual abandon was unusual even in the era of "free love" and what was being touted as the "sexual revolution." For some idiosyncratic reasons of personality I, along with a minority of other adventurous women, resisted contemporary morality about appropriate female sexual behavior and just went nuts. I decided I was well within my rights doing anything men were allowed to do. I knew what many people thought about my unrestrained sexual appetite—and I thought *To hell with them.*

This was not without some costs. Women could still get a "bad reputation" in those days and I definitely ran into that problem. That double standard frosted me. The inequity of it pushed me further in the direction I was already headed. How come a guy could boast about his sexual experience but for some reason think I was "easy" or sluttish for having sex with him? I had not yet fully digested the reality that men needed to have control over women's sexuality but I got the gist of it in my own life.

It was a cultural challenge I was ready to take on. Like everyone I knew, my mother had cautioned me to guard my virginity and do anything I could so that my value in the marriage market would not be damaged. Early on I decided if that was what made me valuable to a man, I could forgo the institution of marriage. I reveled in my role as a sexual rebel.

I was learning a lot from my sexual adventures. I was getting to know people I would never have known any other way.

I learned a lot about sex from ordinary and extraordinary men— and a handful of women. Of course I wanted to know what it was like to be with women as well as men. It was extremely erotic to be trespassing the sexual taboos of that era and learning about what pleased other women besides myself. At one point during the height of my anger at the double standard, I wished I could be gay and just avoid all the politics of heterosexual love. But it is very difficult to will yourself into a sexual attraction, and I never fell in love with a woman, even though I have admired and cared for them.

Sex on Six Continents (Or Around the World Starting with the Art Dealer in New Delhi)

In my year after undergraduate school, I was eager to travel—and for me, that also meant experiencing men all over the world. When I landed in India, it wasn't long before I met a fascinating Indian man named Viendrai who owned an art gallery in Delhi. He was tall, elegantly dressed, and intellectually adept. I liked him enormously, and since I was going to be in Delhi for several days, we met each day for conversation and flirtation. After some lovely nights getting to know one another, we made love in his Delhi gallery. There, on the floor, on satin pillows that he gently laid out for us, he gave me another lesson: the discipline and delights of Tantric sex.

We started by kneeling on the pillows, facing each other, and he placed my hand on his heart and I placed his hand on mine. Our breathing slowly synchronized and we could feel our hearts beating in unison. This was surprisingly intimate and sexy. Then we took our clothes off and did the same thing, this time completely nude, and we kissed. My heart was thumping. The deliberateness of each step, the intense eye contact, and the seriousness with which we proceeded had me weak with excitement. We lay facing each other for awhile, while he traced my body and told me where my energy centers called *chakras* were. Each time he touched me, slowly, deliberately, I felt the energy of my body concentrate beneath his long, tapering, sensitive fingers.

The biggest surprise, however, was when we had intercourse. I was anxious to do what I knew best at that time—athletic, hard, rapid sexual entry, building quickly to orgasm. But he slowed me down and controlled his own response. He not only could decide when to ejaculate, but he could have orgasms without ejaculating. He would have an orgasm, lose his erection momentarily, and then be erect again within a few minutes. I was awed at first, then liberated to be as sexually hungry as I could be. We could just go at it for hours and he could have as many orgasms as I did without being satiated. Unlike a lot of my experiences up to this time, passion did not eclipse conversational intimacy and we talked intermittently and intelligently. I was so impressed with him, I felt blessed having an experience that so completely pleased both my mind and my body. Sex with Viendrai was part lust, part spiritual, and part scientific experiment.

The Playboy in Paris

Viendrai and I had to part since I was going on to other parts of India and eventually to Europe. He told me that I should meet his brother in Paris. Viendrai was one of four brothers, two in India, one in Paris, and one in New York. He mentioned that his brother Ravi was extremely different from him: not at all spiritual, an international playboy, and overly impressed with himself, but that I would find him interesting. I agreed to call him.

I did call Ravi, who met me at a Parisian bistro. He was everything his brother had mentioned, with one addition: He was devastatingly handsome. Tall, thin, with an aquiline face with awesome bone structure and expressive large eyes, he was a heartthrob on any continent. He knew it, of course. Still, despite his natural arrogance and privileged place in the world, he was quite open and engaging with me. I was flattered, of course, to get the attentions of an international playboy. He was the kind you read about being on yachts in the harbor of Monaco. We spent the day together, walking the streets of Paris. The city itself will do the wooing, and by twilight, when the lights make Paris even more magical than it was a few hours before, we were kissing and holding hands. He took me to his hotel, the elegant Bristol on the Right Bank, and I washed up in the marble bathroom thinking that while it was a bit kinky to be involved with two brothers, it wasn't a betrayal of any sort.

Viendrai was in my past. Ravi was my present. And neither would be in my future. It was good to just live this scenario wherever it took me. So I went into the large bedroom, slipped between the silken sheets, and waited to see if Ravi would have the sexual acumen of his less attractive but more intellectual and spiritual brother. He turned out to be a good but conventional lover—and emotionally distant. His lovemaking was like his personality, elegant, impersonal, and proficient but without heart, vulnerability, or, dare I say, soul. When his hands touched my body, I felt like a BMW being serviced by an excellent technician. There was respect, talent, but no personal connection. I had orgasms that satisfied my body but my mind and heart were not engaged. Still, he was bright, fascinating, and just stunning to look at. We liked knowing each other—but we both knew it was not more than that.

It was the kind of relationship that I knew would last only for a short time, and that didn't bother me. Knowing an international playboy was almost like an anthropological interview—captivating but necessarily fleeting. I was glad to have been there, not sorry to leave.

The Hong Kong Harbor

After my European sojourn I wanted to get back to Asia. I flew to Hong Kong and became fascinated by the color and chaos of Hong Kong harbor. I heard that it was possible to rent a small Chinese boat called a *junk* for not much money and get a harbor tour. This turned out to be true, and just by chance, I was the only person who was there for the noon trip. This made the boat trip particularly posh and I was extremely pleased by my luck. I felt even luckier, however, when I came on board and saw that there was a young and good-looking crew. The harbor was beautiful, just about as romantic as it gets—exotic sailing ships sharing the water with cruise liners, fishing boats, and tiny personal local sampans getting their owners from one shore to another. I stayed on deck, taking pictures of it all, and in one picture-taking moment found this adorable young crewmember smiling at me.

In fact, the man in my camera lens was looking at me rather pie-eyed. He was quite gorgeous. Unusually tall for most of the Chinese men I had seen—at least six feet—and well built with lovely black hair, gentle eyes, and a sculpted face. We smiled at each other and I could see longing in his eyes, which I found a very agreeable compliment. I locked eyes with him to show him his interest was appreciated and returned. That was the only way I could convey availability since he spoke not a word of English. Undaunted by a little thing like lack of a shared language, I took his hand and he clasped mine tightly in return. A good sign. I don't know what emboldened me to do this—maybe having the boat to myself had gone to my head—but I led him down into the cabin that I had scoped out earlier and closed—and locked—the door. He was obviously astonished, but made no moves to reopen the door. We were in a small paneled room with a bunk bed, a desk, and not much else.

I started to take my clothes off and he continued to look dumbstruck. I was worried if I was freaking him out or if he was offended or if what I was doing was too risky and he was afraid, perhaps rightly, that he would lose his job. But no, he checked the door, smiled ecstatically—and then took off his clothes. Then he just stood there, waiting for me to do something. I guessed this was probably his first time seeing a nude woman. I think it was a pretty good guess—he was so overwhelmed that he came just while he was looking at me.

I smiled and kissed him and put my clothes back on. Profusely grateful for even that experience, he tried to give me everything of value he had on him: a ring, his t-shirt, his watch. I took nothing, of course, but he was just so happy—he couldn't stop hugging me. The rest of the crew was circumspect but I am sure they couldn't believe what had happened to their friend either. Or maybe they could. Maybe that's just what American young women traveling alone did on these boats. What did I know? I know the image of that young man, in that harbor, looking at me gratefully as I left the boat, was one of my favorite memories I carried with me as I circled the globe.

The Antiques Dealer

My trip around the world went on for months and after a while I found myself in Kyoto, an historic city in Japan. I loved Japanese culture and had taken enough undergraduate credits in medieval Japanese history to think about minoring in it. (The language requirements made that a stillborn fantasy.) Nonetheless, it created a lifelong love of classical

Japanese art. I also appreciated Japanese antiques of any kind, and so I found myself on Shinmonzen Street, then a street with a number of antique dealers on it. At one small shop, I met a handsome dealer named Kazuo. His English was broken but substantial and we started a discussion about Japanese antiquities that became more of a segue to mutual attraction. His shop was small and the American dollar at the time was strong against the yen (the "good old days" for Americans) so I invited him out to lunch. He suggested a nearby noodle shop and seemed very happy about the invitation.

While he educated me about what made one noodle shop superior over another, I noticed how truly handsome he was. He had strong features, strong opinions, and an animated but respectful approach to me. I asked him if he would be my guest for dinner, but he wanted to take me out and I accepted.

We went out to a nontourist place, where carloads of businessmen sat on tatami mats in various stages of being drunk. There were all kinds of drinking games going on and a woman, somewhere between a waitress and a geisha, was egging the men on in that soft but firm style Japanese bar women have perfected. She would kneel down next to the man, flirt with her eyes, giggle, and challenge him to drink shots quickly in succession. I was the only woman in the room besides her and I asked Kazuo why. He told me that Japanese men did not like their wives very much and rarely took them out to dinner. Japanese men wanted their wives at home and not as companions. I asked him if that was what he wanted. He said no. He liked the more egalitarian American model. Clever man.

That night we talked a lot about his life, his goals, and he told me how strongly he felt about me. It was an emotionally intimate evening, and since he was not ordinarily an expressive man, it was clear to me that the time we were spending together was more than just a sexual attraction for him. He was obviously infatuated with me, something I have always thought of as a special situation that required kindness. Besides being flattered, I feel that I should honor someone's emotional involvement. Once a person's heart is open, he (or she) is in a vulnerable situation and I have no desire to hurt anyone whose feelings toward me are loving and hopeful.

Kazuo was gentle and full of compliments. We started to kiss and it became passionate and when I invited him to my bedroom he was ecstatic. In bed he was extremely complimentary. He slowly touched every part of me and extolled everything from my calves to my clavicle. It was as if he was examining a new species and wanted to make sure he noted every part of this new, wondrous creature. He made me feel exceptional, beautiful, and completely flawless. It was a tender and passionate evening—I found him beautiful as well. I would stare at his face and some of my favorite seventeenth-century prints would come to mind.

But Kazuo wasn't just a cultural excursion, he was an exceptional man. He was a man of strong opinions, great enthusiasm, and an intense entrepreneurial spirit. He was handsome, spoke and understood English reasonably well, and was an adoring if somewhat unadventurous lover. He was open to instruction, however, and so it was fun to help him expand his sexual repertoire and be the recipient of his refined sexual technique. I was his introduction to oral sex, and some playful touches like toe or ear lobe sucking. He was very grateful to get any new information and while he was a proud man when he was in business mode, he was an avid and pliant student in bed.

Our parting was sweet and he promised to write. We were delighted in each other. He taught me what it was like to meet someone with an open, undefended heart who could worship me without hesitation. He taught me about his country, its culture and antiques. I hoped I had honored his feelings and I felt that I had taught him a lot in bed, and I hoped his successive lovers would benefit. I hoped we wouldn't lose touch.

The Blonde Adonis

When I got to Athens on my trip, I had to fend off the men in the streets who walked after me and anyone else in a skirt. There were many good-looking men around but that kind of harassment was not a turn-on for me. However, when I got to my hotel and took the elevator up to my room, I encountered a sweet blond Adonis and once again our eyes made the assignation. There was an instant and powerful mutual attraction. He could speak only a few words of English, but as I have indicated, that wasn't a critical problem. In fact, our names weren't important either—and his became lost to me over time. What I do remember was an earthshaking immediate mutual knowledge that we wanted to be with one another. In some kind of sign language we both understood, we agreed to get together after his work ended at 10:00 pm.

We met outside the hotel. I was pretty sure the hotel wouldn't approve of employees going out with their guests. We linked hands. He had the sweetest smile and we walked the streets of Athens as if we were boyfriend and girlfriend. He took me to a charming taverna, where we ate inexpensively. I wanted to pay, of course, but he wouldn't hear of it. He showed me the sights and every so often we would stop and kiss. The time passed quickly and I was surprised when I looked down at my watch and it was 2:00 am. I made noises that perhaps we should walk back but he motioned that he couldn't bear to let me go. Then he led me a bit farther and we arrived at the base of the Parthenon. At this time, it was not roped off and you could go into the center of it. We did, and alone in this huge and monumental structure, under the moonlight, had sex.

His touch was soft, gentle, and his kisses were slow intimate, and romantic. I felt totally comfortable with him and whether or not it was pure fantasy, I felt like we touched something real and tender within each other. I was wearing a skirt and as he reached underneath it and touched me, he pulled my panties to the side and I could feel that I was completely ready for him to enter me. He could feel that, too, and I remember looking into his eyes, both of us smiling broadly and he grasped me under my back and gently lay me down on a marble slab. We kept eye contact as he unzipped his pants and freed his erect penis. By this time, I wanted him badly. Our bodies were completely lined up against one another and I gave him absolute permission with my eyes. When he entered, he glided into me and it felt fantastic, like our bodies were fusing together in the most natural way. What a euphoric feeling it is when you fit someone perfectly!

There are just people who are sexually designed for one another. Plato thought that—and he was actually in my mind since I was near his hometown.

I know this will sound ridiculous for such a passing passion—but it felt like a true connection between us. Our lovemaking was slow and tender. We satisfied each other easily. But of course it was impossible to prolong our relationship. I was leaving the next day and he couldn't speak English! We had gone as far as we could with each other. After sex, we snuggled for awhile and then held hands as he walked me back to my hotel. We looked at each other a long time and said good bye—both of us truly sad to say it.

The Kibbutz

My globetrotting ended in the Middle East. I am not a religious person but I was very curious about this ancient territory that had meant so much to so many people in so many religions. The Six-Day War had not yet happened, and while all the Middle Eastern countries were furious at Israel, things were not at a fever pitch. You could still walk from Jordan across into Israel. I spent time in Egypt and Jordan, and finally did walk from the Jordan checkpoint to the Israeli one. I hung out, learning about the history and culture of this new, embattled country and along the way I met a gorgeous student in a café who introduced himself as Avi and asked if he could join me for conversation.

Our attraction to each other was instant, which flattered the hell out of me because he was a thing to behold. Avi was absolutely beautiful with a head of thick black curly hair, a chiseled face, and a big beautiful smile. He had an infectious laugh and an apparent joie de vivre. Although we shared a religious background, his life was entirely foreign to me. He was a native Israeli and the Israeli struggle to hold on to their nation was the organizing principle of his life. He could not understand why I, an American Jew, would not want to live in Israel and help defend it.

These were significant differences and they kept me from over-romanticizing our time together, but I had to admit I was smitten. He was a fascinating, intelligent, lovely man who also had more sexual charisma than any one human being had the right to own.

After talking for a few hours and then meeting again the next day for lunch and later, dinner, he invited me back to his kibbutz.

I leapt at the chance. The closest I had ever come to a kibbutz was reading *Exodus* and I thought it was high time to get a little more knowledgeable. When he took me back to his bedroom, I forgot about how disparate our location in the world really was. When he took off his clothes, I literally gasped. Not only was his lithe body perfectly muscled, smooth, and graceful, but he had the largest penis I believe I had seen up to that time. I was a little nervous but he knew what he was doing and didn't hurt me.

He was very slow, very seductive, with the pace of a man who knows he knows how to make love with a woman and is orchestrating love-making as opposed to just having an orgasm as quickly as possible. He probably knew, too, that if he entered me quickly it would be painful, as opposed to exciting. We must have made love five times a day during that time together.

The Scare in Beirut

The Beirut I visited was in a golden moment. There was no war, no obvious guerilla movement or dissidence of any kind. The city was described by its citizens as the Switzerland of the Middle East and by all measures I had available that seemed to be the case. I stayed at the Phoenicia, a hotel at the center of the city that many years later I would see burning down during battle. But then it was the center of a cosmopolitan city by the sea, with broad boulevards that reminded me of Paris. I was having a hell of a good time being entertained by friends of friends.

It was in Beirut that the reality of how gender relations are enforced was impressed upon me. I had met up with some people who were invited to a social gathering at the French embassy and they wrangled an invitation for me as well. I did not have a dress worthy of the affair but I put a long black skirt together with a lacy black top I bought in a local shop, and a fancy belt I found in the lobby store, and that made a plausible outfit for a dressy event. I knew no one at the event except my new acquaintances and I quickly lost track of them. I was thinking that this night might turn out to be all about the hors d'oeuvres when a tall, smartly tuxedoed man walked up to me and rattled off something in French. I speak French, albeit badly, and I could catch enough of it to tell him that I was from America and that I thought it was a lovely party. But my accent and halting syntax quickly gave me away, and he smoothly and graciously switched into English. He was a French diplomat, and I gathered he was required to spend a certain amount of time at black-tie events but that he did not like this kind of evening.

We talked a while and flirted a bit and he offered to take me up to the mountain to see the large statue of the Virgin looking down at the lights of the city. I thought it sounded romantic. He was nice looking, quite charming, and I loved his accent. I was not at all averse to imagining a night in his hotel room afterward. However, as we drove up the mountain, he left the main road and took an unpaved road for a mile, stopped the car, and feverishly started kissing me. Taken aback, I withdrew from him, at which time he slapped me hard across the face. I was horrified and stunned. Shocked into a survival response, I calmly told him that he need not worry. I said I would be happy to have sex with him but that I wanted a romantic hotel room. I don't know how I stayed so calm in such a threatening situation but my adrenaline seemed to be supporting my focused approach to diffusing the volatile situation.

He immediately relaxed, resumed his polite and suave demeanor, and turned around, heading the car down the mountain and into the city. When we reached a stoplight, I jumped out of my side of the car and ran like hell. I had been lucky to escape rape or worse. I vowed to remember a number of lessons that night. I promised myself never to put myself in a situation with a man with whom I had little history or trust, where I could not call for help. It was deeply troubling to me that I was so easily taken in by this man's charm and status. I had always trusted my instincts and I had been so wrong about this assailant.

The truth was, as women come to know, that violent men come in all shapes, sizes, and socioeconomic classes. For the rest of the trip I lived by several new rules about personal safety. First, to never get in a car alone with someone unless I knew him well or had many friends in common. Second, to never mistake charm for authenticity. The more charming the guy, the more I swore I would take a wait-and-see position. Third, to never assume that the vision I had of egalitarian interaction was in anyone's head but my own unless I had enough interaction with someone to make a well-informed presumption that we were both on the same page.

Back in the United States: An Experiment

After my trip, it was time to get back to school and my career. Except for my Beirut fiasco, my adventures had all been positive. Still, I had had enough of world travel for a while and it felt good to be pursuing my intellectual goals in New Haven. Of course, this didn't mean I was dropping my need for male companionship.

I was sitting on a bench in the law school cafeteria when he sat next to me. I noticed he was dressed differently from most of the East Coast preppie law students I had met at Yale. He was wearing jeans and a plaid shirt, as if he were just coming from or going to the woods. His face was narrow and quite elegant, in almost startling contrast to his clothes. He had a trimmed, fine beard that framed his almost Shakespearean face, and he radiated friendliness and intelligence. He had dark hair and dark eyes and wasn't my usual physical type, but I was attracted to him. We immediately got into some spirited conversation about politics and he was intense, good-natured, and fervent about his political condemnation of the present administration and the Vietnam War.

He pursued our first meeting and we had some great dates. He owned an extremely battered Toyota van and we would go hiking, fishing, and camping—three activities I hadn't done since I was a kid.

His friends were smart political activists and I enjoyed the intellectual challenge of his circle. Our first sexual moment together took place in a twin bed and it was exciting but quite cramped. Sex was very good and he was an attentive and capable lover—still, I'm not sure I gave his body a chance. I was so attracted to his mind—his quick wit and decisive critiques—that our lovemaking, uncharacteristically for me remained less intense than our mental connection.

This was the man who would be my first husband. We met when he was at Yale Law School and I was taking a combined set of classes in the Law School and in the Sociology Department while I was working on my PhD. It was 1969 and I was definitely tired of sleeping around. I started to get a "been there, done that" feeling about men and sex and wanted a deeper, more committed experience. I picked John because he was noble, smart, always clever and interesting and politically active. He shared my anger about the Vietnam War and in fact, was fighting for conscientious objector status to stay out of the army. His case, which my family helped fund and support, went all the way up to the Supreme Court of the United States and we won it on a five-to-four decision. Those were dramatic and emotional times.

I admired what he stood for and he seemed the sort of person I should marry. But I was thinking more with my head than my heart. It was a way too intellectual match—we were competitive with one another, and I was not really capable of love in the deepest and most profound sense of that word. But what did I know? Outside of a long and passionate relationship in undergraduate school with Tom (my beautiful blond boyfriend), that started out wonderfully and then slowly became devitalized during a protracted end, I had not been been in love. I didn't know what it should feel like. I liked my husband enormously, thought it was love, and found out it wasn't.

We held our relationship together through his fellowship year in Oregon. He was a public defender, and he was trying to make fair legal precedents for poor and disenfranchised people. He was a truly good man and an excellent lawyer and I was proud of what he was doing. However, when I finished my PhD thesis and began my first year of an assistant professorship at the University of Washington, I was totally enveloped in the struggle to be successful as a researcher and teacher. I spent most of my time with my new colleagues at work, and very little with him. We started to act badly with one another and when things noticeably started coming apart we had sustained too much emotional damage to make our marriage last. The damage was in the form of sparring with each other about everything, He would cut me down in public and not consciously realize he had done so, and I would reply in kind. Stories and issues that should have stayed private between us were used as public ammunition.

We were both becoming people we didn't want to be and eventually we needed to stop that humiliating behavior by ending the relationship. We split amicably and we were able to settle our financial partnership by just working it out over a conversation at our dining room table. We were a lot more successful at divorce than marriage. We forgave each other for our past insensitivities to one another and chalked a lot of it up to our mutual and willful ignorance of how to protect and invest in a relationship. We were not meant to be partners, just the extremely good friends we became and remain to this day.

The Venereologist

About a year after my first marriage ended, I met the man I wanted to spend my life with: Ken, a venereologist—in other words, a medical doctor specializing in sexually transmitted diseases. We had, as you can imagine, fascinating pillow talk, but believe me, some of the things he thought were interesting, like photographs of venereal warts that had taken over a person's body, or magnified pictures of pubic lice, were not exactly a turn-on. He was a highly respected STD researcher and we met when we were both on the Governor's Commission on Venereal Disease. How romantic is that? Well, it seemed to do the trick for me. He was cute, with a wiry, toned body, extremely intelligent, quite funny, intensely dedicated to his work, and totally engaging.

I fell deeply in love with him and I was sure he was the man I was meant for. In my twenties, one of the things that I looked for in a lover outside of intelligence and character, was a certain type of sexual charisma. I sought a man with a powerful sex drive and an ability to sexually excite me with a touch or a look. And he had it all. We spent years enjoying our weekends together, always debating perspectives on public health, sex, and relationships.

I loved our dinners out, filled with long debates about the news of the day, the right way to measure a variable, his latest research project or mine, the best sex toys we had seen, or just gossip about people we knew. We were also quite romantic with each other. There would be a lot of eye contact, hand holding, and often some naughty fondling under the table, against a wall on the way to the bathroom or sex in the car because we couldn't wait until we got to one of our places. Once, on a lark, we dropped into a pornographic theater on the way back from dinner and made love right there. If we had been discovered and arrested that would have been the end of my career since I was just an assistant professor and universities don't have a sense of humor about that sort of scandal!

We shared an unstoppable, unquenchable passion for one another—we forgot who we were and what the consequences could be when we wanted each other. We had matched sexual appetites, and couldn't be around each other long before tackling each other.

Both of us took our work very seriously, and he was always willing to hear about what I was working on and wanted me to be deeply engaged with his research. There was an intellectual and physical synergy that was unique in my experience. He had a powerful personality that dominated most of the people he worked with, and that strength and leadership attracted me. He had already become quite famous for his research and his mentoring of the next generation of research stars. He was also a little bit dangerous and that held my attention.

Life with Ken was never boring. On the other hand, he wanted to work almost every minute of every day and I was working hard myself since academic jobs require a promotion to associate professor at the end of six years, or you lose your job. Our demanding careers, especially his, meant severe time constraints and so our time together was precious and not to be taken for granted.

Most of the intimate time I got to spend with him was on his pharmaceutically sponsored lecture tours all over the world. These trips took us to Singapore, Bali, Brazil, Venezuela, Ecuador, Argentina, and other equally exotic destinations. They were intimate, romantic moments in a relationship that had too many argumentative periods and not enough daily time where we just hung out together. Ken had just separated from his wife when I became involved with him and he didn't want to live together. His scars from being in a long, unsatisfactory marriage and a natural disinclination to be more than occasionally intimate were frustrating and ultimately maddening to me.

Our blowups would occur when I would press for more commitment and he would resist. As the years went by I wanted more than "I love you." I wanted to live with him and feel like we had a future together. I also wanted to get married eventually and have children, which was definitely not what he wanted at that time. He had three children and an ex-wife who was furious with him, and the idea of another family and another marriage and more complications didn't attract him in the slightest. He didn't say, however, that he would never want to make a commitment to me—and so, like so many women who don't want to see the truth in front of their nose, I thought he would eventually want the things I wanted rather than lose me.

Around year three we started having a different kind of argument. He came back from a skiing trip in Aspen and said that sentence that no woman wants to hear, "There is something I have to tell you." He told me he had met a woman in Aspen and he had slept with her and was in love with her. I was emotionally destroyed. We had an understanding of monogamy—and I had certainly honored it up to that point. He was a flirtatious kind of guy but I had been so much in love with him—and I had thought he was so much in love with me—that I hadn't questioned what he might be doing when we weren't together. I was distraught but I did one of those ignominious "Please don't leave me, I love you" scenes and so we didn't break up right away. This, by the way, is a form of self-torture I would like to pretend I have never done, since it is so stupid and humiliating that it is even painful to recall. But I did do it and it put me in a jealous frenzy. My general insanity might have gone on longer, but I looked in his bedstead drawer and when I found some letters from her in it and read her totally adoring, childish letters (illustrated on every page with little smiley faces), that was it. How could he appreciate me and love someone who called him diminutive animal names? We broke up—the first of many times. A few months later, he called, apologized profusely, said he loved me and missed me and needed me—that whole song and dance, and I capitulated. But eventually the whole cycle would repeat itself with someone new.

The Unexpected Suitor

While Ken and I could not come to an agreement about what our relationship should be, we had one incident happen that put the question back front and center in my mind. The catalyst came one rainy afternoon in Seattle when I received a call from my parents in Chicago.

Kazuo, the antiques dealer in Kyoto, had turned out to be a very obsessive, impetuous, and emotional man. Even though it had been years since I had seen him in person, with only a few letters exchanged, he showed up in the United States, made an appointment in Chicago with my parents and, without asking me, proceeded to ask my mom and dad for my hand in marriage.

My confused, shocked, and worried mother said in a hushed voice over the phone, "Pepper, your friend Kazuo from Japan is standing in the next room with your father asking if it is okay to marry you."

I gasped.

"Is there something you have forgotten to tell us?" my mother asked in earnest.

"I had no idea this was going to happen," I said. "Please give Kazuo a nice dinner and I will call back in two hours to talk with him. And please tell Dad this is all a huge misunderstanding."

I had been eating lunch with Ken and needed to shorten our afternoon so I could deal with my unwanted suitor. In my series of phone calls with Kazuo it seemed as though he had been fostering some kind of undying love for me for years. Kazuo felt he must marry me and didn't want to take no for an answer.

Two days later he showed up unannounced at my house in Seattle, while Ken was there. It was sad and difficult. It took a few hours to sort things out and finally convince Kazuo that I had moved on to someone else and that he had to go back home. As a dejected, confused, and saddened Kazuo got into the taxi to take him to the airport, I made a vow, then and there, to be much more careful about other people's expectations and what I said, even in a joking manner. But I also thought about how he felt about me as opposed to Ken's on and off protestations of love—and his absolute refusal to make a commitment.

An Ending and a Beginning

The Kazuo episode was the beginning of my reflections about the limits of my relationship with Ken. Ken did love me but not enough. We had had almost five years of heart-searing breakups, passionate reengagements, and bitter fights over his infidelity, and ultimately an end to the whole thing. I had given this relationship my full attention and I thought my best self and it just wasn't going to work out. The rock-bottom event was a trip of his to Hawaii that was near my birthday—and he had decided not to take me. It was such a clear rejection that I had no choice but to respond with a breakup. A real one.

I said, "That's it" and meant it—and he was at the end of the relationship with me as well. The real love affair had been on life support for quite a while and this was just the ceremonial plug-pulling. I cried for a few days but it was a relief, too. What I did take from those five years was a feeling that I had finally discovered how to give my heart—even if it was to an unworthy relationship. l learned what my heart was capable of giving, and it changed the way I looked at sex, love, and commitment. I no longer wanted relationships that were primarily about sex. I wanted to give and get sexual loyalty. I wanted to be in a committed relationship. I wanted to get married to someone I loved deeply and have children. This was all a new way of thinking for me.

Time was no longer endless, no longer completely friendly. I felt a new sense of urgency. I was thirty-three, and if I wanted a husband and children, I had better not invest in fantasy, superficial, or unrequited relationships.

The Clitoritti

I took my dilemma and my heartache to my women's group, a group of women who came to be known as "the Clitoritti." This was a moniker one of the members, Jane, a writer, gave to the ten or so women who comprised the group at that time. Three of the women lived together; first at a place we called Casablanca, then at the second house called Casa Rosa.

It was always open house and we would all stop by at different times of the day to talk about love, sex, rejection, romance, to get a cup of coffee or just to see who was around. At night we would go to Jane's house, which always had a hot tub waiting, and new people to meet. We stripped at the door and jumped into the bubbling warm water, sometimes to meet an interesting man or, most often, to participate in what Jane called "girl soup" which was several women getting parboiled as we talked about life.

Many of them had been telling me to give up on Ken for years, and so when the news got out, we had a meeting with Champagne, congratulations, even gifts! Women dropped by night and day to amuse and distract me. I got more than one impromptu bowl of chicken soup. It made the transition so much easier. These women are each individually wonderful—and collectively indomitable, wise, and the best support system anyone could ever wish for. I felt and feel love and joy in their presence. How could I continue to feel sorry for myself? We had sustained each other through so many romantic vignettes and mistakes that I could come to them without shame. After all we had witnessed:

- Halley throwing a brick through her faithless lover's dashboard window.
- Kim's bisexual boyfriend leaving her for another woman— and man.
- Molly's boyfriend going to her home in Lake Forest to ask her parents' permission to marry her, and going almost directly from there to another woman's house to call and break up with Molly.
- And Dana's lover going back to the lover he had left his ex-wife for after he and Dana had signed a lease to move in with one another.

These same women eventually found other, better men to love, but there was a phase in the life of the group when men turned into bad boys and shocking stories surfaced with regularity. In their company, I had the profound empathy and camaraderie that made it easier to weather disappointment. It made the unpredictability of dating a lot more bearable—and I was buoyed up to reenter the fray when excellent men surfaced in their lives and I felt some reassurance that one would pop up again in mine. Men entered our group as partners of my friends and the Clitoritti was finally witness to positive relationships. I watched my friends start to make lifetime commitments. It got me even more interested in trying to find the love of my life.

Meeting the Viking Prince

He was my perfect sexual template: extraordinarily handsome, very tall, blond and blue-eyed with the looks, according to my fantasy at the time, of a Viking prince. The storybook beginning stops there since he was married (but not to me). He ran for local public office and won the primary, and I worked on his campaign to support a friend who was involved in it. I was rounding thirty-three on my way to thirty-four and I was increasingly feeling those trite but true yearnings for love, marriage, and children. I had pitched in to his campaign because I thought he was a good candidate, but also because this political campaign seemed like a good place to meet a kindred spirit. I never thought about the candidate as a romantic partner; he seemed very married and his wife had a powerful personality that would strike fear into any poacher's heart. However, when I heard they were breaking up, I was immediately interested and determined to ask him out for lunch. Before I could do that, however, we met at a party at my friend Linda's art gallery.

I saw him when I walked in—but I was in no mood to flirt that evening. I felt depressed, still unable to shake my disappointment over the end of my life with Ken. The relationship had been over for about a year, but he had called me that evening, just to say hello. I kept up a brave front while we chatted but even a brief conversation with him would make me break into tears as soon as I had hung up the phone. I had been so convinced he was the perfect man for me, that the loss of that dream still pained me.

In an effort to shake off the blues, I accepted my girlfriend Donna's invitation to leave the gallery and see a movie. A little escapism seemed like a lot better cure for my bad mood than an art gallery cocktail party. However, it turned out to be the wrong choice. The movie was *The Rose*, with Bette Midler and it started in a sad mood and then went to rock bottom. The cheery theme is: a woman who falls in love with her mentor; she surpasses him in fame; he gets self-destructive and kills himself; she goes downhill.

Now totally depressed, I had my friend Donna drop me back at the gallery, where I'd left my car. When I got there only a few people, including my friend Linda the gallery owner, were still there. Among the lingerers, the Viking Prince. My romance receptors were not functioning. I wanted emotional support, not flirtation. Actually I was mostly in the mood to go home, but Linda convinced me that I really needed to come out with them for a late dinner. I did and by chance, it seemed, I was seated next to the now-single, attractive candidate, and he was great company.

After dinner Linda left and I ended up talking with him until five in the morning. We talked about his divorce, his campaign, his architecture practice, our families back in Chicago, and the time just disappeared. When we realized what time it was we both sheepishly agreed that we had had a terrific time just sharing our lives with one another. We kissed good bye in a tentative manner, and I was not sure if we were starting a friendship or preparing to be lovers. I was particularly worried that he was using me as a therapist and I was mistaking it for a more personal kind of intimacy. But I didn't have to worry about it for long. He called me the next morning, which was a Saturday, and we met for lunch. Again, it was an intense meeting, and this time when we kissed there was no mistaking how attracted we were to one another. So we agreed to get together Sunday night.

When he came over Sunday night, he made it clear that his intentions were serious and if we were to get involved I had to stop seeing everyone else. To my amazement (then, and to this day) I agreed.

Half an Adult Lifetime Together

In short order we dated, had sex, he moved in, and two years later we got married. We were together for twenty-three years. More than half an adult lifetime. Most of our marriage went very well and we created two fabulous children. What eventually went wrong? We grew apart. We had conflicts over how to raise our children that became serious disturbances in the relationship, and he became less engaged with his career. I felt that he changed and became a different person from the man I fell in love with. Of course, I played my part in the demise of our marriage, too. My escalating business travel contributed to our stresses and problems. We had become friends, roommates, and co-parents rather than intimate lovers. Like many marriages, it died over some years, slowly but surely.

My talks with my husband about divorce went surprisingly well. He was certainly aware of our problems. He is a very decent man who cared for me and wanted me to be happy. While there were tense moments, and some tears, we both treated one another with respect during our transition in order to make sure our two children would feel emotionally protected and safe. Both our kids, in the last years of high school, were aware of stresses in the marriage and were not surprised when we announced the divorce.

I was lucky. I didn't have to contend with the nastiness that can greatly complicate the transition from married to single status. I also had a satisfying and secure job that helped make me financially secure, and that was a major advantage. This was no accident. I had observed the economic stranglehold my dad had over my mom and I had promised myself that I would never let that happen to me.

▣ *Advice to Myself (And Others)* ▣

How Sexually Adventurous Do You Want To Be?

Reenter the dating world in your comfort zone, not mine, nor anyone else's. However, reevaluating your sexual philosophy and rules after divorce is a good idea. Some women have not been happy with their sexual life for a long time. It does not feel full or satisfying to them. And if this is the way you feel, maybe you should consider broadening your boundaries a bit. For example, think of these familiar "no's" that might be reconsidered:

- I will not travel out of town to meet someone I don't know well and I wouldn't let someone I had only met briefly, or online, travel a significant distance to see me.
- I would never date someone significantly older or younger than me.
- I have never gone to a club where people dance until dawn and I don't intend to.
- I don't like partners significantly shorter or taller than me.
- I am not going to approach someone who I think is attractive in an airport, or a restaurant, or anywhere on the street. I am not encouraging when an attractive stranger approaches me. I don't consciously act available.
- If I lock eyes with someone, I don't act on it. I walk away or avert my eyes.
- I would never go on a singles cruise or to a vacation spot slotted for people looking for sex or romance.
- I don't ask friends to set me up with someone. If someone offers, I decline.
- If I do go on a vacation to some exotic spot, I will stay close to the comfort zone created by the Western-run hotel and not venture out anywhere alone.

All of the above are common feelings and attitudes. They are perfectly reasonable positions. But they may not be necessary ones. Having an adventure means getting a bit over the edge of your comfort zone and that can vary from taking yourself out to a movie and dinner, to trying a nude beach, to wearing significantly tighter jeans. The result? Excitement, pleasure at your own cheekiness, and the possibility of new opportunities presenting themselves when you exceed known territory. You may need a transfusion of courage to begin with, but the more new things you try, the more confident you will become.

Of course, you don't want to put yourself in harm's way, but how risky is it really to go on a date with a younger person or plan a trip with a few friends to an exuberant, prepackaged resort in some exotic locale? Adventure is a relative word, but the concept—venturing into the unknown and untried—is relevant for everyone. I think adventure wakes you up, lets you know yourself better, tests your mettle, and opens up previously inconceivable possibilities.

Recreational Sex Versus Relationship Sex

Despite all the pious writing about the sacred quality of sex and "women's ways of loving," I think there is a place for a sexual adventure outside of a context of love, commitment, or even dating. This is something most males have enjoyed for millennia. I am not advocating this approach for everyone—but I will tell you this: A lot more people have had "hookups" than talk about them.

Young men and women (say, under twenty-five) are more likely to claim bragging rights for drive-by sex, but there are a lot of older people as well who have had sexual encounters for the sheer joy of body contact. If it makes you feel alienated and unhappy—well, by all means only have sex with someone you love and who loves you. But if you need to be temporarily adored every now and then by Julio or Lance—why not?

Finding Your Own Clitoritti—
and Circle of Friends

Half the fun of having an adventure (sometimes *all* the fun of an adventure) is talking about it with my friends. We certainly used to entertain each other in our twenties—and now we still ask each other for reactions and advice. More seriously, when I fell in love and got rejected, or when I went out on a date and I was interested in the guy and he was not interested in me, there was nothing like telling my feelings to one of my closest friends and getting her support and insight.

I cannot imagine my life without these open, frank, and confidential relationships. For over thirty years, about ten of us have met from once a month to once every six months to share our lives with one another. We have been there for each other through marriages, affairs, divorces, obsessional attachments, children's illnesses, and parents' deaths. I include in this circle of decades-long intimates my friends Debra in Connecticut, Laurie in New York, and Janet in Los Angeles, to name just a few. Friends don't have to live next door to be the bedrock of your life.

New friends also enter my life. More than a few times, I have heard people say they have no time for new friends because they barely have time for their old ones—but I don't get that. New friends bring in new vistas, perspectives, and opportunities. They are just as precious in their own way as the women I have known for a lifetime.

When I meet women who do not have several close girlfriends, I am almost speechless. It's as if a woman is telling me that she has cut off several lines of help, entertainment, perspective, and affection for no good reason. True introverts, I know, just don't have this much self to share, and don't want to expose themselves to too many people. Many people have only so much energy and after their husbands or lovers, children, and/or jobs they are used up, and friends become a residual category. I understand it but I can't imagine it. Friends are as important to me as romantic love—and I would urge you to think about how many good friends you have, and if you nurture and keep those friendships current—and if not, why not?

Birth Control and STD Prevention

Dating at any age still requires a strategic approach to health, and that includes birth control if you are still fertile. Birth control is relatively simple; most women's methods don't interfere with sexual pleasure (although I modify that thought when I think of the diaphragms I have flipped across the room, decorating the walls with gel).

But there are many choices that are not rubber, if birth control is the objective.

Dealing with sexually transmitted diseases is another consideration all together. That does require a condom, which does not exactly turn most partners on. Naturally, when we think something will interfere with our pleasure, we become geniuses at denial, thinking of all kinds of ways to avoid the issue of infection and rationalizing that our own chance of getting a dreaded sexually transmitted disease is minimal. But of course, that is exactly the kind of thinking that starts an epidemic. While AIDS is not the death sentence it once was, it still is an incurable and often lethal disease. So motivations to stay healthy should be enough to make negotiating condom use easy—but studies show that only a minority of uncommitted partners use condoms all the time.

We all know why. We all want to be "swept away" and deal with the consequences later. We want to believe that the person we are with couldn't possibly be sick, even if we don't know anything about their past—or, for that matter, their present.

It's not easy to be 100 percent safe, 100 percent of the time. To be honest, I don't have a perfect record myself. But I am working on it—and you should be, too. It helps to keep condoms on you or in your nightstand and if you "get lucky" just take them out in clear view and indicate that they are on the agenda. If that's not your style, use one of the more playful condoms such as flavored, colored—or my personal favorite, Trojan's Elexa, that comes with a vibrating ring that goes over the penis (but is meant for you). Use a good lubricant (latex-safe, of course) and make protection part of your sexually confident approach to your sexual partner. I try to tell myself: If I can't talk about safety and sex with this person, I shouldn't be doing it with this person. That helps.

four

THE MAN WHO MADE ANIMAL NOISES

Who's Out There?

A First Date

In my twenties, I prioritized strong sexual attraction and excitement when it came to dating. In my fifties, I still wanted chemistry but I also prioritized positive energy, self-confidence, good values, respect for intelligence and character, and the ability to love in more than a superficial way. Would that prove a little hard to find?

I had my first official cyberdate with the charming Mario on a Thursday evening after work. We met at a café for a drink. I had exchanged a number of e-mails with Mario and felt as though I knew a lot about him, much more so than any blind date from the pre-Internet world. Our phone conversation had been short but thoroughly enjoyable. Before I entered the café, I did a mental check of my appearance in a more careful, systematic way than I had in years. Hair streaked, styled, and brushed. Nails polished. Makeup subtle yet strategically applied. Outfit that draped stylishly over body now under construction by trainer. New dating underwear, not to be seen on this date but the mere knowledge of which is confidence-building. I felt nervous and excited. And I did not feel fifty or twenty-five. I actually felt about fifteen, when I first started dating. This was a very odd sensation.

I saw Mario, dressed in a dark grey suit, blue shirt, and tie that complemented his southern Italian good looks, sitting at the bar. I was pleased with the way he looked: groomed, put together, nice looking but not so good looking that he was likely to be conceited. He stood up when he saw me, smiled broadly, and shook my hand warmly, as though we had known each other for years. I loved the presumption of easy familiarity.

It turned out that he knew friends of friends and we enjoyed two and a half hours of easy chatting and playful flirtation. Over the course of lattes he would gently tap the back of my hand at random moments.

The odds of a person meeting the love of their life on a first date are at least ten million to one. But I acknowledged that my first cyberdate was an absolute gem of man—a executive in advertising and a smooth conversationalist—and had what appeared a keen interest in me.

As we parted he shook my hand warmly and said he would like to talk in the next few days. I drove home delighted with this pain-less and positive first meeting. I liked the technology that had made meeting a potential boyfriend so easy and effortless. And I waited for Mario's call.

And waited.

A week passed by. Was he in a auto accident? I knew he would call since he had talked about wanting to see my horses, learning more about how a professor also runs a ranch, and other things that showed he was listening and intrigued. He had even raved about my unique-ness and what a great role model I was and how he wanted his daughter to meet me! I had not invented what seemed to be great admiration and interest. After two weekends I called another Italian-American to get insights on what to do.

"Pepper here," I said to my favorite New Yorker.

"Dom's dating service here," my friend responded. "How goes cyberlove?"

"Well, that's what I want to know," I said. "I met this sexy Italian guy who works for an ad agency and he was absolutely effusive, gush-ing compliments and talking about future plans."

"And the problem is?" Dom asked.

"I think he dumped me," I said. "And it's not the rejection that is really bothering me, although I suppose it plays a part in me feeling angry. But what is really confusing me is why a guy who obviously is not interested in pursuing anything with me would make so many references about getting together and dating."

"Yeah. Those smooth marketing types are the worst," Dom said. "It's all so awkward anyway. But these one-shot-only blind dates would be less confusing if the uninterested party would stop with all the gushing compliments and just politely end a thirty-minute rendezvous with a, 'Take care of yourself. It was nice meeting you.'"

"Right," I said, "and none of this, 'We should plan on horseback riding next weekend' and more unnecessary embellishments like that."

"Well, welcome to singlehood," Dom said warmly. "As you tell all your women readers, not for the risk-averse."

Dom was right. Dating, with or without the Internet, was all about risks and rejection. I was a risk taker, albeit a slightly wiser one than I had been before my first cyberdate. Armed with a little more information and caution, on to coffee date number two I went.

The Date That Eats the Cake

The second contender was Ed, the very earnest, cosmopolitan-looking publisher who matched his online picture perfectly. His e-mails were a delight to read, he liked the same restaurants I did, we were also reading some of the same books, and we shared a passion for the appropriate use of words and metaphors. When we finally moved off the Internet and on to phone conversations, he sounded articulate and witty. Sadly, when we met for drinks at a downtown bistro, he was sporting what was for me a potential sex-stopper: a huge diamond pinky ring.

But could I really veto a guy based on bad, huge, garish jewelry? After all, he was literate, smart, and we laughed a lot at our first meeting. At the end of the date I waited for him to say something about getting together again but he didn't. However, he called the next day and said he'd like to see me again.

He was very awkward about how to proceed and said, "The problem for me is that I've never dated much. I hope you will be a little tolerant if I make a few faux pas. I want you to know ahead of time that I am not trying to be rude. I went to all-boys schools when I was young, got married right out of high school, and now that I am single after all these years, I am just no good at small talk and dating etiquette."

I liked his honesty. I accepted a second date for coffee and a stop by a photography exhibit at a downtown gallery. That went well, too, so when he asked me over to his place for dinner the next Saturday night, I accepted. He wanted to cook dinner for me, which I thought was hospitable and generous. I knew he didn't live too far from me and his house proved to be a very modern stylish place overlooking the lake. He had carefully laid out all the ingredients for all of the courses and was a quite knowledgeable cook. After sharing a bottle of wine I was feeling pretty tipsy and everything about the evening was looking rosy. We started necking and it was immediately clear that he had never learned his ABCs of sensual kissing. His mouth smashed against mine and my mind flashed on the Hippocratic oath and the phrase, "Above all, do no harm."

This guy didn't realize he was in the unintentional harm business. He kissed like he wanted to break my teeth and watch me spit them out. He grabbed body parts as if they were on loan and could be removed at any arbitrary moment. He was just plain uncalibrated. I don't think he knew that it was possible to touch more lightly or vary touch and see how it worked. I thought about offering my sexological tips but decided those should wait until I was sure I wanted to really invest time in this guy. I knew that bad kissers can be taught if the student is willing, but I wasn't sure the instructor was willing. I decided just to get through the evening but just gently whispering "softer" and save a lesson for the next time—if I decided to have a next time.

He did respond to some coaching so we went out again, saw a couple of movies together and had a good time. On our sixth date he offered to make a special Mexican dinner for me. I accepted his invitation but promised myself that I wouldn't drink because I wanted to talk to him about how to be gentler with me. That vow got broken early when I saw he had made a pitcher of margaritas. It didn't take long before we were kissing at the table and that sabotaged my plan for a conversation.

Before I could figure out a way to slip in a few tips, he grabbed me awkwardly and started to almost tear my blouse off in what he must have thought was sexy from some scene in a movie. He didn't know, as any woman would have, that I would have paid a lot of money for that shirt and didn't particularly want to see it shredded. I suddenly thought of a friend of mine who buys special cheap underwear for her husband to tear off just so she doesn't regret its demise.

In any case, I broke away from him before he destroyed my blouse and asked for a moment to unbutton it. He kissed my neck while I struggled with the blouse and made it difficult to get the rest of my clothes off. Before I quite had my top off, he laid me down on the floor on my back somewhat roughly. I was regretting that I had pursued this relationship and beginning to plan escape strategies.

I was thinking, *I'm not sure this guy is sexually educable and this isn't a whole lot of fun.*

That is when things got so bizarre I could only gasp and then laugh at what followed. Just as I was going to pull away, put my shirt back on, and say this wasn't working for me, he grabbed a big piece of chocolate cake left over from dinner and proceeded to smear it all over my chest and lick it off. This was not a good feeling. In fact, it was literally crummy.

I thought to myself, *I can either tell this man that he lacks technique, intuition, and is about as sensual as a wrench or I make up some excuse about having something to do with dealing with a family problem.*

"I am so sorry," I said, firmly pulling away from the man with chocolate sauce dripping from his mouth. "But I just remembered I have to take a late night call from my son who said he would be calling from Denver."

He looked like a hurt puppy and I felt instantly sad that I had had to withdraw from him but I had no choice. I was having "flee feelings" and sex was just not possible for me. My sobering and unconvinc-

ing remarks had made him quite subdued and he quietly sat on the
couch while I quickly wiped chocolate sauce off my chest, dressed, and
said good bye. We both knew that was the last time we would see each
other.

Animal Noises

Two dates. Rejected once. Rejecting once. I'm not sure what I found
more distressing. I went back to the profiles and after a few hours on a
Saturday and Sunday afternoon I had new candidates for dating.

I opened up the geographic area I was willing to consider and
after that I was communicating with a lot of men online who were
not living in my area but willing to fly in for date. There was one
man in particular from Alaska that offered to fly down for a weekend. I was flattered. We had shared many weeks of flirtatious e-mails
and phone calls in which the conversations about nature, horses, and
rural life flowed easily. He was a professional man and a partner in
a large firm. An acquaintance of mine had met him briefly and liked
him. I felt a sense of comfort with him, so much so that I agreed to
spend a weekend of wine tasting with him near Seattle and we booked
a bed and breakfast in the country to stay in. We discussed that this did
not imply we would have sex together and I felt that he would honor
my feelings,

This is when I received a lecture on Internet dating and setting
boundaries by my friend Dom. During one of our long phone calls,
Dom, upon hearing that I was going to be meeting "some stranger
from Alaska" at the airport and drive with him all over Washington
State touring the wine country, made me promise to radically limit my
original plans and just meet Mr. Alaska at a restaurant with no commitments beyond that.

"My dear Pepper," Dom said over the phone, "you have to be prepared for worst-case scenarios when you cyberdate. Even with a perfect picture and profile, and a series of warm phone conversations,
any guy you are meeting for the first time could always turn out to be
a sociopath."

"Really, Dom, aren't you being a bit dramatic?"

"Trust me, Pepper," Dom offered in earnest, "Internet dating in New York City teaches us two very vital things."

"Which are?"

"The Net is like the real world, filled with charming yet insane people. Therefore the first date is always in public and only a mutually agreed-upon thirty-minute commitment."

"But I have done that and while I agree with you in general, these short coffees really don't give people an adequate chance to get to know each other enough to make a decision about each other. Plus, this guy is flying a thousand miles to see me. Don't you think thirty minutes is a bit short for that kind of effort!"

"Trust me, if you experience best-case scenario and a guy turns out to be a winner, you get to extend to dinner and dessert."

I agreed with Dom that his advice was appropriate and when I told Mr. Alaska, my new restrictions, to his credit, he agreed to my new terms. If he or I did not feel the right chemistry our date would end after a meal. He was willing to risk airfare and a weekend to see if we were right for each other.

Mr. Alaska met me in baggage claim at the airport—and he was even more handsome than his picture. Plus, he was bright, talkative, and seductive. We had a quick lunch and it was very pleasant and we decided that we liked each other well enough to drive out to the country, stay overnight, and taste a few wines the next day.

But no sooner were we in the car heading east when I discovered that he had a quirk that had not been expressed during lunch. This guy could not restrain himself from making animal noises anytime a reference was made in the conversation to a dog, horse, or duck. In fact, I didn't even have to mention an animal; he just made those noises for his own enjoyment. Somehow in our previous phone calls I must have missed his sound effects when we discussed horses.

As we drove out in the countryside, he saw a horse in a pasture, so he gave the most credible imitation of neighing I've ever heard. It was like old MacDonald's farm. When we arrived to our destination, it was dinnertime and I was honestly afraid that when our steaks came he was going to "moo" in front of the waitress. This finally killed any ardor his looks and intelligence had created and I could not persuade myself to have sex with him. I liked him, though. And I was very sure he would be a gentleman about honoring my wishes to keep the relationship platonic.

We did share a room that night (it had twin double beds) and indeed, he didn't pressure me to have sex with him. I trusted my instincts about what kind of human being he was, and happily, I was right. But Dom had been right, too. Until one actually meets a person in the flesh and chats a bit, you just don't have enough information to know if a coffee date should be extended to dinner and dessert or more. In this case, the date lasted about twenty hours longer than it should have. He wasn't a bad guy, but he was a weird one.

French Fling

As soon as the Frenchman said my name, first in English then in French, I was weak at the knees. I felt like a scene out of the movie *A Fish Called Wanda,* where the sexually aroused woman played by Jamie Lee Curtis needs her lover to say Italian-sounding words in order to have an orgasm. I know it sounds ridiculous, but there is something about the timbre of a man's voice (and a great accent) that is foreplay to me—and to some other people I know. Likewise, if someone's voice has an unpleasant ring to it, it can interrupt what is a perfectly good attraction. But this guy wasn't all accent. He was smart, successful, and stylish. Born in Paris, he lived in San Francisco and had business in Seattle almost weekly. He was one of the few guys I had gone out with who was older than I was. Normally I found men my age less interesting because so many of them were thinking about retirement or were not passionately engaged with their work or their world anymore. This man was educated, worldly, had an interesting and expanding agricultural business, and loved horses.

We went out a few times and I was thinking maybe this could be someone extraordinary. European men, as clichéd as it sounds, do seem to have more of a purchase on charm than the average American. When we kissed on our third date, it was more than perfunctory. He explored my mouth slowly, gently, and with an implicit promise of good things to come. On our fifth date we went out to eat, afterward to a film, and finally came back to an elegant hotel he had reserved for the evening. It was clear he had planned for this first time of ours to be special. We went up to the suite he had already checked out to make sure it was just right and, charming as always, ordered up a first-rate Champagne.

Why was I not turned on?

I don't know how I knew it, but something wasn't right. I have to say, I thought it was just that we had proceeded so gently that it had taken some of the oomph out of it. So I wasn't listening to my instincts. In the bathroom I changed out of my clothes and into a plush terry cloth robe. I was trying to get into a sensual state of mind.

He kissed me once and then chatting about the quality of the Champagne, sat down on the bed to disrobe. He casually took off his dress shirt and draped it over the chair next to the bed. He had on an undershirt, and peeking out of it was the tail end of some tattoo.

Now, I know some people think tattoos are sexy. I, however, am not one of these people. To say I am not a huge fan of tattoos is something like saying the Pope is not a big fan of Madonna.

Tattoos repel me. They unsettle me in some inexplicable way. Nonetheless, I have worked on the more irrational aspects of my repugnance to the point that one tattoo does not a deal break.

I merely mentioned, "You have quite a tattoo."

"Oh," he said with his charming French accent. "I have lots of them."

And then he took off the t-shirt and I was a startled deer in the headlights. He was covered with tattoos. One huge one that covered the entire bicep of his right arm turned out to be the name of his ex-wife, and another on his left arm was the name of his child. A dragon streaked across his clavicle and some other beast was across his shoulder blade. They just kept appearing.

I was stunned. I felt sexually frozen.

He looked at me and realized all was not well.

"Do the tattoos bother you?"

"I am a bit startled, I have to admit."

I wanted to say, "I am horrified and repulsed and while this may not be rational, I just want to run screaming from this room."

He was sensitive to the situation, and asked me if I wanted to stay the night and just sleep.

I nodded affirmatively.

I said, "Just sleeping. That's a good thing. I really think that's a good idea." This was incredibly awkward but I really could not control my reaction. On the other hand, I felt bad for him, and tried to hide the full extent of my distaste for his body art.

We got into opposite sides of the bed and I think he was hoping that I might feel differently in the morning. Fortunately, he fell asleep almost immediately. I was restless and couldn't sleep at all. I couldn't suppress my strong desire to get away from him. I knew he would not feel good about waking up alone but I just could not stay there and I snuck out in the middle of the night, leaving a note saying how sorry I was but the body art was something that I was not able to process right now. Upon arriving home, I e-mailed my apologies again, saying I was terribly sorry but he had just hit a nerve of mine. I felt bad, but I knew I was in the wrong place with the wrong guy.

The Hugger

This date was an improvement in many ways over the previous dates. In e-mail correspondence I had asked how he felt about men wearing jewelry ("didn't wear any"); how long ago the picture on his online profile was taken ("taken last month") and if he had tattoos ("No, should I consider getting one?"). During our first coffee date he appeared to be at ease, attentive, interesting, and interested. He was shorter than average (but everyone is tall enough for me) a few pounds overweight in a way that didn't bother me at all, and he was very well traveled. We talked a lot about places we had been, places we'd like to go, travel horror stories, travel epiphanies. A lot of fun. Our first date ended with an affectionate hug that bordered on the sexual, where he pressed his torso ever-so-slightly almost but not quite inappropriately close to my pelvic region. He was practiced in hugging. His request to set up date number two the next weekend was enthusiastically agreed to. I was interested.

As I was getting ready to go out and meet the hugger for the second date, I saw that I would be delayed and called his cell phone, the only number he had given me. When the cell phone did not pick up nor offer to let me leave a message, I panicked thinking he would think that I was standing him up. I called directory assistance and found his home number.

However, when I called him at his home I found myself talking to a woman who very much believed she was his wife. When he called me later, he insisted there was a difference of opinion about his marital status but I thought it was a good time not to start a relationship with him. And it seemed a good time to take a break from dating and concentrate on work. I wasn't depressed, just a little tired. Then my luck changed.

⊠ Advice to Myself (And Others) ⊠

The Internet Is Your Friend (Don't Turn Your Nose Up at Cyberdating and Romance)

In addition to helping you keep in touch with friends and family all over the world, search for a job, and find the best deals on everything, the Internet is one of the most efficient and safe ways to find romance. I still find a lot of women who think that cyberdating is somehow inferior to bumping into someone at a grocery store or having a blind date set up by a neighbor. I think that's just ridiculous. You get a lot more information about someone you've just met in cyberspace than you do in most other kinds of one-time contact. Those long lists of must-haves and won't-haves, the psychological profiles, and the essay most sites ask applicants to fill out really do tell you a lot.

And while I have just told a number of stories about dates that didn't work out, I could tell a lot more about dates that didn't work out that began in more conventional ways. Or men who I met off the Net who turned out to be something different than represented.

I'm not trying to make the larger point that "it's a jungle out there." I just want to put it on the record that there are bad guys and good guys in the dating world and that cyberspace may have some, too—but not more than its share.

How to Date: Finding First Dates in Cyberspace

For those of you new to the Net, the general structure of online dating is simple: Fill out a questionnaire about your likes and dislikes, describe yourself, describe what you want, write a short optional essay about who you are and what you are looking for. Perhaps fill out a questionnaire that goes into your personality a little deeper, and post a picture. Then you either spend time looking at profiles of available men and send e-mails noting your interest, or you wait for men to contact you. Or you do some initiating and some waiting.

When posting a profile, it's hard not to think of yourself as part of a gallery of faces, chosen or not chosen on the basis of your looks. A crisp, clear, recent picture showing your face and body type is the safest, most honest way to proceed. But make sure it shows off your best attributes. Likewise, you need to see a clear picture of any guy you are considering meeting. Men in sunglasses, or with blurry pics, or pics that don't indicate their body type should be avoided.

You can decide when to post your picture on your profile. If you choose to wait a bit, then choose a few men whose profiles indicate potential compatibility and offer to send a picture if they are interested. I know that there are a good number of men who can be attracted to someone on the basis of what they write about themselves—even if they need to see a picture of you before they will actually agree to a meeting. Never fear, though, quite a few people use personality as their first criteria for picking someone—and have a wide latitude about what kinds of looks they like.

The Phone "Interview"

If you connect well with someone from the relationship site and the e-mail correspondence feels right, then the next step is a phone call. A person's voice tells you a lot, quickly, and either validates or calls into question their e-mail persona. If the first five minutes are awkward and uninteresting, imagine what the date might be like. This is a good time to trust your instincts. If you sense something is not quite right about the guy, don't commit to a date. You are entitled to want more phone time—or to withdraw entirely. At this stage you don't owe each other anything more than politeness.

One additional important thing to remember—don't give someone you haven't vetted your home phone number. If you are unlucky enough to get involved with someone who is a pest, or who doesn't take no for an answer, you might have to change your cell phone number to get rid of him. That would be a pain—but not as much of a pain as having to change your home phone.

Finally Meeting

If your e-mail correspondence and phone call go well, then it's time to meet. As you may remember from dating in your teens, that first meeting can feel awkward. It's normal to be nervous about meeting a total stranger in the hopes of finding a quality connection. In order to relieve anxiety, a lot of women are tempted to talk about their ex-husband, or their bad dates, or their money problems, or their children. These are all miserable ideas. The whole point of the exercise in dating, like the point of any first interview, is to shine and be memorable.

Of course, this is a two-way interview so the other person has to be able to show who he is and how you work off each other. I always feel that first dates should try to lower the pressure as much as possible—plan for a casual coffee or single glass of wine. It is possible, in fact probable, that some dates will be a very bad fit—and so you want to avoid overcommitting by scheduling too much time together. When it goes badly (it's clear you don't have anything in common, or there is zero chemistry, or the other person is just a jerk), time creaks along very slowly. But a thirty-minute coffee date is something almost anyone can get through in a civilized manner.

After the First Date

The harder situation is when a first date goes well, and the guy doesn't call for a second date. This could be due to a number of reasons: He is not attracted to you even though you thought he was, or he felt you were perfectly nice but not a perfect match for him. Most men who are dating at older ages are looking for a serious relationship and very few of them want to date a string of women—even if they would have liked a harem in their twenties. So a perfectly nice date may not result in a followup if they don't sense that you are exactly what they are looking for. Again, a quick rejection doesn't feel good—but it's the style of dating these days. People take their best guess right away and may make the wrong decision prematurely. But if that's their decision, there's nothing to be done about it.

Trying to convince them to try again rarely works. Move on. If he's not calling, he's not for you.

Dating Traditions and Finances

Internet dating still has some very traditional gender expectations, at least with the over-fifty crowd. Men almost always pay for the first date and while some resent paying all the time, the fact is that most men expect to do the heavy lifting. If a woman offers to split the bill, some men will love that, others will find it unnerving. There are men who would dearly love to split expenses—meeting a lot of people gets expensive when one person is picking up all the costs. But in general, you'd never know there was a revolution over gender roles, at least in our age group. Personally, I like to be treated *and* I like to be generous. I think it sets up the relationship to be more mutually respectful to assume early dates are dutch treat and to be pleasantly surprised when the check is paid for. Who pays for what sets up other expectations and it's important to be aware of what your approach to money says about you.

Those First Dates

Dating is, in some real sense, an interview process, and that means that even though two people are initially attracted, further interviews may reveal that you are not his ideal candidate—or he is not yours. This is how the dating game works, but when you are older, you may feel the pressure of age and try to get a commitment early on in the courtship dance. I sometimes think that many people marry the wrong person precipitously because of one too many times when even after fantastic romantic dinners, soul-searching conversations, future plan making, and glorious lovemaking, a rejection comes out of virtually nowhere and the result is emotional devastation. After an experience like that, the next semireasonable person to come along is often snapped up. And generally that's a bad idea with a sad outcome. Running away from dating into marriage doesn't usually work if the marriage wasn't based on what I call the "critical Cs"—compatibility, communication, and chemistry.

But perhaps the impulse to seal the deal prematurely is resisted because we have been there, done that—and suffered for it. We may have had our fabulously romantic courtship but desperately wrong marriage, or our "great for raising children but not so great for anything else" marriage, or some other relationship that we don't want to replicate. We should try our best to remember that marriage per se is no panacea and dating does not have to be hellish. By this time, we should know that jumping into a commitment before we really know each other well is a short-term fix and will not bring us the kind of peace and happiness that we all truly would like to have.

All that said, as a relationship starts to deepen, each woman has to evaluate what is happening to her emotions as each additional date starts to beg for a definition of what is going on between the two of you. Furthermore, when an expectation for more sexual intimacy enters the picture, each person needs to have an internal dialogue about how sex changes the nature of the relationship.

Pacing . . . and Guarding Zippers

Sexuality in the sensuous years is an interesting departure from the musical beds of my twenties. Sex tends to proceed rather slowly. In the 1970s, a large number of Boomers expected some quick sexual connections. These same people are more cautious today—often from the experience of getting into something too quickly and then having trouble getting out. I have met a lot of bruised men in this round of dating—several men who became fathers because their date told them there was "no chance" of her getting pregnant since she was either infertile or on the Pill. Men who had sexual dalliances that turned into psychodramas. Men who experienced nasty divorces, sometimes two or three of them, and who wanted to keep everything superficial for as long as possible, maybe forever.

It was strange to be in a situation where men were guarding their zippers. I kind of liked it—up to a point. The problem is when too many dates go by and you start to think it's not their caution, it's you. And it could be some of both. But I do think a long life of experience has made both men and women cautious—and less sex has reduced sexual expectations. This gives time to get to know each other—and for brains, rather than bodies, to be the lingua franca of mature dating. There is a chance to fall in love with the companionability and erotic intrigue of an evolving relationship instead of being lost in the steaminess of it all. That slower windup, I think, has a lot to say for it. Because once the more serious levels of sex get expedited, that is going to dominate the early parts of a relationship.

Finally Getting Sexual

Everyone, of course, has to find their own pace and evolve in their own way. Still, I do think it is important to eventually get sexual. And I don't think it has to only be in the context of a committed relationship—although if that's your style, that's the way you should proceed. But if years go by without a sexual partner, I'd rethink your guidelines. I am of the opinion that the more sex you get, the more you want. If sex becomes infrequent among older singles, sexual drive reduces as well. For many people, that's a relief. I have heard large numbers of both men and women say they were relieved to be less controlled by their own hormones than they used to be. Granted, an absence of aching need may take some of the pressure off, but it can also reduce the chances of euphoria and bliss.

For the sake of argument, let's say you agree with me, but after a long time of delaying sex in a relationship, it's not clear when to start it. That's why I think sex shouldn't wait forever to begin. I dated one man, a perfectly suitable guy, who was an engineer at an aircraft firm. We had a wonderful time going out to movies and dinner and we were highly companionable. We would kiss, and then since we lived on opposite ends of the county, go back to our respective parts of town. Somehow we established a routine of dinner, movies, kissing—and that was it. It was almost impossible, after a while, to think of a next step. It was almost as if we had missed a launch window. Having sex began to feel inappropriate.

But I wouldn't want to worry you into missing the kissing part and proceeding lockstep directly into intercourse. It's just that there seems to be an arc—when if you are ever going to do it, you do—and if you don't, you stay movie buddies. And that is what happened between my very nice engineer and me. In another phase of my life we would have been in my bed early and often but the two of us evolved into pals. But I suppose that's not the worst of outcomes. We both like horses and chick flicks. Friendships have been founded on a lot less.

Dating: Tips When Things Don't Work Out

WHEN YOU HAVE TO REJECT

I urge you not to jump to conclusions, Give men a chance rather than rapid evaluations and instant rejections. That said, there will be those days that you will meet a man and within the first thirty seconds you know you never wish to see again. The next twenty-nine minutes and thirty seconds of your first date will go by slowly. At the end of this coffee date, if he asks you out again you have some options:

a. You are extremely brave and you just face him and say something like, "You are a really sweet

    (wonderful, bright, interesting, attractive) man
    but we are not matched for the long run."

b. Or, the same sort of thing on e-mail. This requires—let's
    call it what it is—an itty-bitty lie. If someone has asked to
    see you again right at the end of the first coffee you may
    not have the guts—or the heart—to tell him that it isn't
    going to happen. Sometimes the kinder strategy is to say
    something ambiguous ("let's talk about it later"), which gives
    you the time to compose an e-mail that ends it in a very
    complimentary way. If you get really good at these letters you
    can make someone feel really special by gushing about their
    positive qualities while not re-upping for another date.

WHEN YOU HAVE A GUY WHO WON'T TAKE NO FOR AN ANSWER

Okay, there are jerks, drunks, and various socially maladept types whose arrogance is only exceeded by their narcissism. I swear to you that they are the exception rather than the rule, but every once in a while that exception turns up on one's doorstep. It's not impossible to deal with—it's just unpleasant. The majority of men try hard to please, be charming, and back off if that's what you want. When you meet a real lemon it's kind of a shock, since that kind of person is rare. If you are unlucky enough to meet one of these misfits right off the bat, don't despair.

    Just get over it and rest assured that it will definitely get better as you meet more people. If he becomes obnoxious and calls incessantly or, uninvited, shows up at your home or business, you should tell him to stop or you will call the police. That usually gets rid of most men who don't know how to deal with rejection. It is also a service to other women to report these guys to the dating service you found them on because every reputable site will toss them off the site and not let them back on.

WHEN THE GUY MISREPRESENTS HIMSELF

Sometimes people misrepresent themselves. There is not much you can do if you meet someone who is so different from his picture that you can hardly believe he had the chutzpah to show up. Everyone can look a bit different. That is more or less the nature of pictures. But I remember the guy who was at least 100 pounds heavier and twenty years older than his picture. I think that people who totally misrepresent themselves should not be surprised if someone excuses themselves upon first contact. But I wouldn't have the heart to do that, and I don't think most people would. Sometimes the misrepresenting person is somewhere between clueless and delusional and getting upset with them would just be cruel. Fortunately, most men and women are pretty similar to their pictures. Maybe a little heavier or older, but not much.

WHEN THE GUY IS A "SALESMAN"

One unpleasant type of guy in the dating world is the one I call "The Salesman." The Salesman is always selling himself, even if he intends to renege at the last minute. Both men and women can do this bizarre dance. They flirt, charm, set a date—and never intend to fulfill any of it. What I find upsetting is being "set up"—by that I mean treated by an interesting, attentive man as if you are going to be going out again—and then not given a call.

These are the kinds of meetings I don't understand but I think some men just use their charm to get them through the interaction with you and don't know how to calibrate it so that you won't be seriously misled. The result is a sales job that creates a customer when the seller isn't really selling. It's not fun—but it doesn't have to be tragic. I just go back to Don Miguel Ruiz's *Four Agreements: A Practical Guide to Personal Freedom*, one of which is "It's not about you." And it isn't. It's about his style, his tastes, and his needs. This does not reflect on who you are—only who you are in his eyes. If you can remember this as a few missed signals, or inappropriate background or personality types, a lack of interest isn't so beastly.

WHEN THE GUY IS MARRIED

One of the myths about the Internet is that there are these zillions of guys pretending to be single when they really have a wife and six children at home. During the time I have spent looking for love on and off the Net, the incident with a married man that I wrote about in this chapter was the only time in my dating life that someone turned out to be covertly married. Unlike most men who are discretely trying to get a little on the side, this man actually had his picture on his Internet profile for everyone to see. Talk about cheeky!

Generally, a man who is married will not put his picture up on the Web for obvious reasons. The exception might be men (and women) who go to special Web sites for "cheaters." Yes, there is the equivalent of adultery.com where you can efficiently link up with other people who have either "open marriages" or are just plain old running around behind their partner's back. It should be noted that those in open relationships, where the situation is mutually agreed upon, resolutely insist they are not "cheating." For those of you unfamiliar with the sexual buffet on the Internet, the existence of these sites exclusively devoted to adulterers and the people who seek them might shock you. But there really is every type of sexual community on the Web you can think of—and some that are beyond your wildest thoughts as well.

Given those outlets, it's all the stranger when someone goes on a regular dating site and pretends to be single when they are not. I have heard of no incidents about women lying about their marital status— so my guess is that even though it happens, it's much rarer.

I think it's rare for men as well—since a discovery of their marital status on a legitimate relationship site would get them thrown off. But it does happen and it means that women who don't want to be lied to (that would be 99 percent of women) need to take some precautions when they start seeing someone more often and still don't have a lot of information about them. I would say an honest man:

a. will generally (although not always) have a
    home phone as well as a cell phone.
b. can be called very early and very late—and not mind it at all.
c. will introduce you to his children or friends or favorite
    haunts eventually (after a few months of dates and
    professed interest in a long-term relationship).
d. will be affectionate in public places.
e. will be able to see you on Friday nights or Saturday
    nights and will not only see you early in the evening.

If any of these aren't true, I would do a little detective work to
make sure he is who he says he is. Until one has met a few of a date's
friends in social situations and seen his home, you don't really have
all the information you need to really match this man's words with his
life.

five

THE LOVER

Intensity and Passion

The Invitation

It was less than six months after my husband and I had separated. I was, once again, staying late in my university office to prepare for a lecture on sexual desire.

When the phone rang I predicted it would be that writer from a men's magazine trying to push the envelope ("Could you help us create a tracing paper to show where the clitoral nerves are on our oral sex chart?") or one of the prissier women's magazines that couldn't be "tasteful" enough and who wanted to ask, "Could you write about oral sex but never use the words 'oral' or 'sex'?"

The person on the other end of the line, however, introduced herself as Thalia and was organizing a conference for international businesspeople to be held in Bali. She was eager to invite me to present at the conference.

Thalia said, "We were thinking about a talk based on your book, *The Great Sex Weekend*." Then she paused, and in a more serious voice said, "toned down, of course." Before I hung up, I assured Thalia that I would go over content with her and make sure it coincided with her comfort level while I mentally lit a candle to the patron saint of people who travel on other people's money.

As an afterthought, I felt a temporary letdown. I'm going to be in one of the world's most romantic places—alone. The trip was ten months away. That was plenty of time to find a date.

Meanwhile, in Another Part of Town

My ex-husband was having an entirely different experience than I was having on the dating market. As soon as he was reconciled to the fact that we weren't going to stay together, he had gone on a whirlwind search for my replacement. He was living with someone else within three months of our separation. This kind of blew me away since I had delayed leaving our marriage in part because I was convinced he would suffer greatly if I was gone. That thought turned out to be hysterical. He was infatuated almost immediately and would have settled in permanently, except that his first amour nixed that idea right before he was about to move in. Appropriately upset, but undaunted, he was back on the Internet within weeks, and found another woman to love in a few more months.

Within four months (and a few days after our decree became final) he was married to her! I felt a whole lot less irreplaceable very quickly. But I was relieved that I didn't have to worry about him being alone. I had, at least in my own mind, taken care of him for a long time and it was hard for me to stop. I did and do love my ex as a member of my extended family and I didn't want him to get hurt—happily, it turned out he had good instincts and while his courtship of his new wife went at hyperspeed, it turned out he made a great choice. She is a lovely, intelligent, big-hearted woman and they make a happy, contented couple.

I was truly happy for him. I, on the other hand, seemed to be too busy, or too picky, or too something—and wondered if some day I was going to settle for making a commitment with a man who made animal sounds all the time.

Another Work Trip Arises

In this less than sanguine mood, I agreed to join a close girlfriend for a week in the sun. Dee Dee had found a fantastic deal: an all-inclusive week at a resort in the Bahamas, with airfare from New York, for almost nothing. We agreed we would play during the mornings, and work on a book project in the afternoons. Hell of a deal.

I flew to JFK and met Dee Dee at the airport. We were both excited about getting time together and getting some work done in the sun. It seemed, however, that that wasn't going to happen on schedule. We got to the gate of our chartered flight to find out it was delayed because of a heavy fog bank. Nothing was getting in or out. We were told that we were on indefinite hold. Other hapless people booked on the charter were milling around, all of us waiting for more information.

Finally, as the hours ticked by, we were given chits that could be redeemed in one of the restaurants. We trudged over to get something to eat and a group of three male friends walked over there with us. Two were balding guys—one looked like Mr. Clean, the second looked like a Talmudic scholar—and the third was an All-American type, a clean-cut guy with cropped light brown hair, dressed in a jogging suit. I imagined him to be ex, or present, military. He was definitely very cute. He had a compact athletic body, cool blue eyes, and an open, engaging smile.

As the five of us trudged to the restaurant, the cute guy in the jogging suit looked directly at me for longer than is considered polite.

It was about three seconds beyond the social norm. This behavior was extremely unexpected and extremely welcome. He started to chat me up about something with the confidence of a man who knows he's good with women. His attentiveness was amusing to begin with, and then it started to get sexy. He introduced himself as Dennis and his friends as Ryan and Steve. He stuck by my side, helping me with my unwieldy and heavy carry-on bag.

I took a second, more searching look at him, then turned to find Dee Dee looking at me with a grin. She knew my penchant for sexual adventure. I shrugged my shoulders sheepishly and let my helpful fellow traveler carry my bag. I was flattered at what I hoped was a come-on, but I wasn't sure if he was just being very nice—or just bored and looking for someone new to talk to. I thought I would stick around to get more clues.

Laying Over With Dennis

The fog was not moving and neither was our plane, so we settled into the airport restaurant. Dee Dee and I chatted with each other and the trio. There was too much empty time not to have a few drinks before dinner. As I sipped my second glass of wine, I started feeling pretty expansive. I was looking Dennis over much more carefully as the evening progressed. I liked the way his bright blue eyes twinkled mischievously when he smiled. His voice had a slight Midwest twang, and he moved fluidly, like someone who has played a lot of tennis. There was a youthful, boyish energy, a kind of puppy-like playfulness that I found quite adorable. He laughed a lot and he made me laugh with him.

Through a dinner of bad airport food, Dennis continued to focus on me. I found myself returning his attention. Dennis was amazed when I told him the purpose of my trip with Dee Dee.

"You are coming to this resort to work?" he asked, incredulously. It did sound like a lame situation when he put it that way.

His Age/My Age

My guess was that Dennis was a good fifteen to twenty years my junior. That made me think that I wouldn't hold his interest very long when the bikini crowd in their twenties and thirties came on to him. I wasn't being modest, just making a realistic appraisal of his priorities.

I watched Dennis watching me but I was not listening to his playful ranting. It was as though I had turned on a global mute button while I did mathematical calculations.

What am I doing flirting with a man twenty years my junior? I said to myself. What the hell, I was having a lot of fun and this was all just innocent flirtation. I hadn't been with a guy this much younger, but on the other hand, when I was in my thirties I had several adventures with men a lot older than I was. What's so wrong with being the older person in the equation? I figured that just the verbal foreplay would be fun enough to invest some time in this guy.

He was very open and talkative and he told me some in-depth details about his life, including the fact that he was in the midst of getting a divorce, had two kids, and was anxious to be out of his marriage. He had Scandinavian roots—a group I generally expected to be somewhat low-key and spare with words. But not Dennis. He was Mr. High Energy and I appreciated his helping us all pass the time as we waited.

Dennis Comes On Strong

As the wait for takeoff continued in the waiting area, Dee Dee occupied herself with a good novel while Dennis stepped up his efforts to engage me in sexual banter.

"So," he said. "You are a sociologist and you study what?"

Hmmm. Why not see where this takes us.

"I study relationships, sexuality, male and female roles, things like that."

"Sexuality?" he said, slowly rolling the word over his tongue like something especially tasty. "You're kidding me, right?"

"No, I am not. And you should take that as a compliment. Because if I don't want someone to be interested in me, I tell them I'm a dental hygienist with a specialty in plaque."

"Sexuality," he repeated, holding on to the word like a dog tugging at the other end of a towel. "Where do you get your information from?"

"From research. And of course, vast experience." I was challenging him to be intimidated. Wrong guy for that tactic.

"I'd like to hear about all that experience," he said grinning. "So tell me, with all that experience what have you learned about what you like best?" I went into some long rap about sunsets, and dogs and horses, and good books.

He then looked at me seductively and said softly, "No, tell me what really pleases you."

I blushed. He had out-gunned me on the sexual gutsiness scale.

"Okay," Dennis continued, "which movie stars do you find sexy?"

"That would be Dennis Quaid, John Cusak, Ralph Fiennes, Johnny Depp—especially as a pirate, Daniel Day Lewis—especially as a Native American, and Edward Norton." Dennis teased me about my unrequited love for these stars and why it was unhealthy to sublimate all my needs for love and sex in someone unattainable.

"I, for example," he continued with a laugh, "have great looks, know how to please, and am highly available for the right woman."

Then he went a large step further, he leaned over, gently touching my shoulder and said, "Why don't you pretend that I'm the guy in that movie you like so much and see how I'd react to you."

I was starting to breath a little harder. This was sexy and I wanted to play. So Dennis played Dennis Quaid in *The Big Easy* and I flirted with him in his new role. It was all spontaneous and great fun. In any case, this broke the "are we interested in each other" barrier and our conversation changed from aimless flirtation to much more intense sexual signals.

In about two hours we went from whether or not we were going to get physical to how soon we were going to get physical. This suited me fine. At some point, he put his face close to mine and softly said, "I want to spend tonight with you." Then he proceeded to be explicit about what he would do with me during our time together. The menu was elaborate, creative, and hot. I was ready to order up whatever he was serving.

I did not feel threatened in the least. Quite the opposite. I had given Dennis permission to be bold. I wanted to see if he could deliver what he promised. I wasn't worried about whether or not he respected me. I was more worried that he would be all talk and no action.

Changing Seats

The plane, after a six-hour delay, finally got permission to take off. After Dee Dee and I got seated, Dennis and his friends walked by my seat and Dennis whispered that he'd like me to sit with him. I looked at Dee Dee for permission to sit with him for a while. She rolled her eyes then laughed.

"I'm the married lady with the thick novel so you go forth and enjoy. But I want you back before landing."

"I promise."

The plane was not full and Dennis was the only person in his row. Apparently Dennis had kicked his buddies into the plane's hinterlands. As soon as we sat next to each other there was even more chemistry. I told him about my marriages, family, and more details about my work. We were trying to get to know one another—and the additional information added intimacy to an already hot connection.

As the plane hit 30,000 feet, Dennis leaned toward me and said, "There is nothing more wonderful than going down on a woman and I can't believe that some men don't like it."

I smiled and whispered, "If that turns out to be a lie, I will kill you, Dennis."

He laughed. As we talked, we would touch one another very gently, on the hand and the shoulder. At some point, somewhere over the Atlantic, we were holding hands. It felt old-fashioned after what we had been talking about and rather reassured me that he could be affectionate as well as sexual.

Spinning Tales

Dennis offered a foreshadowing of the enormous sexual imagination he owned. He started spinning a fantasy of what he would like to do with me once we were truly alone. In the hands of a lesser man, it would be slimy and inappropriate. But we are talking about a master storyteller here and I had given him permission. I was fully culpable. I encouraged him to tell me more because my whole body was percolating. I could feel my heart beat faster and there was that familiar erotic tension in my pelvic region. There was just a heat force developing between us, right there on the plane, and I believe we were sweating.

For about twenty minutes he spun a fantasy and I was with him in a jungle, completely naked. We were lying on the beach in the sun, putting scented oils all over each other's body, taking time with every bit of skin—ear lobes, the back of the neck, the crook of the elbow, the small of the back—all were attended to, slowly and carefully. A breeze blew over us and birds sung in the sky. We were under a tree and the light was dappled and he began kissing me very slowly at the throat, working his way down my body very carefully, very attentively. Nothing was neglected and when his story reached the point of having touched and kissed every part of my body, he added a list of things he would do next. It was quite a list.

The plane was getting ready to land and I needed to go back and sit with Dee Dee who always got nervous on landings. Dennis and I had arranged to meet after we checked in. This was an ambitious plan since we were arriving at 2:00 am in the morning and there was a thirty-minute bus drive from the airport to the resort, after baggage collection and customs. Once we finally got on the bus, Dennis sat next to his friends and I sat next to Dee Dee and told her that he and I were going to get together in what was left of the night. She couldn't believe I wanted sex more than sleep.

The Rendezvous

When we arrived at the resort there were all kinds of young men and women bubbling around. It was 3:00 am and I was a bit incredulous that all these people were up and enthusiastic. Dancing music was still blaring.

The air was warm and the palm trees rustling. Our room was barely big enough for the two single beds and they were plain rather than charming. It took us another twenty minutes or so to get situated and unpack and by that time it was after 3:30 am.

Dee Dee was reading my mind and so she said, "Okay, so when does Romeo arrive? Do you think he just fell asleep?"

"He'll show up."

Dee Dee laughed. "I admire your optimism and sexual appetite."

"Am I being crazy?"

Looking at the clock, she said the obvious: "Well, it is incredibly late and I can't believe that you have enough energy to do anything but sleep at this hour."

In fact, as the time wore on, it didn't look like I'd get the chance to test my mettle, since it was now almost a quarter to four and Dennis had not shown up as prearranged. *Uh oh*, I thought, *one of these big talkers*. Reluctantly, I started to change into sleeping boxers and a t-shirt, my bedtime uniform. Just about the time I pulled back the sheets, there was a knock at the door.

Dennis, true to his word—although a little late—was at the door. Looking quite adorable, he smiled hospitably at Dee Dee, who was just amazed at our stamina, and he waited outside while I threw on some pants. When I got outside the door, we smiled broadly and actually started giggling. I mean, what a way to start a week in the tropics! Holding hands, we walked down a beautiful pathway in the balmy early morning. The sun wasn't yet up, and it wasn't far away, but we were on our own time schedule. He took me to his room, which was a good ten-minute walk away, and happily, I realized that his roommates had been exiled to some unknown place.

I remembered that most men have an unwritten rule that if any of them have a chance of scoring, everyone has to do whatever it takes to enable that event.

Alone at Last

So there I was in the early hours of the morning with a guy I didn't know six hours before, feeling totally comfortable and sexually aroused. This is perhaps not the safest thing to do in the world but Dennis had passed my stringent criteria.

1. He was not a loner. He was with other friends I had met, who in conversation seemed to back up the stories I had heard.
2. We were at the same hotel and so he was not anonymous.
3. I had his business card.
4. Dee Dee knew where I was.
5. The room had thin walls and even though it was late, people were still within earshot.
6. And finally, this guy just seemed genuine, sweet, and grounded. What can I tell you? I weighed the risks—and this was one of them. Women who want an adventurous life have to take some risks, and usually intuitive skills serve them well. This one seemed likely to be okay.

From the moment we got inside the door, I knew this was going to be a special experience. He kissed me slowly and gently for a long, long time. I was ready to get into bed with him, but then he suggested we take a shower together. Yum.

We undressed each other slowly. Piece by piece, maintaining eye contact. Then we got into the small shower with the warm water running. I turned to him to start soaping him up but he would have none of that.

He said, "Let me take care of you."

"Oooh-kay."

He soaped up a washcloth and then using the cloth and his hand, he lathered up every part of my body. Slowly. He was gentle across my breasts and between my legs but did not linger there. Instead, he paid particular attention to my head and hair and dug his fingers into my scalp in the most sensual and erotic way. I actually buckled at the knees. He rinsed my hair off slowly, languidly, and I relaxed under his care. My body was still a writhing mass of foam when he began to rinse me off. He turned the water to a hotter temperature and soaked the washcloth in it. With long strokes, he wiped off my body. He then turned off the water, and wrapped a towel around me. Slowly, deliberately he patted my body dry, first the front, then on the back. He picked me up and carried me to the bed. I was seconds from an orgasm and we hadn't even begun conventional foreplay.

I wanted him so badly I couldn't see straight. Dennis had condoms on the bedside table. He put one on, but did not enter me right away though I was literally begging for it. Sometimes it's nice not to get what you ask for—at least not right away. He kissed me gently, nibbled at my lips, kissed my ears and neck and worked his way down to my body and kept going south. This further endeared him to me. Unhurried and enthusiastic oral sex followed.

I was totally unprepared, however, for what happened next. It was amazing. Unprecedented. Unbelievably fabulous. When he entered me, he continued the fantasy we had begun on the plane: He had me in another reality. As he moved inside of me we talked to each other, maintained eye contact, and it felt intimate as well as exciting. He kept asking me how I liked each angle, each depth, each slight calibration of speed. I told him what felt good until the pleasure became so intense I really didn't care what he was doing as long as he didn't stop.

When I got to the brink of climax, he held my face and we kept our eyes open looking at each other. I felt like we were entering each other's body and soul. I had a powerful orgasm—and so did he. Afterward he grabbed me tightly and intertwined his body with mine. He said something about how wonderful it was—and fell dead asleep.

Making a Deal

I awoke with the sun streaming in the window. I was disoriented, not sure where I was, what time it was, and how Dennis and I would relate after such a passionate and impulsive evening. After all, intimate exchanges aside, we were strangers. I am enough of a sexual adventurer to enjoy the risky, devil-may-care, act-on-your-impulses feelings that got me into this bed, but I am also someone who wants to talk about the experience we'd shared and find out what this evening meant for the rest of our days here in the Caribbean—if it meant anything at all.

Dennis woke up, properly affectionate and we snuggled in each other's arms for a while. He held me to him very tightly.

After a while, I extracted myself from Dennis's embrace and

asked the question that most guys usually don't warm to: "Can we talk about this?"

To his credit, Dennis didn't physically blanch. I wasn't asking if he loved me or anything ridiculous like that, but I did want to have an idea of how we were going to relate to each over the next week—or, indeed, if we were going to relate at all. I made no presumptions.

I said, "It was terrific. And for my part, I want more."

Fortunately, Dennis was open to talking about what had happened and was articulate and honest about who he was and what he was comfortable with. He said this was his first outing as an about-to-be-single man. He was there to have fun, was just out of a long marriage, and he didn't want a girlfriend. But he did want to see me again. I gave him a pretty similar song and dance—knowing however, that sex like this was one in a million and that I was more attracted to him than I would let on. I sensed that Dennis was thinking what I was thinking: *You are great. We are going to enjoy this. But it is, after all, a tropical fling.*

Dennis asked, "Can we agree to spend our days with whomever we wish but enjoy our nights together? I won't go further than flirting with anyone else."

"That sounds fair."

I already thought he was a unique lover, but I was willing to be realistic about the fleeting nature of tropical romances. I was just glad that he was saying that we would be each other's bed partners every night.

The Day Progresses

I went back to Dee Dee's in time for breakfast, strangely invigorated given the fact that I'd barely had any sleep, and she asked me for all the glorious details. We walked and talked on the way to breakfast and at that time I realized that we were on one of the most beautiful pieces of land I have ever been on—a stretch of beach with trees that jutted out into the water, that was postcard perfect in just about any direction. Breakfast was bountiful—a huge buffet with fresh fruits, good bakery items, hot eggs, and pancakes. We exercised after breakfast and then went back to our room and worked steadily on the proposal through lunch. Things were working out just fine.

The tough part came when I saw Dennis during the day. I realized how the terms of our agreement actually felt to me. It was fine when I had seen him playing basketball with his buddies after breakfast. We waved happily to each other. During lunch, when I saw him walking down a pathway with a lovely young woman—maybe twenty-one at most—waving was definitely not in order.

I watched the young woman looking at Dennis as if he were a god. I can see why she liked this attractive and attentive man. I was surprised by my feelings of insecurity.

If I am already experiencing feelings of possessiveness on day one of my vacation, this will be one hell of a long week.

I had no right to be jealous. We barely knew each other. I felt a little bit like I was back in high school seeing my crush walk through the hall talking to some pretty girl and being really upset by it. There I was—in my fifties—feeling like a fifteen year old again.

The day seemed to go on forever. At one point in the late afternoon, when I took a writing break and went to the pool with Dee Dee just to soak in some rays for a bit, there Dennis was, in the pool, talking intently with a startlingly beautiful young woman while he was holding onto her rubber raft. I was jealous, pure and simple. And slightly embarrassed by my own feelings. I felt woefully uncompetitive in both body and beauty and while I knew this kind of competitive reaction was totally bananas—there it was. I literally bopped my head with my book to try to see if there was any sense left in it. I had just spent a fabulous evening with this guy and there I was, lurking in the background, watching him put the moves on someone half my age.

It felt so . . . well . . . undignified.

Yet I didn't want to flee the pool as if that were his territory and I had no right to be there. I decided to lighten up.

For God's sakes, Pepper, get a grip! I said to myself.

I had just had one evening with him, who cares what he does? I picked up my book and buried myself in it. Some shadow passed over my head. I looked up to see what was blocking my light and there he was, eyes mischievous, a seductive smile on his face.

"I'm just having fun talking to her," Dennis said, rather easily reading my mind. "I'm looking forward to seeing you again tonight after dinner. I've missed you."

"I've missed you, too," I said, feeling a sense of relief. I also admitted it was a little awkward watching him with other women.

He understood but said, "We had agreed that we would both spend our days with whomever we wish as long as it didn't go further than playful flirtation."

Well, that was the deal and it was a fair one, if he was telling me the truth. But, I had my doubts.

He smiled at me and said, "It was a special night we shared and I'm glad that we're going to be together again tonight."

Later at cocktails before dinner, I sat next to an older woman saying to another woman how adorable Dennis was and how he was just what she would like for her daughter!

I felt angry. I just didn't like this feeling of knowing I would be with Dennis at night but couldn't be with him during the day. The more I thought I about this, the angrier I got. I couldn't help but feel that even though I had agreed to be uninvolved with him during the day, it bothered me every time I thought about it, every time I caught a glimpse of him with someone else.

As if on cue, Dennis showed up at the dinner table around dessert time and whispered in my ear that he was free and wanted to be alone with me.

Rethinking "The Deal"

I eagerly excused myself from the table but I was seething inside. I kept quiet on the way to his room and he noticed that I wasn't as vivacious as I had been the night before. When we got back to his room he asked me what was wrong.

I startled myself by saying, "This won't work."

He looked genuinely surprised. "What won't work?"

"You having sex with other women and still having sex with me."

He looked at me quizzically. "What in the world makes you think I'm having sex with other women?"

I mentioned seeing him with young women of starlet quality, taking one on jet skis, whispering in another's ear.

I said, "In all sincerity, you are entitled, of course. I hardly know you. It's reasonable for you to have sex with whomever you wish but it just doesn't feel good to be part of a stable and so I want to bow out."

He smiled and embraced me. "How about a new deal? I am here to flirt, play, and enjoy myself. But I do want to be with you. What if you agree to allow me to be playful and flirtatious during the day—and you have my word that I really am not going to be doing more than that. After all, you aren't available. You are working with Dee Dee all day long. And give me some credit—these women are half my age. I might want to hang with them, but I am not so stupid as to get involved with them. You are the one I want to be with. At night, after dinner with our travel companions, it's just you. I promise not to touch anyone else."

I listened and I felt there was honesty and candor in his voice. He didn't have to offer me any deal at all. He convinced me that I would be all he wanted and needed for the week, and I believed that. For barely two days of knowing each other, it seemed we had traversed a lot of emotional territory. We had a connection. We had a deal. That was enough.

So we got into bed again and master storyteller Dennis created a wonderful fantasy world, each lovemaking session a new fantasy, a new persona, a few new tricks. He made love with me pretending to be one of many men enjoying my body, he and I were on an island, in a tree house, wearing no clothes, just going "natural"—or he was a man I had seen in a store and in the fantasy we start making love in one of the dressing rooms.

Each act of lovemaking had an erotic fantasy where we both played roles. I enjoyed the adventures. In fact I enjoyed it so much, I was in danger of becoming addicted to this sexually gifted guy. He was simply the most imaginative and creative lover I had ever had.

Put that together with a lot of chemistry and similarity in our sexual tastes and personalities and it was exciting sex that kept getting better and better.

One Unique Guy

He really was one of the wonders of the world. Dennis was the only man I have known, since my postcollege trip to India, who was truly multiorgasmic. He could ejaculate several times without any recovery period. A national treasure. Many women can pull this off physiologically because our nerve endings stay under pressure from the blood rushing to our pelvic area even after we've had an orgasm. Our bodies are built for multiple orgasms. Male equipment just doesn't work this way. Blood whooshes in, blood whooshes out. Even young men usually need about twenty minutes to get ready again.

After making love quite a bit, we lay back and started talking, exchanging more information. At one point, he told me he had just celebrated his forty-fifth birthday and he asked if we were about the same age.

Thank God he is not thirty. A twenty-two-year difference would have been just too much to contemplate.

I told him that I was almost eleven years his senior, and he literally fell out of bed.

"You look ten years younger, at least!" he sputtered from the floor.

"I know," I said. "Does my real age make a difference?"

"No. Not at all. You just surprised me."

At first I thought it was just gallantry but since he proceeded to ravish my body with convincing fervor, I chose to believe him.

On the Dance Floor

The next day the same regimen took place. I worked with Dee Dee on our proposal and on breaks I saw that Dennis was everywhere. Mr. Sociability charming young women, their mothers, the attractive staff, as well as creating new buddies to play basketball with—I couldn't quite believe that I was going to remain his favorite choice. I don't know why I cared so much—normally, I would stay as far as I could away from a guy who wanted or needed that much flirtation with women. But I chalked it up to his having been in an unhappy marriage for so long, and for a vulnerability I recognized in myself: a rather adolescent need to be liked and admired.

That night, after a lovely dinner with Dee Dee, I waited in the dining room for Dennis to show up as we had agreed. But he only showed up briefly, saying that his brother was coming down for a few days and he was going to meet him at the airport and take him to the entertainment they were having that night at the resort. He said he'd find me later. I vaguely remembered Dennis talking about his brother joining him at the resort, back in the airport during our fogbound stay. I was curious to meet him.

At some point in the evening, I decided to join the festivities in the disco. A tall, trim, ebony-skinned, forty-something man asked me to dance. As we danced, chatted, and drank, I found out his name was Michel. He was French, had come here from Paris, and had a heavy schedule as a physician in a hospital setting. He had beautiful smooth skin, and looked quite distinguished. I was slightly drunk and feeling uninhibited, and I danced provocatively. We would stop dancing every so often and chat but while my French was serviceable, it wasn't good enough to communicate or understand finer nuances of feeling. I wasn't sure if I sounded like an idiot to him or not. But I was enjoying myself enormously. I forgot about my jealous, suspicious self and started to reconnect with my free spirit.

Then Dennis finally showed up and interceded assertively. I had just come off the dance floor with Michel. I felt someone at my arm and there was Dennis, who simply pulled me away. I hurriedly apologized to the nonplussed Michel. Then Dennis marched me rather quickly away from the disco. I was wondering what was going on here.

Dennis stopped in the middle of the path and kissed me quite passionately. He apologized for not finding me sooner. It was the first inkling I had that perhaps I wasn't the only one who had more than incidental attachment. We walked rather quickly back to his bedroom for a long night of lovemaking.

Nothing Is Simple

The fourth night there was an incident. My home business, running a breeding and boarding stable for horses, needed my critical attention. There had been an incident at the barn between a member of the staff and a boarder and I needed to be an intermediary.

A close friend of mine, Julie, was trying to help calm everyone's rising tempers and she had called me in a momentary meltdown when all parties insisted on being unreasonable. Instead of being able to meet Dennis after dinner as planned, I had to use a phone near the lobby office (since there were no phones in the room) and I ended up talking to Julie for hours trying to be supportive and help her fix things—or as much help as I could be from so far away.

I didn't notice the time go by, but when I did I realized it was really late. When I finally got off the phone, I stopped into the disco looking for Dennis but he wasn't there. Exhausted, I went back to my room, not his. Dee Dee was there and said that Dennis had been there looking for me and seemed upset. I was tired, but I turned around and went back to the disco to see if he was there. He wasn't and I was just about ready to give up when I ran into him on the pathway. He looked very agitated.

"What's wrong?" I asked.

"Where were you?" he said, sounding almost distraught. I was puzzled.

"I was just on the phone for a long time. Things are going sideways with my horse business and I was worried I might have to go home to help straighten things out."

He visibly relaxed. "I was jealous. I was worried you might be with that French guy."

I looked at him, shocked, amused, and flattered. "Don't you think I have my hands full? I'm not the social butterfly; you are! I'm not seeing anyone but you. I don't want to see anyone but you."

He grabbed my hand and started down the long path that led to his room. We walked in silence for several beats. Then he stopped, looked down on me with almost a sad look on his face and said, "This isn't just about sex, is it?"

"No," I said, "it's just not going to be that simple."

That night, our sexual interaction took on a different feel. It felt like making love rather than just making each other intensely aroused. There were no fantasies. Just a lot of kissing, looking into each other's eyes and holding on to each other very tightly. Touching was slow, almost languid. I felt like precious goods and we exchanged words of affection about how lucky we were to have met each other. Locking eyes for long periods of time, we shared tender kisses and slower movements to show our hearts were involved as well as our bodies. It was what we both needed and wanted.

New Feelings

The next day, my mood was a lot different. I felt on an equal footing with Dennis. I felt more secure and I didn't care very much when I saw him sitting with a lovely young woman and her parents. I started talking to Dee Dee about Dennis differently. I raved about his sensitivity, his intelligence, his uncanny ability to analyze other people just from superficial cues, his boyish charm and enthusiasms, and of course, his lovemaking skills. He sounded like a great father to his children, a loyal friend, and a caring adult child to his mother and large extended family. Dee Dee listened and became genuinely worried about me.

"You might be making too much of this" she said with concern. "This could very well just a delightful vacation romance. Why not just enjoy it for what it is and let it go when we get on the plane?"

I knew I should listen to Dee Dee. She was far from judgmental and she had been generous about letting me have all this time with a man—time that ate into some of the time we would have otherwise had together at night. She and I had been friends for a long time and while she was happily married, she was supportive of my decision when I told her I was leaving my marriage, and she was supportive of my renewed entry into the singles life. She found my sexual style a bit scary—and always preached safety—whether that meant knowing whom you were going out with and where you were going—or just the disciplined use of condoms. When she finally felt it had all gone too far, that I was making too much out of a vacation affair, I had to think about what she said.

Reality for Two

It was our last night at the resort. Dennis surprised me by saying he wanted to take me out. He felt we had been too cloistered—just relating intimately in the bedroom—and he wanted to take me on a "proper date." So we dressed up and went to a seafood restaurant downtown, outside of the hotel area.

It actually felt weird to be outside of the resort. We had been in this little bubble of a world, and somehow going outside it made the relationship with Dennis feel more real. The restaurant was right on the water. Dennis had phoned ahead to make sure we had a good table. We faced each other across the table nervously knowing that we were about to have the talk that would illuminate what might happen after summer camp is over—the talk that either kisses off the week or makes it clear that our experience meant something beyond the initial passion.

I felt vulnerable. It's one thing to say and do things that are very intimate in bed. It's another to say them fully sober sitting across a table in a public place. I was confused. I loved being with Dennis but he scared me. He was so charming with women and had a magnetic quality that seemed to attract every female in the room. Did I want to be starting up something with a man that successful with women? Was I just "vacation woman of the week?" Why shouldn't I be able to leave it at that if I was?

We both did a lot of hard swallowing.

Finally I asked him, "What, if anything, do you want from this week to go forward?"

"I want to see you," he said candidly. "But I don't know what I can offer. The last thing I need now is a girlfriend. I don't want my wife to think I left her for a girlfriend—she would become furious and this process of disentangling our lives has been rough enough. I do want to see you but I am not in a place where I can be your boyfriend or anyone else's."

I felt my back muscles tensing up.

"However," he said, "you and I have a special connection. We both know it. No matter what happens that connection is real, maybe unique, and I don't think we could ever not be special together. I want to continue this relationship, whatever it is, but you have to know that it will be a long time before I could make any commitments further than being sure that you and I are special and that I want to see more of you."

My back relaxed. This was not exactly what I wanted to hear, but that was the way it was. All of it had been said on the first day but I had tucked it out of my consciousness because things had become so much more intimate, comfortable and connected. It was ridiculous and even unwise for him to say anything more than this—and yet, we acted like a couple in love, not two people calmly setting boundaries for the next time we saw each other. My eyes were beginning to tear up. It upset me that his speech upset me.

We sat in silence for awhile, holding each other's hands across the table.

I spoke slowly and quietly. "We are going to be going back to our respective cities and it is going to take a lot of work to continue to see each other."

"I know," he said.

"I'm willing to fly to you," I said.

"So am I," he said, squeezing my hand tightly. "But I am in a major struggle to hold on to the company I started and that needs every bit of attention I can give it."

"I understand. I have to deal with my teaching schedule, my kids' adjustment to college, and all the issues that are going on at the stables and my ranch business at home. Neither of us lives a simple life, but I want to see you as much as we can manage."

"I do, too. But I'm worried about how much time I have to give."

I suddenly felt anxious. I realized there was the possibility, however slight, that I would never see Dennis again.

Almost on cue, as if to calm my nervousness, Dennis said, "I want to make an actual date to see you in New York when I'm there for work."

Relief! Having an actual date to look forward to made me feel like the Caribbean wasn't going to be the beginning and end of this relationship.

Back in Seattle

When I got home from the Caribbean, I could think of almost nothing but Dennis. I thought about the way he touched me, and especially about the intimacy we created that increased every day. Resorting to a Hallmark cliché, I found myself thinking of what we shared as a soul mate connection. I e-mailed him about how overwhelmed I felt, and his response was . . . nothing.

A week passed. I was not feeling patient. I knew breaking the traditional code of dating prerogatives had cost me in the past but I was hoping that with Dennis it would be different. Nevertheless, I proceeded with caution.

Ten days, however, was about as cautious as I could manage. I finally called Dennis to find out what was going on. I felt disappointed and angry. I thought our romantic week and straightforward discussions deserved at least a response to my e-mail, even if it was a "leave me alone" response. As Dennis's number rang and rang, I got more and more nervous.

Should I leave a message, and then be ignored? Did I . . . ?

My thoughts were interrupted when Dennis answered the phone and said in a warm, familiar tone, "Hello." I realized then that I had almost hoped that someone would answer the phone saying that Dennis was in the hospital. Knowing that he was there, easily available by phone, easily able to call, made me feel a whole lot worse. Why couldn't he have contacted me in some small way after being intimate daily for a week?

I said, "Hi Dennis. It's Pepper. I'm wondering why I haven't heard from you."

I immediately wanted to rip my tongue out.

That's right, start off in a punitive tone—that always turns men on.

I couldn't believe that I had immediately said something to put just about any guy on the defensive. I realized that I was a lot more hurt and angry than I had let myself realize.

He said, "Pepper, it's great to hear from you." Then he added with the slightest hint of sarcasm, "Perhaps you could have a more charming opening line?" He defused my embarrassment with a chuckle.

"I'm sorry," I said. "Your are right. How about 'It's great to hear your voice, Dennis'?"

"Ah, much better," said Dennis. "Now that makes me want to hold you and put my tongue in various tender places." Before I could respond to that clever way of derailing the need for an explanation of his silence, he continued with a less playful voice.

"Pepper," he said, "things have been very difficult this week but I'm sorry I haven't called. I have been working eighteen hours a day, there are some problems with our funding. To top it all off, divorce proceedings have been brutal. So go easy on me, okay?" My tone and feelings softened.

I should have known Dennis would have a good reason for not calling. This is the man I remember. We talked for a long time recalling some of the best moments of our trip together and filling each other in on our lives since then. I relaxed; there was an easy familiarity between us that reassured me that our connection still held. As Dennis freely shared the details of the problems he was having with his business and the divorce negotiations, I lost any feelings of being uncared for that I had been harboring.

Dennis's Rule of Three

We always seemed to be leaving messages for each other and it would usually take four or more calls back and forth before an actual conversation would take place. Part of the reason was that he was embroiled in trying to save his company and he was on the phone all the time talking to people. Sometimes he was just so upset with the way things were going that he didn't feel like talking. I began to expect that it would take days for him to get back to me with a phone call.

While I understood that his life was in turmoil, it was still hard not to feel pangs of insecurity when days would pass before a return call. Still, I was so sure no one else was in his life that it never occurred to me that he might also be seeing other women. This feeling lasted for a few weeks. Then I changed. I don't know why but I convinced myself that Dennis did have another woman in his life. And this thought made me anxious, a state of mind that does no one any good.

During one of our weekly phone calls a few weeks later I asked him, "Are you dating other women?"

Without a pause Dennis said, "Yes."

I didn't know what to say next. He lived in another city. Why had I thought he might *not* be dating other women? I didn't quite have a follow-up statement ready, so I said the best thing I could.

"Oh."

"Pepper," Dennis said matter-of-factly, "we live in separate cities. You are lonely and I am lonely. I don't want you to see anyone else, but of course you should. And while some part of me would dearly love to have a girlfriend, and if you lived here it would probably be irresistible, you don't live here. So I do something to be less lonely and also to keep myself from getting in trouble. I have my Rule of Three."

He always disarmed me. I could hardly argue with his dating logic. He had never told me anything different. But I still wanted to feel special. A little alarm rang in my head.

"What is the Rule of Three?" I asked.

Dennis chuckled, since he knew I could not resist asking and answered, "It may not seem like it but it's the best thing for you and me.

What I do is consistently try to date three women, never one woman. Three women is enough to let every women know I am not serious and I'm not going to be. If each of the women I see knows of the two others, I am making it very clear I am not in a position to make any kind of commitment."

It made sense if he wasn't giving me a serious amount of bullshit.

I said, "So there are two women you are dating there and I fit into the third slot?" There was a certain amount of bitchiness in my tone. There I was, hurt and expressing it the wrong way again.

Dennis chose to ignore my tone and reassured me. "No, actually you are in a category by yourself. You are not one of the three women I am dating here. You are someone I didn't expect to find and didn't want to find, at least not now. I have told you, I can't have a real girlfriend right now. I want one desperately. I was born to be married. I like the comfort of being married. But I am watching the end of a marriage, which even though I want it to end and have wanted it to end for a long time, is very painful. And my business is a big trouble. So I am not in a place to be involved—I wouldn't even know what my real motives were."

I was listening closely.

"But I can tell you this . . . totally honestly," he said, "you are my 'gold standard.' You are who I would want to be with if I could be with someone. I don't know our present much less our future. But I feel that we will always be involved with each other, somehow in some way."

This was not exactly the impassioned need for me I fantasized about hearing from him.

I said, "I don't really understand what this means about us. I don't know how you want me to feel about you or what place you want in my life. I don't understand if there are four number ones, or if there are three number twos and I get some special category, like Best Cinematography."

He responded speaking slowly, with carefully chosen words in a tone that was gentle yet firm. "You are special to me. I told you. But you don't live here and furthermore, even if you did, I would have to say this same thing: I am in no position to make a real commitment at this stage of my life. I am just ending a long marriage. I have financial problems. But I am really looking forward to continuing to have a relationship with you and can't wait to see you in New York."

His candor hurt but God knows I had made him spell everything out in capital letters. I got it. At least he wasn't a game-player. He was honest and being careful to clearly communicate his intentions and his boundaries. He was in a different emotional space and time of his life than I was and I resolved to be careful and limit my attachment to him. I had made him state his position over and over and I think it had finally gotten hammered into my reluctant brain: There were no loopholes in his position; he was not available for a monogamous, committed relationship. Unless I wanted to be pitiful even in my own eyes, I had better moderate my emotions. But as is true in most truly romantic situations, that is easier said than done. I felt a huge pull toward him.

Into Therapy

This situation was emotionally dangerous. I was making this vacation romance into something more than it was capable of being. I advise other people to talk to an objective listener and I felt that I needed help sorting this out, too.

At the door to the counselor's office, a small, youthful looking woman with straight hair that was kept off her face by a headband greeted me. That didn't inspire confidence. Nonetheless, she was highly recommended so I lectured myself on jumping to conclusions and got myself ready to bring her up to date on why I was there. After I answered a few basic intake questions I sat back in the comfy chair across from her and waited to see how she would begin.

She said, "So, tell me a little about what prompted this visit."

"Oh, God. How far back do I start? I have always thought that seeing a therapist was easy but starting was like slogging through mud." I continued, "I have recently gotten divorced, about six months ago—and that is a done deal."

The therapist was listening closely. Then I began my monologue.

"But I am surprised at how quickly I've become infatuated with someone I met on vacation and that I've become convinced, way too soon, that this is the man that I am truly meant to be with. I know, with what few rational senses I have left, that it is way too early for me to feel this way. I also know that I should back off because he is clear about not wanting to make a commitment to me or anyone else while he's going through several important crises in his life. I am thinking that something more primal is going on here that is expressing itself in my infatuation with this guy. I am worried that I have some unresolved issues from my marriage that I don't know about. Maybe it's just the great sex that is making me think love instead of affair. In other words, I'm confused and worried that I am delusional, acting like a love-sick teenager, and going to get hurt and lose respect for myself in the bargain."

The therapist listened to my stream of consciousness but, appropriately, she asked questions since it was too early to offer answers. She wanted to know more about what it was that drew me to Dennis and what was really creating the sexual fixation. She asked whether I always had intense reactions to relationships and if not, why this instance was different. She also wondered why I chose to accept the terms he offered—and did I really understand their significance? A key question was whether or not I was relationship material right now, regardless of whether or not this guy was right for me.

All good things to think about, of course. She did advise me, as I would have advised other women when they return home from vacation with the "love of their life" story:

a. You have seen this guy out of context and you don't know who he would be, or who you would be with him, in everyday life.
b. You are just divorced; this relationship may be about your emotional needs and not be much about him at all.
c. Give it a break, lower your emotional temperature, and just watch what happens.

After our first fifty-minute session I felt relieved that I was thinking a bit more and fretting a bit less. I felt I had made a good decision to seek counseling and had received some very practical guidance. Of course, the bottom line was that I was absolutely infatuated and not particularly amenable to hearing good sense. But I was making a stab at it.

Dating Dennis

My weekly phone calls with Dennis continued, although, to my chagrin, they were mostly initiated by me. This went on for a month or so until Dennis asked me to firm up our first post-Caribbean dates.

"I need to go to New York City to meet with some investors. I'll fly in from Denver to meet with them. My days will be completely taken up and I wouldn't be able to be with you until after five but it would make me very happy if you would come. I can promise you that I will wine and dine you and in general make your evenings worthwhile." That last sentence was said with a lascivious emphasis on the word "worthwhile."

I smiled. This last sentence was so Dennis.

"That would work out great," I said. "I need to go see editors, agents, other friends . . . there's a zillion things I've been meaning to do in New York. I can cash in some miles and I could come on a Friday and stay the weekend."

When I hung up the phone I realized I could feel my heart beating hard, and my hand was sweaty. Three weeks later I was heading out to meet Dennis. When my taxi dropped me off in front of the Plaza Hotel on Central Park my heart was pounding. I walked into the lobby and Dennis was waiting for me. He was beautifully dressed in a stylish suit and tie, and had just come back from his business meeting. I thought about what great taste he had. Clothes aren't that important to me, but I had to admit that when a guy really puts himself together well, it has an effect on my physical reaction to him.

We embraced. I liked the feel of his jacket. All my senses were alive and kicking my logic to the basement.

"Get ready for something great," he said as we entered the elevator.

He kissed me immediately after the door closed.

"Yes, this is great," I murmured.

"Yes, it is," he smiled and said. "But this is not the great thing I promised. You have to wait to see the room for that."

I looked askance.

Never underestimate the aphrodisiac effect of a great stage setting! Our room qualified as a sensual backdrop for any erotic fantasy. Our home for three nights was one of the large ornate rooms on the second floor that looked directly over Central Park. It was really a huge room for a New York hotel and it was handsomely furnished in a kind of Louis the Fourteenth style that somehow escaped feeling garish. There was a fireplace and an extremely high ceiling. A big marble bathroom with a tub that could fit two made it a perfect place for us.

While I was taking this all in, Dennis put his arms around me and we took a few minutes to nuzzle, watching a horse and carriage trot by our window. It was a beautiful day and at that moment, the whole city seemed to be designed for lovers.

Dennis let go of me and started loosening his tie. He took off his coat, laid it on the chair next to the fireplace and turned to face me. He kissed me slowly and touched my face, my neck, and my shoulders and looked at me for long seconds at a time. The kissing created a space where we just floated. Time seemed irrelevant.

Dennis was a traditionalist when it came to kissing. He didn't hurry any of it. I just relaxed into the sensuality of being mouth to mouth, eyes meeting part of the time, stroking each other's back, neck, hair, and face. Knowing I was tired from my flight, Dennis ran a bath, put some bath salts in it, and slowly took off my clothes while we waited for the tub to fill up. Then he slowly undressed and we both climbed into the warm, sweetly scented water. We shampooed each other's hair and kissed and stroked each other's bodies. I loved the fact that we were taking this kind of time with one another. I knew that both of us wanted to do this on the first meeting after the Caribbean tryst.

When we got out of the bathtub, we kissed slowly. I reached to touch him more erotically but he moved away from me and laid me on my back, while he slowly worked his way down my body with his tongue and hands. This was just as delicious as my fantasies had been. Dennis was very knowledgeable about women's bodies. He knew that you could just enter a woman, and if she was excited, that would feel terrific. But he also knew, that if you teased a woman, stroked her, licked her, stimulated her with your fingers and your tongue, you could make her into a sexual maniac. So Dennis took his time, knowing that his reward would be a totally frenzied woman, begging for it, and explosive when that itch was scratched.

And that's where he got me. So excited that I couldn't bear waiting any more. But that didn't mean he was going to satisfy me just because I was insanely ready. I knew from my experience with him in the Caribbean that he liked to bring me to the edge, let me hang there, and then not let me have an orgasm until he was good and ready to give it to me. He wanted me to love the process as well as the orgasm and he liked me to do the same thing with him as well. So I did, even though I really wanted him inside of me. He told me exactly what he wanted me to do, which was a turn-on because I hate wondering if I am doing what the guy needs. Dennis would tell me exactly what to do, which was exciting and gave me confidence that I was being a good lover.

We both had orgasms orally but with Dennis that was just foreplay. We rested and touched each other languidly after that and he briefly fell asleep. Then he started touching me again, revving up my passion again and this time, he asked me to climb on top of him and ride him. He got very, very close, then pulled me off of him and entered me. Every stroke inside me got me close. He waited until I had your basic wall-shaking, screaming orgasm, and then he had his own. When it was over, we realized that he had gripped the headboard of the bed so tightly that he had taken it off the bed.

I fell asleep next to Dennis thinking, *This was as passionate and as personal as the Caribbean. I feel reassured and comforted and so sexually fulfilled that it is scary. No wonder I feel addicted to this guy. Sex like this happens only a few times in a lifetime.*

Actually, if you ever get sex like this in your life you are one lucky lady.

The rest of the weekend was a series of intimate tableaus: long dinners, great conversation at the dining table and during our long baths together, and both nightly and morning lovemaking.

In Love

By the end of the long weekend I felt in love. After three days of romance and great sex I didn't want to say good bye. But good bye had to be said.

Sunday afternoon we took a short run in Central Park and after a shower, we headed toward the airports, Dennis to LaGuardia, me to Kennedy.

I didn't want to ruin anything so I just said, "This couldn't have been better."

Dennis said, "I agree. I'll call you tomorrow." We kissed passionately and soulfully. And that was it. No big promises, revelations or plans. But no disastrous pulling away either.

As my taxi took me to my airport I realized that my insecurities about Dennis, his Rule of Three, and our future somehow faded. I was going to enjoy him and whatever would be, would be.

Months of Dennis

Over the next few months, our trips to New York became fairly regular and they all had the same great outline. A gorgeous room, extended lovemaking, and dining in wonderful restaurants. We shared romantic moments, having breakfast in a dive around the corner from the Plaza, jogging in Central Park in the mornings, or walking home from some Broadway show. They were perfect weekends from beginning to end.

I was more than smitten. But I was careful not to try to push it somewhere Dennis clearly didn't want it to go. We didn't talk much about his "other life" and I didn't talk about my life in Seattle—partially because I didn't have three guys to trot out and partially because he had told me that he didn't want to know. He said it would make him jealous and he knew that was ridiculous but nonetheless, he would feel that way. So we kept a curtain drawn about what was happening elsewhere.

Fantasy Life

I was also totally addicted to Dennis's kind of lovemaking. I loved the erotic storytelling he was able to invent in bed.

"Pepper," Dennis whispered to me, holding me tightly under the sheets, "I have taken you to a private men's club. Men are admiring you. You can tell that they are looking at you . . ." Dennis would weave his erotic fantasies and I would love it.

We learned what to say to each other, and what wouldn't work. I could tell him when a story trespassed my boundaries or wasn't sexy to me. He would tell me what fantasies he liked. As a result, we refined our lovemaking to the point that we remained sexually supercharged every time we were together. Sometimes it was almost unbearably erotic.

Catching a Cab

One time, after too much Champagne, we were riding back from dinner in a taxi. It was right when the theaters let out and the streets were crowded with other taxis, commuters, buses, and the general intense confusion that is New York City in Times Square at 11:00 pm. Bright lights and noise all around us, but I was concentrating on what was happening inside our cab. Dennis was kissing my neck and started unbuttoning my blouse.

I was so aroused, the idea of his touching my breast in a semipublic situation was a turn-on.

Dennis not only unbuttoned my blouse, but also unhooked my bra.

He touched me and nibbled at my breasts, which was easily seen if the driver looked back. Under the influence of a serious amount of wine, I not only allowed it, I enjoyed it. I figured if the driver wanted to kick us out of his cab, he was entitled. But no outrage seemed to be coming from the front seat. I imagined he was watching. I was just drunk enough so that was exciting. But Dennis didn't spend all his attention on my breasts.

He whispered to me, "Take off your panties." I moaned and did just that. I wasn't wearing any panty hose, which made it a lot easier. It suddenly flashed on me that Dennis had asked me not to wear panty hose. He did that every now and then because it was a turn-on to both of us to know that I wasn't wearing underwear. But this time was obviously different. That devil had been planning this seduction in a taxi all along.

He pulled my skirt up and started touching me. I was insanely turned on. We were getting wildly passionate in a taxicab, right in the middle of downtown Manhattan. For a split second I thought, *What am I doing?* Then I said it out loud,

"Dennis. What are we doing?"

"Don't think," he said. "Just let me take care of you."

I can't believe I let him. But right there in the taxi club, with buses passing by and who knows who was looking at us, I had an orgasm. Here I was in my mid-fifties and doing things I would have considered over-the-top edgy in my twenties. We gave the taxi driver a big tip. He looked quite happy.

Back at the university, I worked hard, harder than usual, since most of my sexual energy was reserved for my trips to New York and occasionally to Denver to see Dennis. He had also come to Seattle a couple of times and met a few of my friends. He liked my life there and he liked the city. It made me think this whole thing might come together someday. Our relationship had been going on for six months or so and I was perfectly happy with it.

This is what I deserve and this is what I want.

When I thought about our future together, I kept thinking, "It will work out."

Love

After about nine months of weekends in New York City and other places, and almost daily phone calls, our relationship had deepened, or so I felt. He invited me home more often and we took some trips together. One trip, we rented a medium-size cabin cruiser boat, small enough for a single person to captain. He wanted to do something special that weekend and so the plan was to visit some friends in the Midwest and take a trip down the St. Croix River. Unfortunately, it started to rain like mad, so we had to pull over to the side and had a picnic in the boat's small cabin. We kissed and made love in our cramped but cozy space. Afterward we sat on the little bed. He then drew away from me and moved to the far end of the bed.

He took a long look at me, and said, "I love you."

I felt like I had been holding my breath for almost a whole year without knowing it. I had not let myself think about how much I wanted to hear those words—and hearing them allowed a huge rush of emotion. I heard my heart beating. I felt my pulse. The world seemed to pause for a moment in order to let those words have the attention of the universe.

He said, "Pepper, you really are the gold standard. We are fated to be together. I have known that for a while now."

I remembered him using the gold standard phrase before. I wondered how often he had said "I love you" to a woman. He continued as if he had read my thoughts.

He said, "I have never told another women I loved her except my ex-wife."

We looked at each other, neither one of us wanting to disrupt our eye contact. I touched his hand and he took my hand in his.

"That means so much to me," I said.

I knew this was a big thing for him. It was for me, too.

I said, "I love you, too." And I did.

A Turn of Events

Disaster struck Dennis's business. The venture capitalists pulled the plug and sold the business out from under him. He had a lot of paper debt and basically he lost everything he owned. His home. His savings.

Dennis was devastated. He went into what I would call a clinical depression. He had trouble functioning and he withdrew from a lot of people, even me, to some extent.

One night on the phone, he called in the middle of a real tailspin. "Pepper, I feel like I am at the edge of an abyss. And what is scaring me is that the abyss looks good and I feel like jumping in would be a release from all these problems."

That scared me.

For the first time in this terrible process he was going through, he sounded self-destructive. I told him I was going to talk to his family and he didn't try to dissuade me.

I kept in touch by phone and didn't push for visits. I waited for Dennis to get his life together. His mental health improved but the economics of his life started to strain our relationship. He had desperate financial problems. I lent him a little money to help tide him over and he hated having to accept that. It weighed on him. He began consulting and made enough to cover his basic obligations but not much more. If we were going to get together, it had to be on my dime and that became awkward for both of us. When we started seeing each other again, we would keep it simple and not do things that cost much money. I did not care the least about extravagant Manhattan getaways. I just wanted to be with Dennis.

His visits became less frequent and his phone calls irregular.

True to his word, his Rule of Three held steadfast. But I tolerated it less well. I thought by this time we would have a commitment and things weren't getting better. I still loved him but I could feel my emotions changing. I began to doubt that we would ever really be together. I began to distance myself from my most intense feelings about him. Most important, I started to do some online dating again.

Bali Beckons

Months were flying by and my trip to the speaking engagement in Bali was coming closer. I was not sure what to do about having a traveling companion. Dennis was still my obvious preference but I didn't know if the trip was something that would be good for us. I e-mailed Dom and asked him what he thought of the idea of taking Dennis and he responded with one of his typical "best case/worst case" responses.

> Dearest Pepper:
> Best case: You have a fabulous time with peak romantic and sexual experience with a totally emotionally available and stable Dennis. Worst case: Dennis becomes moody, keeps stating how this romantic adventure does not mean he can become involved with you in a significant way—you react with insecurity and hurt—and it's a total disaster.
>
> If you can live with worst-case scenario—go for it!
> Ciao,
> Dom

I pondered worst case. Then best case. Then called Dennis and said, "The organizers will pay for both of our tickets and all other expenses would be paid for the two of us as well." Still, Dennis hesitated. He was busy. He had some important career possibilities. He couldn't make up his mind. Finally, at the eleventh hour he said, "Okay, I can't miss this. I'll go."

I was pleased, even touched, because I knew getting away was hard for him, but his equivocation had taken its toll on me. I was happy to go with Dennis but was tired of everything being so hard—having to beg for his time. When he said yes it put us back on some kind of track, though I didn't know which one.

To Bali

After setting down in Denpasar, we made our way through baggage claim and customs. We were met by a driver from the Ritz Carlton at Jimbaran Bay, a short ride from the airport. The road twisted and turned past some not particularly beautiful vegetation, until we entered what was obviously an elegant area of resorts. At one point we turned off the street into the private road leading to entrance of the hotel, passed giant urns and groomed plantings, and stopped at the lobby area. Sarong-clad porters welcomed us. After we walked through the large doors to the hotel grounds, Dennis and I saw a stunning vista: terraced ponds, beautifully landscaped gardens, and the endless blue sea beyond. The air was fragrant with flowers, the sun sparkled on the ocean, and I was, to quote a New Age expression—blissed out. And all of this is on someone else's tab. Life is good.

Sex and Setting

Our room had a beautiful big white bed and the room colors were soothing. This was going to be a wonderful vacation.

After we unpacked, Dennis and I headed to the preconference party. Upon entering the party room, which was filled with lightly inebriated, relaxed-looking, tanned business types from both the West and the East, we were offered very pretty tropical concoctions. We sipped our drinks and I went over to the speaker's table to get my own materials and instructions for the conference. An elegant woman wearing a nametag that said "Thalia" was at the welcome table and she introduced herself and greeted me warmly.

She said, "I have something special for you from the hotel manager" and handed me an envelope.

I opened it right away and found a gift certificate for a massage treatment called "Couples Massage."

I asked Thalia, "And is there a special way couples are massaged here on Bali?"

"It's a very wonderful experience for two people with two massage therapists." Thalia said, "But if you would like to exchange it for some other spa treatment it would be no problem."

Fat chance of that! I thought. The offer felt a little like some of the fantasies Dennis would tell me. I knew this wasn't going to involve sex—but could anything be more sensual than having this treatment together?

Dennis was intrigued by the gift and said, "If you make the massage appointment for tomorrow, I will take care of your treatment for tonight." My knees went weak. We went to our room and I barely got through the door when he pinned me against the wall. Our bodies molded together perfectly. As always the pleasure was intense and emotionally connected.

Two Hearts and Two Masseuses

My lecture on *The Great Sex Weekend*, a book I cowrote on how to rejuvenate sexuality in long-term relationships, went well and I was eager to meet Dennis for our massage.

I found Dennis inside the spa's small, simple, but elegant waiting room. We smiled seductively at each other.

Two lovely Balinese masseuses came to take us, individually, to dressing rooms to shower. Dressed in robes, we were taken to an enclosed space, an outdoor room made private by high wooden fences and climbing flowers.

Each of the women helping us was exceptionally beautiful. I was sure that Dennis was thinking that if these women are planning something erotic, he was up for it. Of course, the women were quite proper and instead of laying hands on us immediately, they directed us into a large warm pool that was bigger than a conventional hot tub and probably could have accommodated six or more people. The women motioned for us to disrobe and enter the pool. Then they left us alone. We took off our robes and stepped into the swirling warm water that was topped with masses of rose petals. I moved next to Dennis's body which, like most middle-aged bodies, packed a few extra pounds—as did mine. I wished I had kept the toned body I had when I first met him. He was closer to his earlier weight and shape than I was. But he treated me as if I was irresistible and as a result, I felt irresistible.

We cuddled and kissed. I was longing to take proper advantage of this sensual scene but I wasn't sure about how long we had this pool or how close the masseuses were. I didn't want to embarrass them or us. The women eventually did come back to get us and handed us our robes.

We were taken into a room that was open to the garden, the warm, fresh breeze caressing us. Two massage tables were lined up, parallel to each other, and we were put on the tables, tummy down, close enough for us to hold hands. The women carefully draped our bodies with small towels that kept our lower torsos covered. Then they went to work on our bodies. We were covered with yogurt mixed with a spicy perfume, and this was rubbed into our skin for about an hour. Then we were rinsed off with warm water. As we almost drifted into sleep, we were told to turn over and my breasts and pelvic area was covered with small but adequate towels. Then more lotion was reapplied. This was a more classic massage oil with a strong Indonesian aromatic scent called Champaka. I found it almost intoxicating. Another hour massage followed.

Finally, the masseuses told us the treatment was over, helped us sit up on the table, helped us on with our robes and offered us ginger tea. Dennis and I looked at each other with wide grins. The three-hour couple's massage was more than mildly erotic. Being nude together in front of these talented, exquisite women may not have been intended as actual foreplay but it worked very well for that purpose.

We floated back to our room and began another long passionate evening together.

Trouble in Paradise

The next day I was completely busy with the conference and Dennis had to fend for himself. I noticed that he was hanging around some lovely local women who were selling crafts and luxury items to the conference attendees. One of them was particularly sexy and of course that was the one I saw Dennis with more than a few times. He was doing his Dennis thing—flirting, charming whomever he chose to shine his light on, and it really upset me. Not only did I feel I deserved to be free from jealousy at this meeting, I felt that it reflected badly on me if anyone else from the conference noticed that my boyfriend was all over another woman. After all, here I am lecturing to all of them about love and relationships, and my boyfriend is putting on a fairly public show with someone else. I felt humiliated—and while I tried to control my feelings with a "that's just Dennis's way" explanation to myself, it didn't work.

When I walked out of the morning session for a break, I saw him having lunch with this extremely sexy woman who was touching his arm; I had trouble not making a scene then and there. By the time dinner came around, I was verging on homicidal. I went back to the room and waited for him. He was hours late.

My imagination was working overtime and when he finally arrived, my eyes were cold, steely and he took one look at me and said "What?"

"You know what! You were all over that woman all day and not only did it hurt my feelings, I felt publicly humiliated."

"You are making way too much of this, Pepper. And I was all alone all day. Why shouldn't I find some companionship? It was harmless."

"Oh, this is my fault because I had to work? And I don't believe it was harmless."

The conversation went downhill from there. I questioned his "Rule of Three" he had steadfastly hung onto. He got defensive. I felt it was time for us not to see other people. He said he was in no position to make a commitment until he got his finances back in shape. I told him all he needed was a regular job and that I didn't care if he made a lot of money. That made him really angry.

"Listen, Pepper. I am who I am. A nine-to-five job would never work for me. Who are you to tell me how I should make a living?" I was listening wide-eyed as Dennis smoldered.

"I can't hold down a regular job and also create another company—and that is what I need to do and nothing, not even you, can get in the way."

It was our first real fight and it was awful. It scared us both. We mutually backed down from our harsh words and managed to have a warmer dinner. Later in bed, we held on to each other extra tight that night but did not make love. The cab ride to the airport the next morning had a sad feel to it and although we kissed good bye sweetly, we both knew that something had been fractured and we left Bali more fragile than we had entered it.

Another Change

After I returned from Asia, my feelings toward Dennis continued the transition they had been taking before the trip. We were still great together when we could actually get together. But our fight had revealed some serious tensions and flaws in the relationship. I was suddenly aware that I had been angry with Dennis for a long time. I was angry because he felt that until his finances were in order, he couldn't be my partner. And that made me angry because he wouldn't get a regular job to earn a steady income so that we could be a real couple. I was angry that after almost a year of knowing him, his Rule of Three hadn't turned into a Rule of One—me. There was too much distance, too many frustrations, jealousies, and economic problems to keep the romantic relationship from disintegrating.

There wasn't some sudden event that made me give up on Dennis. But more and more time passed between visits and more of our lives were unshared. We never officially "broke up" but we became much more minor characters in each other's life.

Lessons

As I prepared to enter the dating scene again, I thought long and hard about my history with Dennis and I did not want to replicate its problems. I did not want to be with someone who was economically marginal and unable to do things with me. I did not want someone who was emotionally unavailable and unwilling to make a monogamous commitment. That said, I thought about all the gifts this relationship had that I hated to lose. I had learned so much from being with Dennis. I had felt adored. (A pretty amazing trick when you think about it, given his full social calendar.) I had learned a lot about being imaginative and open about my fantasies during sex. Dennis had helped me learn better communication skills inside and outside of bed. I had never had a more intimate relationship in my life. He had wonderful enthusiasms and these encouraged and validated my own. I always felt I could be myself with him. We loved each other's personalities as well as our electric physical connection.

Dennis had also shown me that I had unconsciously gotten bossy and that I had to cut it out. I had been the "boy" so long in both my long and short-term relationships that I was used to leading and I had trouble following.

Dennis was adept at telling me when I overstepped boundaries. I learned how to show more trust and respect and give up control some of the time. Dennis knew how to handle me without being paternalistic or condescending. I had learned a lot about life, love, and sex from Dennis and even though my dream of being lifetime soul mates wasn't working out, I was grateful to have had this relationship with him. I wanted to keep the good stuff and get rid of the Rule of Three, the long distance, and the economic divide. No matter what happened, I felt emotionally richer for having been with Dennis and I treasured his presence in my life even if it wasn't going to be as my lover or partner forever.

◪ Advice to Myself (And Others) ◪

Rebound Versus Reality

Everyone talks about the rebound effect. It's real. If you have been used to being with someone, it can feel terribly lonely—even if you were the leaving party. If you were left—there is likely to be a significant wound to your ego and that, coupled with the loss of someone you loved, has sent a number of people into a tailspin. I wasn't like that—it took a long time for my marriage to unwind, and I was ready to be on my own. But I remember what it was like long ago when I broke up with Ken, the venereologist I was with for five years. The pain was palpable. I was surprised when I woke up the morning after we had broken up and the first thing I felt was a pounding headache and then, nausea. I didn't want to get out of bed. I had all the signs of acute depression. It might be one of the few times in my life I lost my appetite. So I know that it can be literally painful to lose someone you love. I know that unless you fight to regain your equanimity and joy, feelings of emotional emptiness can undermine the pleasures of everyday life.

It's only natural to want to end the pain by falling in love with someone else. If the pain is intense, so is the urge to get rid of it. Unwanted emotions include anxiety, unfulfilled craving for companionship, and the need to feel worthy again. If depression doesn't take hold, another deep emotion—infatuation—is a welcome relief.

On the other hand, soon after a relationship ends, it just might happen that you meet someone who is wonderful for you. Not all emotional connections after a divorce are necessarily false. I knew that Dennis and I had a real connection—it was just hard to believe in, given the timing. What I did, and what I think is a good approach, is to honor the feeling—but not make any steps that are permanent (i.e. moving to his home town, installing him in my house, eloping). It is a narrow rope to walk, since falling on either side (too quick a commitment versus not being at all open to the relationship) could be a costly mistake. The point being—let yourself feel what you feel—but enjoy it for a long time before you can even begin to think you know what is really going on between the two of you. In the meantime, take in your circle of trusted friends' advice, but don't let their caution totally deter you. The heart, for all its foolishness, has some hidden wisdoms—some canny intuitions that are worth respect. I wouldn't be afraid to love too soon—I would just not sign any papers.

Vacation Sex and Vacation Love?

Vacation sex is just that—a connection out of time and space, often under the best most romantic conditions that could possibly exist. It is easy to construct a fantasy love affair where you believe that romance will conquer all and that the guy you have just met is not only the greatest lover in the world but has the heart of the Dalai Lama. That perception is probably going to last a week, max, but hey, that's what vacation love affairs are for: getaways from reality, and enjoying any fantasy you want. The way you experience him that week can be wonderful and there is no reason to compromise vacation euphoria by doing a postmortem on it while it's still going on. Stay in the present and enjoy it. As a single woman, whom are you betraying or disappointing? Your mother? Puleeese.

The only thing to remind your hormone-altered brain is that even if the person you have met is someone terrific "in real life," what happens in Bali is probably not transferable to Brooklyn. On vacation, stress is minimal, and we have the time and the emotional largess to be the most attentive and accomplished of lovers. Back at home, our daily cycle changes everything. Still, I have known people who found each other on the other end of the earth from home. For example, I met a couple who got married after serendipitously meeting each other in Katmandu. Twenty-five years later they are still happily together, living in Minneapolis with two almost grown children. Vacation romances can blossom into lifetime commitments. But my guess is most of them don't.

So what? Why not just enjoy a vacation romance as it happens, love the connection—and not feel it was a waste if it doesn't go forward? Only you, of course, can formulate your own equation of risk, romance, and potential pain to see what you want to do. If you can deal with the fact your love affair will almost certainly extinguish with your last Mai Tai, I would urge you to be receptive to vacation romance. But if your ego is not particularly resilient and your heart is easily punctured, spending time reading a good novel by the pool might be a better choice.

The Safety Issue

There are two kinds of safety to think about—one is having a condom on you or near all the time, even if you are going on a trip that seems to offer no romantic temptations or possibilities. Life is not predictable and who wants to miss a great event—or take a bad chance—by not having condoms at the ready. Be prepared to stick up for yourself if the guy protests. Be prepared to leave if he get really snitty about it.

Secondly, you also have to plan for the unlikely, but possible, vulnerability to sexual assault or physical violence. Do not go to someone's hotel room, do not get into someone's car, when you don't know the man well (or he isn't a friend of someone you know). Let any brand-new vacation date, no matter how sweet he appears, know that there are friends who know where you are, who you are with, and when you expect to get back.

Possessiveness, Insecurity, and Jealousy

Just because something is a vacation fling doesn't mean intense emotions can't be generated. Becoming physically and emotionally intimate with someone who was a total stranger six hours earlier can feel very vulnerable, leading to feelings of insecurity, which easily leads to jealously. The fact is that a fling can get serious even when it's ridiculous to imagine that serious feelings are at stake. A quick connection is a connection all the same, and if you are passionate or impulsive

(I can be both) you can get in over your head and lose your sense of proportion pretty damn quick. This is fine if all the characters in the play conform to their storybook roles and everyone who should end up together, does end up together, and is actually who you'd hope they'd be. Sometimes that approximates what happens. Sometimes it doesn't.

Just remind yourself: Strong emotions can happen quickly and surprise you. Be aware that there may be some emotional costs to what started out as a romp. I have never been sorry about meeting Dennis but the insecurity, jealousy, and possessiveness I felt during our weeks together were no fun. Sometimes that's the cost of admission.

Long-Distance Lovers

Of course, there is also the issue of trying to stay connected, committed, and monogamous with a long-distance lover. It hasn't worked for me so far, but I do know many people it *has* worked for. I know a couple who met in Sweden, commuted for two years between Sweden and Washington State, and ended up getting married and raising a family. I know a number of success stories—but it took an almost fanatical belief in the relationship and not an incidental amount of money. One of the main problems, however, is that because seeing each other is a big effort and not a daily event, there is pressure to make it perfect when together, to have great sex and a lot of it, and not to rock the boat with issues and problems. In between visits, there is the issue of maintaining trust, controlling jealous fantasies, and dealing with the lack of day-to-day communication and shared experiences. Not for the faint of heart, but ever the optimist, I would never give someone up just because the distance was difficult.

Monogamous Versus Nonmonogamous Lovers

Most mature women get to a point where they are ready to reevaluate some of the rules about love and sex that they held throughout their lives. Monogamy in relationships, however, may be one rule you never thought you would ever reconsider. Still, it's worth a discussion here.

Nonmonogamy isn't for everyone—in fact, it's not for most people. But there are some times in your life that insisting on monogamy puts pressure on a relationship before it is ready to support such a commitment. When Dennis and I first met we were wild about each other—but we were also in different cities and there was no short-term way we could see each other often.

I suppose each person could insist on monogamy anyhow—but that is hard to sustain for years apart. Furthermore, even if you are infatuated, it doesn't mean both people are ready to be sexually loyal when they can't see each other for long periods of time. Some people insist on nothing less than monogamy no matter what—and if both people can do it, that is certainly the most secure way to build trust and commitment. But I don't think it's preferable to say you will be monogamous—and then not be.

I believe in honesty—or at least a "don't ask, don't tell" rule that each member of the couple fully understands and accepts. I think both men and women want someone they care about to be exclusive with them—but men tend to be a little less thorough about carrying it out. Most women don't have much trouble being monogamous and they presume it as a condition for a continuing relationship. If that is who you are, it is who you are. But consider this, especially about a long-distance lover or a lover you care about but are not ready to marry or live with: Putting monogamy down as a condition may end a relationship prematurely, before it gets to a point where monogamy is a natural evolution of both partner's emotions and conditions permit a more constant relationship. If your lover doesn't want to lose you, but the cost of maintaining monogamy over long distances and rare moments together becomes greater over time, it becomes likelier that your partner will lie about what is really happening in his life away from you. If those lies get exposed, loss of trust and feelings of betrayal may be much more damaging than holding off on a monogamous contract.

These days and at these ages, monogamy is something that cannot be assumed: It must be discussed. I didn't like Dennis's "Rule of Three" but I did admire that he was honest enough to talk about it, and I could make my own decisions with full information. He felt that the rule kept him from getting involved with any one woman who was competitive to our connection—and maybe it did. In any case, I think you live one contract at a time and that might mean not making assumptions or hard and fast rules about monogamy. I know it's true that one person cannot dictate conditions and assume they will be followed. What you need is an open and clear agreement about what kind of relationship you are in. I have certainly been in relationships where monogamy was expected and monogamy was real on both sides. But that isn't always the case and you need to discuss your expectations and see if both of you are on the same page—and if not, if any compromise or change is possible.

Differences in Finances

People differ about the role of money in relationships. I have more than a few women friends who are major breadwinners in their relationship and they find it a comfortable arrangement. Single women in their prime, however, have often worked hard to recover financially from divorce, or, as someone who never married, carefully managed money in order to stay financially solvent. Naturally, they feel protective about keeping themselves economically secure and independent. On the other hand, if finances are shaky, older women might be motivated to find someone wealthy, or at least someone who can pitch in and help contribute to financial security in the coming years. Many of us didn't prioritize money in our first marriages or when we were single and childless, but over the years economic needs surface and money is no longer a minor consideration. We know if we need a man who can take care of himself (or not). We may select someone who can help support or enhance the lifestyle we are living.

Money is also a significant issue to men in the marriage market. Many dating men explicitly say in their profiles online that they are not interested in having a woman who is financially dependent on them; others talk about not having a lot of money and if that's what a woman is interested in, she should go elsewhere. Some men, just like some women, are looking for a partner who will make life financially easier. On the other hand, a number of men's online profiles entice women with statements about their economic success and their desire to "spoil" a partner.

This is such tricky business. We all want to be loved for ourselves, and in a traditional relationship men expect that in addition to being loved for who they are, being a "good provider" will make them more attractive on the dating market. But women are not used to the difficulties they may face as the more economically secure person in a relationship. We are not generally flattered if someone finds us more enticing because we have money. Many men would find being able to take care of a woman who needs economic help endearing. Fewer women would like to be in that position. We have to be honest with ourselves and figure out how we want money to work in our relationships at this stage of our lives.

Specific choices arise when a woman has significantly more discretionary cash than her partner. For example, if you want to travel to India and have the ability to travel to India, and he only has the ability to travel to Indiana—you have four choices available:

1. You go to Indiana together (and feel bad about missing India or get over missing India).
2. You treat him to India as a gift.
3. You think of all money as couple money and you go where your combined money can take you and stop thinking about it as his and yours. You may or may not be able to afford tickets for two to India or Indiana. (This is the model many married couples sharing one bank account have.)
4. You go to India alone and have a wonderful time—but that might defeat the idea of being a couple, and being able to share that experience together.

There are also sensitive situations when you meet a man with more income or wealth than you have. A lot of older guys have been the main earner earlier in life and they vary in how they want to deal with money in their next relationship. They might want to continue in their traditional role, paying for most or all large expenses, or they may want to split expenses equitably or equally. Things that seem minor, like who will pay for a trip, a dinner, or a purchase, require some discussion—and it can be awkward or off-putting. Decisions about how money is spent can have a strong ripple effect on the whole relationship. If you aren't used to sharing economic responsibility, a man's desire to split costs may feel ungenerous. If someone doesn't want to take care of you financially, it may have emotional symbolism as well. However, if you feel, as many feminists do, that allowing a man to be the economic leader gives him too much control in other realms of the relationship, sharing economic costs may appeal to you.

This is uncharted territory for many women. In traditional relationships, no negotiation is necessary. He pays, she is grateful and shows it in a number of ways. But if it's untraditional—you are the high earner, or he wants you to share economic responsibility—you may be surprised that you resent this new deal. Role reversal isn't that easy. Finding an easy way to be "equal" isn't automatic, either. I have found that I can be generous and enjoy taking a man I'm dating out to dinner or on a vacation. But I have also found I have my limits and some kind of economic reciprocity is necessary for me in a relationship.

Honestly, I don't think there is a right or wrong pattern here, but you do need to know yourself, be honest about what works for you, and figure out what would work in a long-term relationship as well as a short-term one. If you are going to be the one who pays more, you need to make sure you are not going to resent it. You will also need to be sure your man can accept your generosity without feeling diminished. Money is more than money. It can be seen as power, dominance, control, or success. Now that we've opened up all the options about who pays what, we need to talk more openly about money, just like sex, and see if the way we use it is compatible with a potential partner.

Men in Crisis and Other
Unavailable Lovers

Can a relationship weather a lover's personal storm? For example, if he loses a job, is going through a tumultuous custody battle, or is having a crisis about whether or not to change his career. It sure puts a burden on things. I believe it is possible to get through these tough spots (just as a lover might be there as we endure crises of our own) but when we are the observers rather than the sufferer I think it is important to know the limits of what we can do. As women we might try to "mother" someone—and we know how much adult men love that! We need to step back, and that saves us from being resentful when they don't follow our advice or let us participate fully.

Its also not clear if a full-blown crisis will prevent a man from being intimate. The advice I would give from my own experience is step back more, be emotionally supportive during the tough period, and wait to see who this person is under ordinary circumstances. Of course, turbulence can go on so long that neither you nor he may be able to sustain a relationship, but sometimes things do go back to normal and then you can really see who you are together. It may be better—or not.

And of course the same cautions apply when it's *you* in crisis. Sometimes we can incorporate a man into our life to help us through major problems and sometimes we just can't. A supportive man should be able to come forward—or give space—when you ask him to respond to your needs when you are under pressure. On the other hand, if you are a complete mess, it's unfair to ask anyone who you just met to cope with an extreme crisis. Put things on ice until you are in a stronger, stabilized place.

Having a Lover Who Makes You Feel Irresistible

A man who makes you feel irresistible is a treasure. Most women, including myself, have to wrestle with some kind of body image issue. It's not something that's easy to discuss. By the time we are fifty only a small percentage of women are perfectly fit, perfectly slim, and thrilled with the image they see in their mirror. Most of us, including women whom the rest of us would envy, do not feel as sexually alluring as we might have twenty-five or even ten years ago.

But that doesn't mean we aren't still sexy, great to look at, and arousing to the men we are with. We need to feel that reflected desire, however, and we also need to accept our bodies and faces and feel worthy of being wanted. I am not against diet, exercise, plastic surgery, talented hairdressers, and makeup artists—whatever we want to make us feel good about how we look. I think we owe it to a partner and to ourselves to stay as fit, healthy, and attractive as we can (and they owe it to us). But ultimately it is an interior sense of sensuality and sexiness that we have to create and believe in. This will be relatively easy if our feelings are reinforced by a partner who convinces us that we are desirable. However, it is almost impossible if we are with a constant critic. Stay away from men whose passion is modest to missing, and who have a penchant for critical commentary.

None of us are immune to rejection—but what helps is to remember that even if some men don't want us, other men will. Finding a man who remains sexually ardent through thick and thin is not a small thing. Such men are not impossible to find, and these men have the talent to make us feel like the sexiest thing on earth. Look for them and think very hard about being with any man who is less than adoring to you. We can be desired at any age—and it is the response to that desire that inflames our own emotions and releases us to be our fullest sexual selves.

About Fantasy

It's too bad so many people deny themselves the fun of fantasy play. I think men are more adept at using their erotic imagination: They are more likely to masturbate, masturbate often, and use fantasy to sustain their sexual tension until ejaculation. A national study done in 1995 by a team of demographers and sociologists at the National Opinion Research Center showed that less than half of all women (in the United States) masturbate, many fewer masturbate regularly, and the favorite fantasy is replaying some behavior with a partner that has already taken place. But fantasy can enrich sex even more if it is used to explore behaviors and situations that might never be desirable in real life but still hold an erotic charge—for example, fantasies of group sex or sex with a taboo or unlikely person.

Alone in the privacy of your bubble bath, fantasy can place you and the man of your dreams in a gondola in Venice, atop the Eiffel Tower necking with fireworks exploding around you, on a pristine beach in Bali being lathered in coconut oil by a Javanese tour guide, or just strolling down a garden path hand in hand. With or without a lover as the focus, fantasy is an integral part of being sexually adventurous.

About Sex and Setting

The Caribbean and Bali are exactly the kind of places I would recommend for a couple looking for a getaway to help rekindle passion. One should never underestimate the power of a staged setting to heat up sexual desires. After all, fancy hotels pay designers hundreds of thousands of dollars to create a mood—they obviously think it's worth their money to create a backdrop for romance. They know that while the tropics offer balmy evenings, a big sky, bright stars, and gorgeous vistas, amorous feelings can often be destroyed by even one jarring note. Toilets that run all night, garish room decor, or voices heard through the walls might not deter all lovers, but many women would just not be able to proceed with passion if all these dissonant noises or room defects were present.

Still, you can inoculate yourself against most little mood-spoilers if you decide to. You can open yourself up to possibilities not present in your original plan. You can seduce yourself by necking in the pool, sipping sweet drinks out of one shared straw, and letting yourself remember the great luck of life that allowed you to be together in a setting like this one.

But is a Bali-type getaway necessary? I don't think so. I think people can create very sexy environments in their own bedrooms and bathrooms if they just take the time and keep everyday concerns and distractions at bay. If possible, I would make the bedroom a private, childfree haven except for certain limited hours. This is easier for older than younger women but the point is to keep the bedroom a place for intimate conversations and sexual play and nothing else. If possible, get rid of the television or ban it during hours that have romantic potential. Buy great sheets, have candles everywhere—and use them. Equip your bathtub and shower with scented bath oils, body washes, and shampoos. In my opinion, no bedroom or bathroom should be without a dimmer and flowers and romantic music. Let the bedroom be a stage setting so that the same inspiration that a place like Bali encourages can be available at home.

six

HUGE HANDS

Seductive Toxic Relationships

Flying

I was invited to present at the International Academy of Sex Research meeting in Paris, and of course I accepted. The prospect of a long plane trip became a little more attractive when I was upgraded from business to first class because of my frequent flyer status. When I got on the plane in Chicago, I was also quite tickled to see that the man who sat down next to me was extremely attractive, handsomely dressed, and had rugged leading-man good looks, rather like a young James Coburn. I tried not to stare at him but he had a fascinating face. He had a kind of uber-sexuality, and by that I mean he projected a type of male magnetism that athletes and actors often have. Sitting next to someone who oozed such a large amount of testosterone-soaked charisma was almost uncomfortably sexy. I noticed his broad shoulders, short, well-cut hair, and exceptionally large hands. His hands were almost too big even for his six-foot-one-ish frame. And I quickly scanned for the most important detail of all: no wedding band on his huge ring finger. That, however, was the end of the good news.

He was maddeningly indifferent to me and simply refused to notice me even when I got up to go the bathroom, or asked him what time it was. I decided to play with the situation and see if my work would capture his attention even if I hadn't.

I very carefully took out all my resource material, placing my books, *The Great Sex Weekend* and another called *Everything You Know About Love and Sex is Wrong*, on my tray table and began writing my sex column, answering some juicy questions on my laptop. I noticed from the corner of my eye that my seatmate had ceased to enter figures into the spreadsheet on his computer, and was peering over my shoulder. I pretended not to notice.

In a short period of time, he asked me, "You seem quite busy with work. What do you do for a living?"

"I work as a sociology professor and sexologist."

"A sexologist?"

"Yes, the study of sexual behavior," I said in my best professional voice. "As you might imagine, it's really quite fascinating. It's more than just looking at how Tab A fits into Slot B. I study relationships, laws, cultural norms, identity formation—things like that. It's nice to love your work!" I smiled somewhat seductively after that last sentence.

"Really?" the man replied, grinning broadly.

"Yes, amazingly, I actually get paid to study sex. And right now, I'm on my way to give a lecture in Paris on female sexuality," I said. "Do you think that's like bringing coal to Newcastle?"

Now he seemed quite engaged. The flight attendant offered us wine and our conversation flowed easily to dinner. He had several martinis and became unguarded and chatty. I could feel some chemistry starting. For me, this would be measured by my increased heartbeat, perhaps a bit of flush around the cheeks, and how much eye contact I maintain (and is returned). I was getting a lot of eye contact from this guy whose name, quite fittingly, was Hugh.

Huge Hands

My new travel mate Hugh (whom I had secretly nicknamed Huge Hands) had become a very attentive seatmate. The wine and martinis kept coming throughout the flight. Our conversation grew more flirtatious, helped by the liberal lubrication of free alcohol and the length of the flight.

I am not much of a drinker and rarely have more than two glasses of wine but I hadn't been high in a long time so I thought, *What the hell, I'm not driving!*

Hugh seemed to down it all with aplomb and so I happily accepted the offer of another drink each time it was offered by the attentive steward. I was quite buzzed and having fun with the feeling.

I learned that Huge Hands was single, had been married twice, lived in Detroit, and seemed to be a very successful businessman working in the area of mergers and acquisitions of large companies in trouble.

I found him a challenging person to talk to. He was very bright, much more politically conservative than myself, and unwilling to give an inch on political or intellectual disagreements even as we flirted with one another. I liked the challenge of taking him on, even if I found some of his political ideas slightly to greatly repugnant. We agreed on a certain number of central values however, and I found his strong opinions worth understanding. He listened to my point of view closely, often because he was just waiting to refute it, but I liked having this worthy opponent. We were able to agree to disagree and the conversation got animated more than heated.

We took a break from our debates while he watched a movie and I listened to music and wrote. We kept ourselves occupied with all the amenities and services that first class provided. I was very aware of his presence next to me. I was getting ready to bed down for the night, when I became conscious of the fact that I was in an open dormitory miles up in the sky and only inches away from a handsome guy with a extremely well-proportioned body. He had taken off his coat and tie and dress shirt and was in a t-shirt that showed a well-developed chest. He looked really good. I closed my eyes and fantasized about a way to convert this fortuitous seating into a new iteration of the "Mile High Club." I kept my fantasy to myself, however, and I decided against pursuing anything more than flirtatious banter with my seatmate.

Huge Hands made a quip: "What are you going to wear to bed?"

I joked back, "Nothing but what nature gave me." He looked surprised, pleased.

I smiled, saying, "Just kidding." But we both gave each other a wicked laugh. It seemed that we might have had a little thing going, but regardless, there was no place to put it into play.

The Next Morning

After brushing my teeth, pulling my hair back into a ponytail, and putting on fresh clothes, I returned to my charming seatmate. Huge Hands and I had breakfast in our little courting cabin. I was sorry that I was going to lose such an interesting conversationalist. He was going on to Asia. A small compensation: He gave me his business card—which had his direct number penciled on the back. He promised to look me up if he ever got to Seattle. I held my hand out to shake and Hugh held it in both of his large hands rather tenderly.

He said, "It's been a real pleasure. I hope to see you again." A charge went right through his hands to mine. Seeing him again had just become a real goal. I gave him a card with all my numbers on it and told him a call would be really, really welcome.

My Role Model

The conference went well and I spent some wonderful time with Nadi, a French friend of mine in her late seventies. She was exactly, in almost all respects, what I would hope to be at her age. Role models of how to be every bit a woman in your seventies and eighties are rare and I prized her as a mentor. She was chic, slim, sexy, effervescent, and in such great shape that I had to hurry to keep up with her pace when we strolled the streets. In her heels, short skirt, and gamine haircut, only her snow-white hair gave Nadi's age away at all. She was just a bundle of energy—enthusiastic about her cooking, children, friends, and politics. I was touched by her affection for me and she and I had fun together, talking about love, current events, and books.

I loved hearing her stories about being a young woman who had fallen deeply in love with an important older man.

She had been what I suppose some people would call a mistress and others might call the great amour of a man who was highly placed in French society. He had been head of an international agency and a member of the most famous literary circle in France. Nadi was twenty years younger than her lover, but it was a true love match and eventually they lived together, had a son, and loved each other deeply until his death some twenty years ago. She never loved another man again. It was one of those great passions that could not be replicated. Nadi had never had the desire to be with anyone else again.

Nadi and I had countless conversations about this relationship, about love and about men. Ahead of her time, she lived the independent life of a liberated woman. She had a successful career as a conservator of historical sites and culture and she experienced a profound love in her life. I hoped to stay as vital and attractive as she had and in many ways, I looked to her, and to French women in general, on how to be an older woman. However, as romantic and sympathetic as her own romantic history had been, I knew I had not stopped at one great love, nor would I ever be content to have passion and love only in the past tense. I fervently hoped that I would have another great love in my life.

But one grand passion, that consumed her from the age of twenty to the day she lost him, was the way it worked for Nadi. When he died, no one could ever touch her heart like that again. I wanted to love that deeply, I wanted to experience a total immersion in someone else. But even if the man I loved and lost was not replaceable, I couldn't quite imagine losing my desire for companionship, physical closeness, for intimacy. Nadine and I had countless discussions about her philosophy of life versus mine and while she was immovably uninterested in romance for herself, she was always very interested in my love life. When I was serious about someone I would bring him to meet her if it was at all possible. Bringing a man home to Nadi was like bringing someone to meet my actual mother. However, my mom had passed away more than a decade earlier, so it meant even more to me when Nadi referred to me as her American daughter and welcomed the people I cared about into her home. I could love more than one man in my life—and I could love more than one mother.

During my stay with her, we strolled the streets of Paris near her apartment and talked about my life since my marriage. I said, "I still find myself thinking about Dennis. Nadine, what am I going to do about that?"

Nadi gave me her best French look of "Ah, what can we do with the heart." Then she said, "So your heart is with him. But it will get better. And, I know you. You will love again. There will be a new man."

I said, "But the wear and tear is difficult. Sometimes I wish I could be like you. Have one great love and then devote myself to family and friends and other things."

Nadine stared at me and said, "Do you think that my loss goes away? That I feel no pain thinking about the man I loved for so long and under such difficult conditions? I could not have another man because I am still full of love and I think about him all the time. That is not what I would wish for you. I have my son whom I love very much and my grandchildren and this is enough for me. But I do not think that is who you are. You need love again. Maybe again and again. And I will always be delighted to meet them."

I laughed and hugged her. So French. So practical in so many ways. But also so romantic. She was right, her path was not my path. But I could not help being taken with her magnificent loyalty and depth of emotion. I said good bye to Nadi reluctantly, promising to be back within a year. I was lucky to have Nadi in my life; I just wished I could have her wise and reassuring counsel more often.

Back in Seattle

The flight back home was way less exciting than the flight to Paris. I had no intriguing seatmate to flirt with so I worked and napped. When I returned home though I found a nice surprise: a message on my phone from Huge Hands. I hadn't forgotten about him either—his devilish grin, his sharp blue eyes, and his overall sexiness.

I began a nice cyber–pen pal relationship with Huge Hands and that felt right for me. I would write breezy accounts of my day and he would write one-line zingers back at me—often smart and increasingly erotic. I would say something about how busy my day was and he would just ignore my chitchat and cut to the chase: "I want you. What are you wearing? What aren't you wearing? When are we going to get together?"

The Layover

After weeks and weeks of cyberflirting and phone calls, I was happy to be able to tell Huge Hands that I could arrange a four-hour stay in Detroit on my way to a meeting in New York. He was satisfyingly excited about the prospect of seeing me again. I arranged to meet him outside the United baggage claim. He'd be in a car and we'd go to a nearby bar and talk for a few hours. He picked me up in a bright blue convertible and when I slid next to him he took one look at me and kissed me passionately on the lips. I loved it.

We had been engaging in verbal foreplay for more than a month now and kissing seemed absolutely right. We couldn't stop kissing. It finally dawned on us that we were necking in front of a busy doorway, unconscious that we were holding up a line of cars. Hugh then gained enough presence of mind to drive to the bar.

At the bar, we continued to mix talking with passionate kissing. I didn't have much time to think but when I did I was aware of how little I knew about him. He had told me about his previous law practice (and I had Googled him as part of my due diligence), his education, some of his business deals, and a lot about his past marriages. But I didn't know much about his character. I liked the way he raved about his children and how involved in their lives he seemed to be. That all seemed reassuring.

Hugh was kind of a piece of work though. He was cocksure of himself in just about every category. I liked talking with someone who made me have to think quickly and stay sharp. I liked the challenge of a big personality.

Our first meeting in the sports bar, however, was very little about intellect and a whole lot about lust. We must have been quite the sight, kissing intently at the table, in the parking lot, pressed against the hood of the car. I had trouble catching my breath much less watching the clock—but I couldn't miss my connecting flight so I pulled away from him in time to get back to my next plane. I had to run to get back through security and to the end of the United section of the airport. It was a very sexy beginning.

In my plane seat, sweating from my sprint, I felt a bit hyper, the way I often do when I've met someone who sexually interests me. Still, I wasn't thinking of him as boyfriend material. I had made a decision that my next boyfriend would be local and not only was Hugh not local, he was insanely busy, traveling all the time, and hardly available for an intimate relationship. I also thought that a part of him had ice water in his veins and told him so.

"But, Pepper," Hugh had protested, "I cry at movies and symphonies. I've got this big female side." I didn't believe it. But he was very sexy and he continued to e-mail and call me late at night. Those late-night phone calls were especially warm and sexy, and increasingly affectionate. I looked forward to them.

The Next Time

Once we had had a taste of each other, we both wanted more. This time I was willing to meet him at a hotel in New York when we were both there for business. I arrived at the hotel lobby and he was waiting for me, with a big smile on his face. I have to say that one of the reasons I was so hooked into him was that salacious, mischievous grin he owned. We kissed hello. He already had the room key and he took my luggage and we went directly upstairs.

As soon as I walked into the room he was undressing me before I could say anything. I liked this kind of passionate-no-holds-barred-move. Sometimes I'd really rather not talk. And this was one of those times. Nothing had to be verbally negotiated with Hugh. Our eyes, our bodies and our hands were signaling that we were both entirely enthusiastic about having sex as soon as possible.

While we were kissing we would stop long enough to take off another article of clothing until we were both in our underwear. I thought he had one of the most beautiful bodies I had ever seen. He had been an athlete all his life and even though he was in his early fifties he had a tight tummy and no discernable extra weight. I tried not to think about how my body compared to his. I wasn't at my worst but I wasn't at my best.

Foreplay was fabulous. He clearly enjoyed giving oral sex and I definitely enjoyed giving it, too. And that stereotype about men with huge hands proved to be true. However, when we got to the time that intercourse would have been a good idea, he could not sustain an erection. At this point, I decided to sensitively address what was happening. I pulled away from him a bit, kissed him and said with a seductive smile, "This doesn't seem to be working. Is there anything I should be doing for you?"

He laughed and said, "Sometimes it works. Sometimes it doesn't. But I have an interesting alternative I think you will like." He proceeded to start kissing my thighs and worked his way back to oral sex which made me totally pleased with him.

The Many Months of Hugh

Over the next six months we continued to meet in various American cities and a couple of times he joined me when I was working in some exotic locales such as Antigua or Mexico. We continued our long debates on politics and culture through meals and late nights in bed after sex. Hugh was always interested in sex and in particular giving and receiving oral sex but he could have intercourse only for a short time. It was hard for him to sustain an erection for an entire lovemaking session. Our sex ended with him masturbating himself to orgasm—it was almost the only way he could have a climax. I liked watching—I thought it was sexy. He would hold me and kiss me while he touched himself and it felt very intimate.

I believe that there is no "right" way to have sex—and whatever makes my partner happy and satisfied is just fine with me. Sometimes I would help him and add a few other sensations with my mouth or hand. Other times I would just cuddle into him and touch his chest— which was a big turn-on to him. Most men think of their nipples as just body decoration, but this was not the case with Hugh. His nipples were highly sensitive and often a necessary part of getting him to the point of an orgasm.

One night I asked him about his sexual pattern. "I'm wondering about the fact that you usually prefer to finish lovemaking by masturbating. How did that start?"

He laughed when I turned into a sex expert and started interviewing him.

"All right, Pepper, start taking notes," he joshed, but then turned serious. "My first marriage got hostile early on and we stopped having sex. I was married over twenty years and for about ten of those, my main sexual outlet was masturbation."

"I see. Well, my theory is that you have learned to come like that for so long that it is hard for you to have an orgasm any other way."

He didn't quite agree with my theory—but he didn't have a better explanation. To his credit, he was open to and interested in my theories even if he was going to debate them. Hugh was always willing to talk about his sexual habits and those of other people. He would very carefully ask me what I needed and do it. Besides having huge hands, he had a huge ego and never really seemed to be embarrassed about whether or not he got an erection. I liked that kind of sexual chutzpah.

Love?

As the months accumulated, Hugh starting exhibiting a very unusual and perplexing way of telling me he cared about me. When we saw each other, there were almost never any serious emotional promises or feelings mentioned. In fact, quite the opposite. He felt we lived too far away from each other to get serious unless I was willing to move to Detroit, and I was not. Most of the time he made it very clear that while we were great together, this was a recreational relationship and we both should just enjoy it for what it was. I was more attached than that, but I accepted and understood the terms of the relationship.

But one night he called at midnight and said, "Pepper, I love you."

"Could you repeat that? I don't think I heard you right." I wasn't kidding; I could not imagine tough-as-nails Hugh was telling me he loved me.

He said it again. "I love you."

I really couldn't quite believe it. "Once more, please."

"I love you."

It moved me. I had had feelings for him but had only whispered them to myself because I hadn't thought they'd be welcome. Our dating had been fun and sexy, but he had given me every reason to believe that even if we'd lived in the same city, we probably weren't life partner material—and living in different cities made it easy to just enjoy the good times together and not start talking about mortgages.

I had started to feel like I loved him, too, but there was a distance between us that was not only geographic. He never talked about me coming to live in his section of the world and he definitely did not want to come and live in mine. I didn't think he had enough heart for me. Our connection was hot and cold.

Nonetheless, when we had had a particularly romantic time somewhere, I would occasionally fantasize out loud about the possibility of us living in the same city and sharing more of a life together. He would quickly tell me that we had no future together beyond what we currently had. When he said this I felt sad—but there was almost some relief. He was such a protected guy and so inflexible in his opinions and lifestyle, I knew that if he had wanted to be my partner there would always have been a struggle of wills and perhaps a minimum of emotional generosity. So to some extent, his own emotional limits made it safe for me to care about him.

Many times, late at night on the phone, he said he loved me and told me he had never been as close to anyone else in his life. He would say that we were soul mates, meant to be together, and that ultimately we had to end up together. This went on and became so common that I came to expect these late night confessionals. Yet we would find a weekend together and there was rarely talk of love. Confusingly, after he returned home he would call me up, always late at night, and tell me again how we were meant to be together, how we were soul mates, how I was his best friend and unique in his life and in his emotional attachment, and on and on.

Sometimes I would point out this dichotomy and during a phone call, indicate that I thought what he really wanted was just a great physical friendship.

Insulted, he would say, "How can you say that? You are my best friend in the world. We are soul mates, meant to be together. I love you."

I would start to think I misjudged him. That he was just only brave enough to say these things at night. But then the next time we spoke during the day or saw each other he would seem detached and disinterested. When I would broach going to another level in the relationship, he would back off. I just didn't know how to explain his ambivalent and inconsistent behavior. I would have chucked the relationship if this had happened with someone in my home town.

Hugh was sexy, smart, challenging, and exciting—we had enormous fun together. I figured that I could handle the lack of emotional consistency if I could just keep him in a "special friends" category. It was pretty clear he wasn't planning on being with me on a day-to-day basis, so unless I wanted to be a masochist, I needed to keep him in a special category: someone I "loved" but kept boxed in a special category labeled "fantasy lover."

I also kept dating other men. Against the odds for this kind of relationship, Hugh and I stayed connected and we talked or e-mailed every couple of weeks. I had given up on anything serious with him but I did have a soft spot in my heart for him. Still, I wasn't surprised when one night he called to say he'd met someone. What did surprise me is that he said, "I have met someone and she does not want me to see anyone else—especially you. I have to do what she wants. But I don't want to lose you."

I said, in all earnestness, "I am happy for you. I didn't see a future for us as lovers but I have always hoped we would stay close friends. Why is she so sensitive about our friendship? Shouldn't she trust you enough so that if you say you are committed to her, she should assume you are?" Hugh was silent.

"If this is what you want, I'll respect that boundary and support your relationship 100 percent." I really was kind of pissed off. If his girlfriend loved him and if he loved her, it seems to me she should trust him. I didn't like the idea of someone telling Hugh whom to be friends with. I did understand that perhaps she was insecure. Actually, when I thought about it, if Hugh was my guy, I'd feel a bit insecure, too. He was such a randy man.

Problems

This new situation proved unexpectedly problematic and unsettling. From time to time, Hugh would call me, always late at night, to tell me he loved me and then say he wanted to see me. At first I thought something powerful was driving him to me and that his love for me may be deeper than I had supposed. But the next day or two would pass and he would call up, apologize for his outburst and recoil from his own statements. I told him not to call me up and tell me he loved me. I didn't want to be a part of his midnight fantasies anymore.

"If you want to be faithful, Hugh, be faithful. Don't jerk me around like this."

If he continued to do this I knew one or the other bad thing would happen. Either he would start up with me again and that would be a dead end—or he would ruin our friendship by being indulgent about his feelings and not thinking about how these protestations of love confused me.

I told him, "You shouldn't tell me you love me. It would be better for me and for your relationship to keep our friendship platonic now."

"I agree. We just need to be friends." And that sentiment lasted until the next midnight call.

After a few weeks he called me again, and this time told me, "I love you and can't live without you. I need to see you."

"Hugh, what are you doing? Either you love this lady or you don't. I don't think this is good. I don't understand why you are calling me and then saying you love her and need to stay with her. What do you want to do?"

"I don't know. I love you both. I just can't not see you."

And then, of course, this call was followed by contrite e-mails and further calls saying he should never have said those things. After a couple of these calls, I should have told him to put up or shut up and get lost. This was advice I would have given any woman. But I let it go on too long. His powerful, magnetic presence was still an aphrodisiac for me and I started to think that maybe he really had some very significant feelings for me and that I should see him again and see what was going on. Late one night, he pressed me to come see him for a visit when he was doing business in Portland.

"I need some days with you. I think I love you very much. I need to see you badly."

Finally, I said, "Okay, I'll get a plane ticket." I spent hours thinking about the situation, which had a complex morality, to say the least. My advice to any woman in this situation would be to block Hugh's calls and move on. But I was not following good common sense advice. Knowing I was not being wise, I called my close friend Janet, who had known me since undergraduate school and had met Hugh a couple of times and had a good take on him. She thought I was taking a major risk—but she also thought that Hugh was struggling with a genuine attachment to me and if I still had some feelings for him I should go see what was going on inside of him. She also felt that I was much more attached than I let on. It was clear that I was not ready to retire the guy without a last examination of the relationship.

I decided that maybe there was something here that Hugh had recognized between us that I should honor by considering seriously, too. We were very good together. We had an indomitable sexual attraction and we had been terrific companions. It sounded more and more like he was breaking up with his girlfriend.

The day before I was supposed to leave Hugh called me up and left a message on my answering service that said, "I can't see you. I need to be loyal to my relationship."

I was beyond furious. I was sick of this and the call was the nail in whatever coffin we had been unconsciously building. I was angry at him and myself. I wanted to stop this stupid, destructive dance we were doing together.

I called him at his house and he said, "Be careful, because she's here."

"Screw that!" I yelled. "You've got to stop this. It's disrespectful of both me and your girlfriend when you behave this way. Stop calling me or I'm going to talk to your girlfriend about what's been going on with you and me. You are an insensitive schmuck playing with my feelings and betraying her as well. She should know who you really are." And I hung up.

"It's Fran"

A few days later, my cell phone rang while I was in a cab. It was a woman who said, in blunt tones that indicated I knew her, "It's Fran calling."

"Fran? I'm sorry, I don't know who this is."

"Oh, yes, you do. I'm Hugh's girlfriend." I was stunned. I assumed he would know that I was just angry when I talked to him and I had no intention of calling his girlfriend. I was now in an awkward situation.

"How can you do this to Hugh and me? Why are you after my boyfriend?"

"Excuse me, Fran. I was content to just be friends with him once he told me he was seeing you. But he has been calling me at least weekly to tell me he loves me, and wants to see me. Frankly, I haven't known what to think. I assumed the two of you are on the skids. Then he calls me later on and says he wants to preserve his relationship with you and that we should just stay friends. This has happened multiple times. He calls and tells me he can't live without me, and then he calls again to tell me to forget his last call. I am totally confused about what is going on and I am angry and tired of his inconsistent and inconsiderate treatment of me. I called him because I didn't want it to go on anymore."

Fran was silent for a moment, then said, "Hugh has a terrible drinking problem. When he is drinking heavily he starts calling people late at night and saying things while he is totally drunk that he can scarcely remember. He is good at camouflaging that he is that drunk, but he will have polished off an entire bottle of Scotch. I have arranged interventions to get him to stop and admit he has a problem and get help. His whole family has had to do interventions."

I was twice stunned, even speechless as I listened to these revelations. It had the ring of truth. I remembered that when he called me he would often repeat parts of his protestations of love over and over until I would accept them. It was so unlike the way he spoke to me when we were together. This new piece of information clarified everything for me. I felt embarrassed to be so clueless. I told Fran, in all earnestness, that I was sorry for any and all of my part in this, and that I had not realized that he had been drunk when he was declaring his love for me. I had just gotten angry and tired of being emotionally set up and didn't imagine he could be acting the way he was with me and still have a serious commitment to her. I had absolutely no idea that he had been drunk when he was talking to me.

Well, I take that back. I did have a suspicion once that he might be drinking and I asked him if he was drunk and he scoffed at the suggestion. However, I wondered about it. I suddenly recalled how many martinis he had put away on our first plane ride together and I remembered thinking that while he had gotten more gregarious, he did not seem to be drunk, which meant he had to be pretty experienced at downing martinis.

More Lessons

Now that I could understand Hugh's behavior better, I had to look again at my own. I had been almost willfully stupid. I was humbled by my own denial. In my own (weak) defense, I have never been much of a drinker and had not been around an alcoholic (or at least known I was around an alcoholic), and so didn't know what to look for. But now it was clear and I felt bad about not understanding and not having better boundaries for myself.

That was the end of it. I never heard from Hugh again. No surprise there. I was both relieved and sad. We had had a chance to change into a lifetime friendship if we'd played it right—but we did not, and he had become a toxic person in my life. So now I had to review what this whole business had really been about.

Before I found out about Hugh's alcoholism, I would have described our long-distance affair as hot, a lot of fun, a challenging connection with deep affection, maybe even love. Now, I had to reassess everything. I can't know what Hugh was actually feeling, but I thought long and hard about why I had stayed attached to him. I think I was overly impressed with his intellect and his alpha personality and I was not self-protective enough when it was clear that he didn't care about how his actions affected me.

I had let my hormones create an artificial bond between us. He had never offered me himself in a real way—but I had let our mutual sexual attraction and romantic trips get in the way of analyzing his behavior more carefully. He had called me his "best friend" and his "soul mate" and told me time and time again that if I ever needed anything he would always be there for me—but that was either alcohol talking or he didn't know what intimacy and friendship were about. I had no idea about the biggest secret of his life—his runaway drinking. And, because I was lost in the romance of it all, I ignored clues that I could have put together if I'd tried hard enough.

It was a disappointing end to a relationship that had had its high moments as well as the last low ones. I cared enough for Hugh to hope he and Fran figured out a way to cure his alcoholism. And I cared enough for myself to never accept that kind of treatment from anyone again.

✦ Advice to Myself (And Others) ✦

Drinking Problems

I have been, at times, very naive about people's drinking habits. I grew up in a home where it seems to me that the first time I saw my parents drink more than one drink was when they were in their fifties. I had my own first drink at eighteen, overdid it, became as sick as a very sick dog, and never went near bourbon again. I am not always sure of the signs of drunkenness, but I catch on when people slur their words and say the same sentence over and over. But it has to be extreme for me to "get it."

What were the signs that I missed and you might look for, too?

a. Erratic behavior
b. Melodramatic protestations of love or commitment—
uttered many times, and recanted or denied at others
c. Big changes in attitude and behavior when drinking
d. Calls, especially late at night, that are different in
content and emotion than other times of the day
e. In the male case, continuing impotence in an
otherwise healthy and sexually interested man

Hugh did all of these and more and I still wasn't getting it. He was such a confident person, he seemed so sure of his opinions, his intellectual and personal authority, and he was so impressive over- all, that the idea of him with an out-of-control addiction just didn't make sense. But in fact, each of the first four items on the list de- scribed him. And I think the fifth may have been true as well. His inability to have an erection much of the time might have been in large part alcohol-related. Alcohol constricts blood vessels and over time can damage a man's ability to have a strong erection. I thought Hugh was a great lover with or without an erection, and so I didn't spend much time thinking about it. I attributed much of his erectile problems to his dysfunctional sexual life with his second ex-wife but in retrospect I think alcohol was very much involved. I remember that he went through a period of time when he was perfectly able to have a hard erection, and while I thought at the time he might be taking one of the erectile function drugs, it occurs to me now that he may have merely stopped drinking for a while.

Erectile Dysfunction

Alcohol isn't the only reason for male impotence. As men get older, an increasing number of them will have trouble getting and keeping erections. I personally don't think it's that big of a deal—if you can talk about it. There are a number of ways to have excellent, passionate sex that don't require a hard penis—but none of them will work as well as they could if one part of your mind and one part of his mind is worrying about what is or is not happening between his legs. In Hugh's case, I have to admit that I was a bit sorry when his penis worked perfectly because then he preferred intercourse and cut down on the extensive foreplay he usually engaged in. I missed those long, luxurious sessions of oral sex.

There was also the curious fact that he could almost never have an orgasm during intercourse and rarely by any other means than his own hand. He had gotten used to having orgasms touching himself—and that was the way he preferred to climax. That would not have been my first preference but it didn't get in the way of a passionate sex life. There are a lot of ways to make love, and I think older men and women have to get out of thinking that if it isn't intercourse, it isn't worth it. Not so, by a long shot. I was extremely turned on and our sex life was very satisfying. Ultimately I think it is the psychological dynamics (healthy or not) as well as technique that make a relationship hot.

Toxic People

If you met Hugh you wouldn't know he was toxic. I don't think *he* knew he was toxic. He was handsome, articulate, extraordinarily bright and opinionated, and he had become ultra successful at every-thing he had done in his work life. (His marriages that turned hostile and sexless were another story.) But he was a master at intermittent reinforcement—hot now, cold then, hot later, cold following that—a kind of pattern that keeps a lover emotionally hooked. He didn't want me enough to really try to create a relationship, but whenever I would get distant, he would come on strong.

Certainly, in his case some of this was due to his drinking prob-lem. But men, whether alcoholic or not, can be just plain emotionally unhealthy. At times Hugh made me feel like a sexual convenience. Sex would be immediate, quick, and impersonal. We would meet in some city and we'd walk through the door of our hotel room, and before the door had shut he had slammed his mouth against mine and had his clothes and mine off within minutes of arrival. I loved the passion, but over time, the lack of romance got to me. When I had enough of it to withdraw he would turn into the most romantic of lovers and arrange for a room with a fireplace, great Champagne and long, luxurious lovemaking. Then, instead of a new level of intimacy getting established, he would disappear for a while and not take my calls. Then he'd call out of the blue, late at night, and tell me he loved me and couldn't live without me. I would decide not to see him again, and then he'd beg, cajole, and be seductive.

I know you may be saying—Pepper, what were you thinking? You should know better. How could you put up with such a hot and cold rela-tionship? I don't have an adequate defense except to mumble something about how hot he was, and how effective intermittent reinforcement is. (You may remember that if you took a Psych 101 course.)

Worse, unfortunately, I am so not alone in this kind of revolving door syndrome. I hear the same type of story I have just told you over and over from all kinds of women.

Toxic men can be unusually seductive and tempting. We know that they are not good for us—we just have trouble weaning ourselves from them. Still, the important thing to remember is that life with one of these guys can never be good—and love can never be real. So the best way not to sustain damage is to get out early. Is that hard to do? Very. Especially because it is hard to leave an unhealthy but exciting relationship for no relationship at all. Still, that's a leap worth taking. It's far better to be single than allow oneself to be emotionally abused.

What constitutes abuse? A man who doesn't show love in his everyday treatment of you. A man who systematically disregards the impact his acts will have on your ego and heart. Sex under these circumstances may look like making love, but this kind of lover is selfishly romantic, interested only in sustaining his own fantasies and needs.

It's sad for me to come to this conclusion over this relationship. Hugh used to tell me he would be there for me forever, that he would do anything for me, and that I was his best friend and I wanted to believe him. However, a friend would not have continued to make those calls, or sabotaged our friendship by pursuing me after he had made a commitment elsewhere. I take a chunk of the blame here—I could, and should, have kept saying no. But if you are enamored, it's hard to resist what you think might be your lover's real change of heart and sudden understanding of your uniqueness as a partner. Well, there is enough "blame" to go around—but the bottom line here is that getting out of a toxic relationship is like breaking an addiction: extremely difficult to do, but absolutely necessary for your self-respect and emotional health.

Gambling on Someone Becoming Who You Want Them To Be

Do most adults radically change? Not really. So why do we expect our lovers to become someone other than the person they are? I believe that this sometimes is attributable to the fact that many of us have a savior complex. By that I mean we think we are the one person in the world that can save someone from himself (or herself). We have the conceit that we alone hold the key to this person's innermost needs, and that we can provide love and show them how to love, if we only stick it out through whatever traumatic tests come our way.

We think that this guy has problems—but we can solve them.

We will just tinker with this and that and voilà! He will love us as he has loved no one before. He will give up his past philandering, he will regret the pain he has caused us, he will understand how unique and fabulous we truly are, and he will start to get all warm and fuzzy and pop the question and be a model husband for ever after. A series of statements like that should make us all gag.

It's so patently illogical and self-deluding—and yet how many of us have tried again and again to make a relationship something it was not—and after many ups and down, realized it would never be what we wanted it to be. In my experience, you get what you got. Occasionally traumas change a person (a near-death experience, a loss of their livelihood, an unexpected divorce, a cataclysmic event like the World Trade Center), but that is so much rarer than the status quo with little blips of reform or insight. In general, people are who they are, and we are who we are. While some therapists who do couples counseling will try to change the behavior of one or both parties in order to save a relationship, others urge toleration and acceptance as a more likely solution. I tend to side with this latter group more often than not.

Going from Lover to Friend

I have remained close friends with just about every man I have ever been seriously involved with—but it doesn't work unless the transition to friendship includes genuine care for each other's feelings and vulnerabilities. If the embers of love are still alive and one or both people stay seductive, it endangers the establishment of a new kind of relationship. It makes me sad to say this, but not all great love affairs can transition into something else.

Hugh and I did not make the transition to friendship, but it's a process worth discussing. I think that if there has been a great love affair, there are often the seeds of a great friendship. The tendency, however, is that if you are hurt because you were ultimately rejected as a life partner, you may be tempted to react strongly and bitterly against the person who has disappointed your hopes and heart. I understand that, but I think it helps to think of it this way: If this person has loved you and tried his best to be a good partner, it's not his fault if his heart can't go the distance.

If there is still respect and admiration, why not give yourself the time and distance you need to get over your heartache—and then resume the friendship part of the relationship when you are able to do that. There might be limits, especially if they are now in love with someone else. But sooner or later your heart will forget about how much it needed this person, and you will be able to reclaim some memories and connection that are still sweet and are a good foundation for friendship.

Practically, that means meeting for lunch instead of dinner, or having dinner early without romantic trappings. It means being able eventually to discuss the new people in your life—and be happy for each other. If you know you are special to one another, your close and deep friendship is a considerable consolation for the loss of romantic love. If you break up with honesty, communication, and respect for each other, if you feel you love their character and past treatment of you, then these feelings can carry toward a friendship. Sure, you may have to forgive a few of his trespasses (or vice versa) and the feelings of rejection (that is part of any breakup) but if you can get beyond that, the friendship can be real, durable, and profound.

seven

THE COMMITMENT

Love and Compromise

Ups and Downs

It was not quite three years since I separated from my husband. I was finding dating a roller coaster—up, down, high, low, thrilling, scary, and ultimately exhausting. The hot and cold relationships with Dennis and Hugh had taken a lot out of me.

Setting New Criteria

One quiet Sunday evening after working at the ranch all day, I decided to go back online. A profile that caught my eye featured a picture of a good-looking man, blond-haired, green-eyed, with a sweet smile. He was fifty-two, younger than me, which usually worked out just fine. I read his profile slowly. He had a University of Washington undergraduate and business degree, and the personal statement he had written about himself sounded like someone I wanted to know. He worked as a consultant to the aerospace industry. He had done some therapy to help him over the end of his marriage and felt that he knew himself and what he wanted. I liked his candor about seeking counseling and I admired his ability to be self-reflective. He wrote that he was ready to create a meaningful, committed relationship with someone. He was also involved with horses. I was thrilled to think I might find someone who loved horses even half as much as I did. I was intrigued and sent him a message linked to my profile that went something like this.

Hello there.

I live on a horse ranch just like you do. I am affiliated with the University of Washington and I really liked the way you described your personal growth over the last few years. I am a professor, writer and rider and I think we might have a number of things in common. I am enclosing my profile and if you like what you read let me know, and I'll send you a picture.

Sincerely,
Rosebud

He e-mailed back the same day.

Dear Rosebud:

You sound great and I'd love to talk. In fact, I think I know who you are. If you will give me your cell phone, I'll call you. If you would rather call me, here's my number.

Sincerely,
Ted 843

I e-mailed him my picture and thought, *I wonder what Ted's response will be. I wonder if he really does know who I am . . . and if he does, whether that's a good or bad thing?*

His speedy response indicated he was interested so we arranged for a time to talk on the phone. I called him and his voice was friendly, confident, and attractive. He was lively, easy, and fun. I liked this guy. Then he gave me a zinger.

"Pepper, I have to tell you that I remember you from when I was an undergraduate," he said sweetly.

"Really?" I said cautiously. I was thinking, *Uh oh.*

"Yes, really, you were my professor in Soc 352."

"How old are you?" I asked, worried about the fact that maybe he was younger than he said or looked.

"Fifty-two. Don't worry. I dropped out for a while and came back later. I was an older student. I only talked to you once very briefly about an assignment. It was a huge class."

Oh, no. I had been his professor! This may not be good. On the other hand, that had been twenty-five years ago. I guess enough time had gone by, and he wasn't that much younger than me.

I said, "Well, I apologize for not answering your question. I just needed about twenty-five years to think it over."

We both laughed and we agreed to meet a couple of days later for dinner. We knew we had enough in common to skip the usual thirty-minute interview date over coffee. I was excited to see him even though I could not remember meeting him. Almost all my under-graduate classes were large and it was rare that I would get to know a student well enough to pick him or her out of a crowd.

A Chance Encounter

In the meantime, I had Sheila, a friend and fellow sex expert, visiting and I planned on entertaining her the next day. We were going to a charity fund-raiser being held on a boat. I thought Sheila would enjoy the cruise around the Puget Sound on a bright sunny day, so the two us went for the three-hour trip.

Sheila and I were among the first guests on the yacht. As soon as we walked in we hugged the hostess and were sent to the bar to get drinks and mingle. There were only a few people there. Among them was a sort of sad-looking, nicely dressed, tall guy, standing alone. He appeared to be feeling awkward, as if he was looking for his wife who had deserted him during this party that he really didn't want to be at. Sheila and I chatted him up a bit, but I wasn't really in the mood to meet new people and she and I drifted over to various other guests who started to fill up the boat. I clung to a group of old friends, enjoying this rare opportunity to have several hours of the pleasure of their company while we sailed beautiful Puget Sound.

As the time went on I began to get nervous about getting back in time for a horse breeding that was to take place at my ranch. I edged toward the front of the boat to make sure I got out quickly when she docked. The sad-looking tall guy, still without a wife by his side but looking less sad, was there and so I talked to him a little. Somewhere in the conversation it turned out he had horses and my ears perked up.

I asked, "What kind of horses do you own. Race horses?"

He looked at me strangely and said, "Why would you pick race horses?"

Chagrined at my own stupid assumption, I said, "Well, it's that kind of crowd here."

Then he looked at me, with a mischievous look in his eyes that I rather liked and made me reassess him. "Pepper, you know what kind of horses I have. We talked about it."

I stood there stupefied. I racked my brain. When could I have talked to this guy? I didn't recognize him at all. I had to apologize.

"I am so sorry. I don't recognize you. Did we talk along time ago?"

"No," he said. "Not a long time ago. Very recently."

Now I was totally baffled. He, on the other hand, was smiling, clearly enjoying the advantage.

"Pepper, I'm Ted. Or Ted 843 online."

It took me a full ten seconds to get it. Very long seconds. Then it hit me. He was the guy I was supposed to have dinner with the next night. He looked like his picture now that he was smiling. I recognized him. I was horribly embarrassed.

"I am so sorry," I sputtered. "I just didn't recognize you, Ted."

"No need to apologize. I'm just happy to see you again after all these years."

"Well, Ted, you are being very forgiving."

He grinned.

"I have really messed up. I would certainly understand if you didn't want to have dinner with me tomorrow night—but I hope that you will."

"Of course," he said, quite graciously. "I'm really looking forward to catching up."

Our First Date

The next night, as I dressed for the date, I thought about what I should wear. Ted had looked stylish but casual and so I decided to do the same. He asked me to meet him at an Italian restaurant in a part of town I was totally unfamiliar with. So I put on a really nice shirt with black pants and figured that couldn't offend anyone. I took such great care to be on time that I got to the restaurant a full half-hour ahead of time. There was a big statue of a rearing horse in the front of the place, which I took to be a good omen.

I walked in, happy to get there before him so I could settle in—but he was already there. A half an hour early, too! This was also a good sign. The restaurant, despite the odd horse statue, turned out to have superb food. He ordered expensive wine and even though I knew nothing about wine at the time, I thought the bottle he picked was particularly delicious. The time flew by in the way it does when you really click with someone. We talked about our lives twenty-five years earlier when we first "met," his experience in grad school, horses, our kids, and our family backgrounds.

As Ted talked I thought about how well we were connecting. My pet theory about believing I know right away if I am attracted to some-one or not was clearly being disproved. This was a man I had not given a second thought or glance to when I saw him on the boat. Yet here I was totally engaged by him and definitely physically attracted.

After the dinner, he walked me to my car and I asked, "Ted, I enjoyed that very much. Would you like to go horseback riding next weekend?"

He replied, "That would be great. Should I bring my saddle?"

I found that a totally endearing remark. I love a man who has a saddle to bring!

"Sure," I said. "How about you come Sunday morning and I'll provide the horses and lunch."

"That would be really nice," Ted said. He then bent down and gave me kiss on the cheek.

I was a little taken aback. It was such a decorous kiss. I didn't need a big passionate kiss but I didn't know what this little peck meant. If he was thinking about me as his teacher, this was not going to be fun.

We talked a little during the week and Sunday he showed up at my ranch house, saddle in hand. He looked great in jeans. When I watched the competent way he tacked up the horse I gave him, a fabulous gelding named Bellagio, I thought to myself, *This is sexy. It's been a long time since I've groomed horses with a date.*

I could literally feel my attraction for Ted growing. Funny what turns out to be foreplay.

We had a great ride and then I pulled together a couple of sandwiches for lunch at the house. Ted had never ridden a gaited horse before and so much of our discussion was about the merits of gaited horses compared to Arabs, which is the breed he liked and had shown in Western Pleasure competition. Eventually he had to leave because he was meeting his daughter for a special dinner. As I was saying good bye to him he gently bent down and kissed me quickly on the lips. I loved the way he kissed me this time.

I walked him to his car and he asked me, "Would you like to go out to a wine tasting next weekend?"

"Yes," I said. "But I'm pretty ignorant about wines so I won't be able to give any knowledgeable opinions."

He smiled and said, "There's no right answer. It's about discovering what you like."

"That's what I'm doing right now," I quipped.

And then, most amazingly, I remembered him from all those years ago. A good-looking student coming up after class to ask me some question. It stunned me that I could recall him. He saw me deep in thought and, almost as if he read my mind said, "Well, I've known you for twenty-five years and now you're getting to know me. I think we've been taking it slow enough—time to speed this up a bit."

I liked this guy.

Dating Ted

Ted picked me up at my home. He was very flattering about my taste and that pleased me. I liked his taste, too—and noticed that once again, he picked and wore clothes well. I don't normally notice how a man dresses but Ted had a signature of casual elegance and I really appreciated it.

It took us forever to find the wine tasting venue, but neither of us got upset and I found that I wanted to lengthen the time we'd have together any way we could—even if that meant getting lost. When we finally got there the wine tasting had just started, and they were featuring German whites—a kind of wine neither of us knew much about. The wine tasting date was not only fun, Ted's own enthusiasm for the enterprise got me more than situationally interested in the industry and products. He guided me through some of the basic ways to smell and taste wine and ultimately opened up the world of collecting and discussing fine wines to me. I didn't have the greatest palate in the world, but I became more knowledgeable and that led to a continuing interest in wine, especially red wines, especially syrahs. More important, that date led to a series of dates—each one as interesting and as much fun at the last.

The Friendship Evolves

We took drives out in the country, went to movies and plays and had great fun discussing them, and we began to meet each other's friends. He showed me around the business he owned and ran which was impressive not only because it was successful, but also because he had created this from a dead-end start—a boy who had left home at seventeen without a dollar in his pocket, who had gone from a struggle to survive to a man who put himself through the UW and gotten a BA and a Masters in business. After college, he created his own company. I admired his incredible discipline, ambition, passion for his work, and intelligent decision making. I started asking his advice on some major decisions of my own, prized his counsel, and when my own fledgling business, a boarding stable, had some big problems, I leaned on him for emotional and practical support.

I thought we made a great team and I felt stronger with him in my life. I was beginning to fall in love with him and the thought of us as a couple made me giddy with pleasure. Still, I was a bit worried: Various trips he had to take and then I had to take slowed down some of our sexual momentum. We had become much more intimate but we still had not made love.

After the seventh date ended with some more passionate kissing, but no sign of any other interest in going further, I thought this was frustrating and a little worrisome. It is was clear Ted did not want to have sex with me yet. Actually, I hoped it was only a matter of "yet." I hoped he was attracted enough to want me.

I was feeling quite attached and I loved his company. I didn't want to be just his friend or companion for excursions.

"How's it going with Ted?" Dom asked one Wednesday night over the phone.

I was doing my usual multitasking. I balanced my cell phone and a latte while I retrieved e-mail messages.

"Well, I am beginning to worry about whether we will ever have sex."

"What number date is next weekend?" Dom asked.

"Nine. But I do think there might be something smart about putting sex off as long as it eventually arrives."

"What makes you say this?"

"I think I sometimes use sex to distance myself from people, rather than become emotionally intimate," I said. "Once you sleep with someone, sex often becomes something you do in the relationship, instead of talking and deepening the psychological and emotional connection. Not sleeping with Ted is allowing us get to know each other."

"This sounds like a new dating mode for you."

"It is."

Our Roles

After a few more weeks of dating, I was getting a little hurt, and slightly insulted, about Ted's lack of sexual interest beyond good bye kisses. But I didn't want to push it because I knew that rarely helped and that it would be especially wrong for this guy. He was not the kind of man you could push. His early split from his parents and family had made him extremely self-reliant. He was also an interesting mix of traditional and liberal attitudes about women. He was at ease with my desire to pay my own way some of the time (we alternated who paid for dinner most of the time) and he liked my assertive style and devotion to my work.

Nonetheless, it was clear to me that there were some male prerogatives, like driving, or initiating physical contact, that he preferred to keep in place. I noticed other things that made me hesitant to take the sexual lead. When we ate dinner out, he would ask me what I wanted and then usually ordered for both of us. When I visited his consulting firm, it was clear that he had a top-down management style. He liked leadership and control and while he was pleased with my accomplishments and personality, it was clear to me that he needed to be the leader in this, or any, relationship. I felt very respected and he took my opinion seriously and often acted on my advice, so his approach didn't bother me. But waiting to be wanted was not my strong suit.

In any case, by this time I wanted him to want me enough to make the first moves. He knew my sexual temperament—he'd heard my lectures! It became clear to me he was holding off consciously and for specific reasons. I respected his right to go at whatever pace he wanted. My new mantra was: *This is a new mode. There is no need to rush.*

Finally, he made a move toward more intimacy. Ted invited me to visit him for a five-day visit on his annual fishing excursion to the British Columbian wilderness. I accepted immediately, and about a month later I found myself taking two seaplanes for five hours to get to where prime salmon-fishing waters had lured him. As my plane circled in over a gorgeous heavily treed bay, my heart started beating harder as I sighted him waiting for me at the dock. He was dressed in a yellow all-weather coat and he looked relaxed and handsome.

I have to count this as one of the most romantic moments of my life.

We kissed as I got out of the plane, and he took my things and we went to the cabin cruiser he had rented for the month. It was cozy but not at all fancy, designed more for fishing than luxury cruising. I liked the feel of it but as soon as we'd thrown down my gear, we were quickly off on the smaller skiff to see the salmon fishing waters—and be alone. His son was on board the bigger boat helping Ted take care of the various clients he had invited for fishing during the other weeks of his month-long stay.

I was glad to be whisked away. Ted and I needed to reconnect privately.

Alone in the calm waters, he stopped the boat. He looked at me and I got up and walked over to him. We looked at each other for a while and smiled and then kissed slowly and with emotion. Then his kisses intensified and I felt permission to let myself go. We started kissing passionately and I melted into him, the scenery, the water lapping at the boat, the entire environment just became part of that kiss. He held me tightly and his hands stroked my back.

We pulled away from each other after about five minutes of this and he said, "Let's go back to the boat. My son has to go to the local fishing tackle store for a couple of hours and we can have the boat to ourselves."

We motored back, and I kept my hand on his thigh for the entire time. We kept gazing at each other and the look was warm as well as sexually excited.

The Moment

This was the feeling I had longed for and it thrilled me to feel him give himself to me in a way he had not before. When we got to where the big boat was moored, he checked to make sure his son was nowhere around and we went into the small master bedroom. I was thrown off a bit, though, by that bedroom. As soon as I entered it, I was greeted with a sour, musty smell that told me there was probably a serious mold problem.

I didn't want to say anything right then and ruin the moment. But perhaps I should have. The smell permeated my brain and as thrilled as I was to be with him, I found myself unable to fully let go and be in the moment.

Ted took off my clothes. Then his. He looked great to me. He worked hard on his body and it showed. He was lean, not particularly muscular but toned. After so long a buildup it was kind of embarrassing to see him without clothes and I was unusually nervous. I felt there was a lot at stake here and I wasn't sure how to proceed. To be safe I waited for his lead.

He lay down on the bed and I lay down next to him. It was a bit cramped—the bed took up most of the room and we smiled and laughed a bit at the awkwardness of it all. Both nude, we faced each other, my shorter, heavier body pressed against his longer, leaner one. It felt great.

We kissed and looked into each other's eyes and then it struck me. I cannot believe I forgot condoms! I started to do what I have told other people not to do—make a deal with a higher power: God, if you can just give me a pass this one time. That felt presumptuous so I just started to rationalize.

Okay, I know I am healthy. I had just had a checkup a couple of weeks ago. I believe Ted is not sleeping with anyone else. At least I don't think he's the kind of guy to have a lot of partners. This is probably okay.

Ted continued kissing me but I couldn't stop thinking about the condom.

I thought, *Okay, Pepper, this is not a good calculation to make and it really is just a rationalization not to spoil the moment. Maybe Ted will produce a condom. But maybe he figures since I'm the expert, he'll just wait and see if I produce one.*

I made a decision: I will just put my trust in Ted.

Ted and I moved slowly with one another. My heart was there but my head was not cooperating. My heart was so full, the actual things we did seemed less notable than our emotional connection. It certainly was making love rather than having sex. But between the mold smell and my anger at myself for not having condoms ready, I wasn't fully present. I could hear people out on the dock and I knew the room was not soundproof. I was way too conscious of the outside world and it just wasn't an ideal way to start our sexual relationship.

Ted was trying to be a careful, sensitive lover but then I thought I heard noise outside the door.

That did it for me; I knew I wasn't going to be able to have an orgasm. Usually, although not always, I make a lot of noise when I come—it's just the way I am. I was too intimidated to feel free to do that—but Ted was working diligently to give me an orgasm. I knew it was impossible and so I did something that I never did again with him, but that seemed the most useful choice given the situation: I did a very good—but fake—rendition of an orgasm.

I couldn't hide some of this nervousness and it was just not a stellar session in bed. I sensed that Ted was disappointed, too. After so much waiting, I had wanted our first time in bed to be perfect. But it wasn't. Still, we cuddled and felt close to each other and napped in bed until we heard a lot of banging around in the galley which meant his son had returned to his boat and we should get up so I could be polite.

A Second Chance

The next morning Ted and I made love but we were still off balance and I did not have an orgasm. I sensed that Ted took this rather personally. While we were making love he asked me if I had had an orgasm yet. I was making a lot of noises (everything felt great) so it might have been hard to know whether or not one of them was an orgasm or not.

I said, "No, but it doesn't matter. I am just loving this."

Ted looked worried and said, "What should I do for you to have an orgasm?"

I replied, "I don't need one. I am really just enjoying making love to you right now." But I could tell from his expression that this was not a satisfactory answer.

So I told him how to touch me and kiss me and that did the trick. Still, it wasn't quite what it could be since I was aware that I was doing this more for his benefit and the benefit of the relationship than my own needs.

I lay there snuggled in his arms, so happy to be with him. It was hard to know exactly what was going on in Ted's mind, but it seemed that he might feel that whether I had an orgasm not only reflected badly on him, it reflected badly on us as a couple. I didn't want that feeling to gain traction. There was no lack of passion or desire on my part but just thinking about how important my orgasm was to him made me think too much, rather than feel the sensations in my body. I needed to get out of this mess. So the next time he started to touch me, I told him how to give me an easy, quick orgasm and he seemed pretty happy with the result.

While Ted took a shower I thought about what was not quite clicking between Ted and me. What was true was that I needed to be totally in the moment to have an orgasm during intercourse and there were a lot of distractions keeping my mind in more than one place. Also, I felt it normally takes a while with a new partner to figure out how to fit together, how to respond to each other's sexual habits, and how to relax enough to be easily orgasmic.

I was feeling pressure for the sex to be perfect, some of that probably self-imposed, I was actually scared that I wouldn't have an orgasm each of those first times we made love. Still, by the second day, it was getting easier and I felt we were learning each other's bodies and getting in excellent sync.

After a perfectly lovely day at sea, Ted and I ended our third night with a romantic dinner and another chance at lovemaking while we were alone on the boat. By this time I was used to the boat's bedroom, we had gotten rid of the moldy mattress, and I was entranced with Ted. I had also worked up a big desire for him. We made love. I had an orgasm that rocked my body and we fell asleep in each other's arms. I felt Ted was happy, but I was relying on my instincts. He didn't talk much about his feelings. I wanted to be totally honest and intimate with him and I figured now that we were sexually adjusted to each other I would be able to fess up about my acting performance so that we wouldn't have any lies between us. Ted had stressed that he wanted a deeply intimate relationship and I agreed, which to me meant no secrets, open hearts and truth, however difficult that might be.

The days passed and I found myself enjoying Ted's company more and more. In bed, however, the unspoken expectation of timely orgasms remained.

I was tired of going over and over this same territory in my brain. While Ted slept I found myself wide awake thinking about the situation. I have never felt that kind of pressure in any other relationship. I had to get Ted to see it as no big deal. It was not about technique, or desire, or anything but the random readiness of my body. I began to understand the performance pressure most men have felt during the course of their sexual lives

The Talk

On the fourth day Ted and I took the big boat on an expedition into a beautiful inlet off the ocean. There was some tension about entering the inlet: It was impassable at low tide, turbulent at high tide. You had to get through it at just the right time of day. It was exciting watching Ted captain the boat and we celebrated not getting into big trouble. That night we dropped anchor in this idyllic and quiet pool of water and put out crab pots. When we picked them up they were full of crabs. Ted expertly prepared them and we gorged ourselves on the sweetest crab I have ever tasted. I loved seeing Ted's big, happy smile of satisfaction. All was right with the world and Ted and I joked and talked and had an easy camaraderie. We anchored on the boat overnight and held each other and looked at the stars without speaking for a long time. The air was full of promise and comfort.

The next morning Ted and I took the skiff and went to explore the marshlands, a beautiful cove where the water met the land and entered it, narrowing down into meandering rivulets of water. The more our little boat moved down these tiny rivers penetrating the land, the thicker the marsh became and after a while we were poling rather than floating our way in. The skiff grounded a few times and we had to jump out of the boat or put paddles into the water to push ourselves out. As we followed a narrower and narrower slip of water, we came across places where very big bears had obviously been sleeping. I was really hoping those bears weren't close and I tried not to look nervous, but I was. Ted got us out of the area without incident and I realized how much I trusted him to protect me. I relaxed under his obviously competent leadership and allowed myself to just enjoy this gorgeous inlet. I kept feeling so blessed to be invited into this pristine environment.

That night when Ted and I had returned to the big boat moored at the dock, I decided to see if I could lower the pressure a little bit on the whole orgasm question. I felt so comfortable with him. A little open discussion on this seemed possible now.

I said, "Ted, I just love making love with you. I wanted you out there in the reeds, and while we were eating the crab. There hasn't been a moment on this trip that I didn't want to reach for you. I'm just so happy to be here."

Ted smiled and kissed me.

"I just want to talk about one thing, if I might."

He looked serious and said, "Shoot."

"Well, it's about having orgasms," I said.

Ted looked a bit surprised, but rebounded fast. "Okay," he said, in a somewhat measured tone. "I know there's something going on there. Do you usually have a lot of trouble having orgasms?"

I looked at him. The easy way out would have been to say orgasms were hard for me and then he would have understood. But they weren't that hard and I was thinking this was a relationship that could go on forever and we had both talked about the importance of honesty for intimacy. So I wanted to open up, tell all, and start from there.

So I said, "Well, no. I don't have a lot of trouble having orgasms. I'm just like most other women. I don't have an orgasm every time I have sex."

He said, "Well, I don't know. My experience has been that every woman I have ever been with has had an orgasm every time."

I looked at him, assuming he was joking. He was not.

I said, "I don't think that's right. Most women in the studies that I know about don't have orgasms every single time they make love."

He said, "They do with me."

Uh oh, I thought.

I said, "How do you know?"

He said, "I can tell."

I said, "Could you tell with me?"

He said, "What do you mean?"

"I mean that while all the other orgasms I've had with you were real, the first one was not. Could you tell the difference?"

He looked absolutely shocked and a little angry.

"No. But why would you fake an orgasm? I think that's a really wrong thing to do."

"I agree, Ted," I said. "And I don't need to fake them with you and I don't want to."

Ted was staring at me.

I said, "But I felt such pressure the first time and there were so many distractions, I just decided to please you instead of ending our lovemaking in a way that distressed you."

He was not happy. First, because I had faked it. Second, I think, because he hadn't known I'd faked it. We talked longer, and he seemed to understand—and I assured him that everything else had been as he thought it had been, which it had, and that I was easily orgasmic with him, but I didn't want to feel that if I didn't have an orgasm each time that he would feel something was wrong with me or with us.

He took it all in and we kissed and cuddled afterward. But telling him about that first faked orgasm was a very bad idea.

Rethinking My Strategy

I had the feeling that honesty about sexuality with Ted was going to be a pretty dicey affair. He had his ideas about how women functioned sexually, and sex expert or not, he wasn't taking my opinion about female sexuality when it contradicted his perceptions of his own experience. My lesson from all that was that sometimes honesty is not the best policy, depending on whom you were with.

I thought about how Dennis could hear just about anything I had to tell him, and integrate the information without one thought of it being personal. Ted may not have meant to punish me for my honesty, but he did. I think revelation made him reevaluate our whole sex life—and maybe me. I started walking on eggshells when it came to sexual conversation or feedback. All my life I have been very open about sex—and now, with someone I cared deeply about, I felt I needed to keep a lot inside.

The Next Time

That night, as we made love, we were both pretty self-conscious, but amazingly enough, I did have an orgasm. I never know what my body is going to do. I would have bet a hundred dollars against having an orgasm that night and I would have lost.

Despite our problems in bed, the rest of the week was magical and it also gave me one of the most beautiful, spiritual, and romantic moments of my life. Ted had promised me that we would see some whales, and he is a man of his word.

It was late in the day when we finally set off to see the whales. So even though there was some fog coming in, Ted and I jumped into the skiff and headed off to a bay where he had seen whales gathering. The waves were wild but not dangerous and as we cut across the bay into the open water I was bursting with pleasure and affection for this new man in my life. Along the way, we stopped at a lovely little island to explore it and almost got trapped there. The water was changing direction and if we stayed there even a few seconds longer we would not have been able to push the boat back out. Ted, his beloved golden retriever Sandy, and I would have been stuck there overnight. The possibility was so great that I had to think about how I felt about it.

The truth is that I felt so safe with Ted that I wouldn't mind being trapped on an island with him. I craved time and adventure with him.

But we did get out and off we went to find the whales. By the time we got there, however, the fog had become a thick blanket over us; we only could venture inside of it a short way or we might become disoriented. The fog opened up enough to give us a glimmer of sky and so we tentatively penetrated deeper into the sea. The mist was magical and except for a tunnel to the light, we were enveloped in it. We turned off our motor, the fog threatening to wrap around us, but the search for the whales emboldened us to stay put. We sat there for a moment in the pearl grey quiet of the day, and waves lapped against our skiff as if we were on a lake instead of the ocean.

Then, breaking the silence, I heard all around me the blowholes of the whales, creating a symphony of the most extraordinary sound. We sat transfixed, listening as long as we could. We were awed at the magic of that moment, alone in the mist together, the invisible whales singing to each other, allowing us be their audience. I was so grateful to be there. However, the fog was becoming dense and I started feeling uneasy. Ted decided it was safest to leave right away and started the motor. The noise ended the ethereal moment we had shared, and we headed for the funnel that led to the light that now scoped down to just a tiny window of blue horizon. As we cleared the grip of the fog we found ourselves right behind a gigantic gray whale, its fluke disappearing as we came near. We followed him for twenty minutes, the whale diving and surfacing regularly, Ted and I watched—rapt and silent, delighted.

I looked at Ted captaining our little skiff. I was falling in love with him by the minute.

Our last night together, the lovemaking was intense, heartfelt, and satisfying. When I looked in his eyes I saw the same deep affection there that I felt for him. I felt passion take me in a way that I had not experienced with him before. I felt that sex would not be a problem for our future.

The next morning I stood at the dock waiting to board my seaplane home. Ted was holding me. I felt in love, and I didn't want to leave.

I didn't say anything about love but I told him I didn't want to go. Ted said, "Don't."

Of course we both knew that I had to. He had clients coming in. But I loved being asked to stay.

While we were waiting for the plane to arrive, a beautiful woman appeared on the dock. She was going to be picked up by a slightly later plane. I had a flash of jealous reaction to her presence. Where was my insecurity coming from? Ted was a trustworthy guy. If he was giving me this attention, I didn't imagine he was going to be hanging around with other women at the same time. I was pretty sure, but not totally confident, that Ted was not looking around now for someone else. But I had been wrong before about men's emotional or physical monogamy. I decided to trust my instincts about what kind of person he was.

Ted and I talked and kissed and made plans to see each other in three weeks when he came home from his fishing trip. The seaplane arrived and I boarded. It made a circle around the bay and then soared out over the mountaintops and then left, I caught a last glimpse of him standing at the dock and my heart was aching.

An Understanding

When Ted came back and picked me up at my house several weeks later, I was thrilled to see him. We went out for a special dinner at his favorite restaurant.

Not one to suppress much, I asked, "Where are we as a couple?"

He smiled and said, "Well, I assume that if we are going to see each other seriously we won't be seeing anyone else. If I concentrate on you, I assume you will concentrate on me."

My first thought was *I am only too happy to agree.* I was ready for a serious, monogamous relationship.

My second thought was to call Dennis. Even though we were no longer intensely pursuing each other, we hadn't closed any doors and I needed to do that.

I told Ted I would tie up some loose ends in my life and then he would be at the center of it. I spent the night with him in his house and, for the first time, left a few clothes, a toothbrush, and some other personal items. As I did, I remembered thinking in almost a euphoric frame of mind, "I have a boyfriend!"

Weekend After Weekend

We started seeing each other on every weekend and I loved our routine. Usually, although not always, we would stay at least one of the nights at his place, a cute farmhouse situated on a heavily treed piece of land on Vashon Island, which is within commuting distance of Seattle. We would rise early, make love, and he would usually make me a healthy breakfast. He was disciplined about his exercise and his eating, and his regime influenced me to do better myself. I started eating smaller portions and less protein, signed up with his trainer at his gym and enjoyed our runs and walks together. (Well, almost together. He was way more fit than I was and so he would do a quick loop by himself before he would rejoin me.) He would work on his land or do some things with his friends or golf while I would write, or we would have dinner with an especially interesting couple who were his best friends. He was more relaxed at his farm than at my ranch. He was a creature of habit, plus he was a light sleeper and my dogs (I always had a small pack of them) would jump on the bed, or bark, or in some way make a nuisance of themselves that didn't bother me but disrupted his sleep.

Our relationship grew informal, the way relationships do when people get serious about each other. Sometimes we would have a spontaneous lunch during the week. Our long conversations over meals would cover his work challenges and my own, and a running commentary on everyone we knew. I loved the fact that he liked to analyze personalities and people with me. I felt he was trying to be open about everything and I liked the fact that he let me participate in his decision making about family and business issues. I brought him problems, too. I trusted his judgment. During one of these conversations Ted mentioned he had just come from his therapist. Long ago, as a scared young kid on his own, finding a counselor had been a lifesaver and he had continued to take time to download his thoughts and issues to a therapist throughout his life. I thought that was an incredibly smart thing to do.

We talked about the therapeutic process and I shared my experiences when I left my first marriage and how helpful those sessions had been for me. I respected a man who could look at his inner life, his most complex feelings, and keep analyzing the impact his childhood had on his adulthood. He was trusting and open with me and I just kept falling more and more in love with him for who he was and who he tried to be.

So the relationship deepened. We got to know each other's families. Ted's and my weekend dates became a little harder to manage over time. We struggled occasionally over whether we would be at my place in the foothills of the mountains or at his island home. Our commutes took a couple of hours each way, which was a drag but there was nothing to be done about it. He wasn't asking me to move in, and he didn't like being away from his house too long. We had a lot in common but we also had two very separate properties and lives to maintain. And we both enjoyed being in our respective houses the most. We had settled in in other ways, though. We were getting to know each other's friends, going to restaurants that felt like "our" spots, and our lovemaking was regular and satisfying if not edgy or risk-taking in any way.

Over the months I got to really know Ted. His strengths were many. He felt things deeply, he was intelligent and diligent, and had a will to achieve that was volcanic in its power. He had several passions that I had known nothing about before I met him and I loved learning new things with him about wine, business, and fishing.

He was however, not without his faults. He had a lot of anger in him. Most of the time he was happy and calm—but when he erupted, even though it wasn't at me, it was upsetting. His traumatic childhood had left some emotional scars. Occasionally, some of those family issues would present themselves and his anger over them would be so intense that anything I said would get me in trouble. It was clear I had to be very careful when there was anything going on that concerned his family, ex-wife, or three grown children. Sometimes he would ask for my advice and thank me gratefully for my insights. But other times he would shut me out and it made me wonder if he would allow our relationship to deepen into a real partnership.

A Dynamic

Ted's anger brought up some tough family memories for me as well. I had a dad who could erupt in anger, and if you dared to take him on in any way—for example, tell him you thought he was wrong—he would go into what sometimes seemed to me a dangerous rage. I had a few severe spankings from him as a child. When I would try to defy him, my mother would intercede and tell me that I needed to let him get his way for the moment and she would find a way to get me what I needed later.

I didn't like that kind of manipulative approach. I liked taking things head-on and saying what I thought, peer to peer. I could certainly do that with Ted. He didn't want a doormat or "yes" person. And he didn't get angry often, and almost never with me. I wasn't afraid of him. But I recognized that he had that kind of molten anger inside him and it dismayed me. When he was really upset, he didn't want me to comfort him. If I wasn't careful, he saw my attempts to be helpful as a kind of maternal meddling and an attempt to infantilize him. I certainly didn't want to be that kind of person. I had to choose my words carefully and the best choice was to give him a wide berth until he was in a better mood. That hurt and frustrated me.

I felt closest to him when he would open up, let me in, consult with and confide in me. For example, partly in response to my urging, we flew to Denver and visited one of his sisters, whom he had not visited in a long time. They had good long walks and talks together and I liked her and her husband very much. On the way home he was truly appreciative of my support and participation in that part of his life. That made me feel needed and valuable and the whole trip made me feel we had shared something special. When we were collecting our baggage in Seattle to go to our different homes, he took me by the shoulders, looked steadily in my eyes.

"Pepper," he said seriously, "I want you to know that this trip has been a turning point in our relationship." He pulled me closer. "I love you. I feel like we have become something together that is different from where we were before."

And then he kissed me tenderly and we held each other in the way you do when you are alone in the world together, no matter how many other people are around, no matter how much noise is being generated as backdrop. You are in a precious bubble and you stay inside of it until you break your embrace.

There was no moment in all the time we had been together that I felt closer to him.

Control

But things didn't change radically after that perfect moment. The unity of purpose and feeling we shared at that moment didn't stand as a new foundation for our relationship. There were more times than not when he wanted to deal with his problems himself in his way. And his way was to think about it privately and talk about it after the fact, when he had already decided what to do.

Ted had a big ego but a tender ego. It took me a long time to figure that out. I think he was actually very shy. I sensed that my attachment to literally hundreds of people gave Ted the creeps. He liked one-on-one interaction and felt most comfortable concentrating on a very small number of close friends. I thought every new person I met was a potential addition to my circle of intimates.

Competition

There was also some conscious—and unconscious—competition between us. Once, during a dinner party at my house with some of my
closest friends in Seattle and some of Ted's close friends from the
island, I was talking a lot, trying—I thought—to make everyone feel
more at home and help make the two groups knit together.

Ted turned to me when he came in to put a dish at the head of the
table and loudly proclaimed, "You really need to be the center of attention, don't you?"

There was a stony silence at the table from my friends.

I responded in a joking manner, "Well, yes, I do. But I am willing
to give it over to any one else who needs it."

Inside I was hurt, humiliated, and deeply angry.

About twenty minutes later I was alone with Ted in the kitchen. I
felt betrayed and embarrassed.

I said, "How could you do that?

He said, "What?"

"What?" I looked at him to see if he was being snide. He was
not.

"Humiliating me in front of everyone. Insulting me and putting
me down."

He said, "Oh, don't be so sensitive. I was just kidding around."

I looked at him again and said, "Ted, you were not just kidding
around. And if you think you were, I'd really like to talk later about
why I didn't think it was funny. We need to support each other in
public and in private. If you think I'm grandstanding or behaving in a
way you don't like, tell me. But tell me later in private and I can work
on it."

He said, "I'm very sorry." And he was. Later in bed, he deeply
apologized and said that he had never meant to put me down and
that the last thing he wanted to do was humiliate me in front of my
friends. We explored the possibility that he was angry with me at
some deeper level he wasn't consciously aware of, and he promised
me he would consider that theory, although he didn't see anger as

the cause of his remark. There was some tension in the room between the couple he had invited and my clique, and perhaps he had become defensive in their behalf. In any case, we talked through it and I felt reassured that he wouldn't do something like that again. Ted was a quick study and he had a strong respect for ethical and civilized behavior. When he trespassed his own standards, he was the first to admit and correct it.

A Vacation

About ten months into the relationship, Ted and I decided to take a vacation to Cabo San Lucas together with his three adult children. As it turned out, the all-inclusive resort had a lot of advantages. It was right on the beach and offered something for everyone in our group. We had great adventures there: horseback riding on the beach, going into the water on horseback and swimming, and motor scootering to some old churches, which was hot and sweaty work but absolutely fascinating.

On our second day, Ted's children got tickets for all of us to a Black Eyed Peas performance in a club in downtown Cabo. I felt like a teenager as Ted and I waited in line, starting at 10:00 pm with tickets already in hand, for two hours. The concert didn't start for at least an hour after that. In line, we enjoyed ourselves chatting and mingling with the crowd of Mexican and Anglo mostly twenty-something concertgoers and groupies.

We both were excited. He reminisced about other rock and roll shows he'd gone to. As we waited and waited, we made a game of evaluating the hundreds of people we were watching in the long twisting lines ahead of us.

"I think the girl in the go-go boots, with the see-through handkerchief top is particularly fetching," Ted remarked.

"Yes, I can see that, but I only rank her as an 8 compared to that Lolita ten people ahead of her. Besides having waist-length dreadlocks, she also has a plastic skirt on that trumps the handkerchief top."

"Well, you have a point there, but don't you think the man with the painted body and Daisy Dukes deserves to win this contest?" I looked and sure enough, Ted had picked a winner—nothing could outrank that guy.

We amused ourselves in this fashion until the interminable line finally started to move. Happy and impressed with our ability to stay up for this show, we wrapped our arms around each other, intrigued with what would happen next. When his kids went to explore the line a bit before it disappeared he grabbed me and kissed me.

He held me in his arms and looked down and said, sotto voce, "Life is always fun with you, Pepper. Thanks for agreeing to the trip, the concert, and for sharing this time with my kids. I just want you to know I appreciate it all." Ted could be endearing at the world-class level.

At one o'clock the band rocked and we stayed and drank and danced until about six in the morning. It was sexy, exhilarating, and exhausting. I was surprised that I could still stay up that late and have the energy to dance till dawn. I loved the press of hundreds of sweaty bodies, doing their thing individually and together, collectively creating a community. It was a satisfying and totally engrossing evening. When we finally gave up and walked into the awakening world outside the club we all were quite mellow. We were sleepy, but happy in the car and parted ways when his son and daughter went into their room and we went to ours.

Ted and I cuddled on the bed. I thought how good I felt with the man holding me in his arms. I felt deeply connected to Ted for many reasons—I loved his strength, his innate wisdom, his curiosity and enthusiasm for life, and the way he interacted with his children. I liked our bantering and I liked the way he treated me during these adventures we enjoyed together. I have always felt that an important ingredient in compatibility is having similar endurance and levels of energy. The fact that both Ted and I seemed to have boundless energy, especially for our ages, was an important bond to me.

I hugged Ted and whispered a soft "I love you." He murmured, "I love you, too" and almost simultaneously passed out. I was right behind him.

A Year

The months went by and soon it was almost exactly a year that we had been together. I thought that our sex life improved immensely. We made love more often, we would create slow Sundays where the day was about our morning coffee, feeding the dogs, and then going back to bed and making love. But it wasn't exactly as Ted would have it. Something was missing. He told me that there was a level of passion he had experienced before that was not present between us. It hurt to hear that. But it motivated me to figure out just why it wasn't what I knew it could be. I thought our sex life was getting better and better. It was a little freer, a little more experimental. I figured if we need a bottle of Champagne to get more feverish, I was up for it. I knew some great vacations together were coming up and I promised myself I would devote some real time to lovemaking and intimacy.

What I couldn't deny was that there was some truth to what Ted was saying. I think the reserve in me came from a reserve in him. Even though we had told each other many times that we loved each other, I didn't feel that he was consistently committed to me. That kind of noncommittal feeling had not necessarily inhibited me in other relationships, but it did with Ted. I often felt judged in and out of bed, in a way that made me feel insecure about how he felt about me. That could fuel passion or prevent it—and more often it was the latter. It didn't prevent pleasure—but it sometimes kept me from going over the top.

But I thought we were developing in the right direction. I had become easily orgasmic with him and I felt things were getting sexier all the time. We had had a few nights in bed where it got wild and crazy. I wasn't worried about this aspect of our relationship. I thought we had plenty of time to elaborate our relationship.

Off to Paris

A couple of months later, things weren't so easy. Ted was traveling and I was traveling. Plans we had made to go fishing or go on a trip with my brothers had fallen through. He said he had too many issues at work to go. I needed to take a trip to Europe and I pledged to myself that I would stay home after that and spend a lot of time with Ted getting things back on track. Still, as I made preparations to go visit The Hague and Paris and Provence for a week with my nineteen-year-old daughter, I was just a tad nervous. Too many plans with Ted had been cancelled. Something felt wrong.

I was upset that he wouldn't be joining me and my brothers when I got back, but Ted had said, "I can't because of work." When my participation in a big fishing trip was cancelled I asked Ted if there was something going on.

Ted said, "No, it won't work this time. I don't have the boat this year. They only had so many rooms. I need my son to help me with the clients and so he'll be sharing the room with me—so unless it's really important, I think its just too difficult if you come."

I listened to this with a sinking heart. The Ted I knew would have found a way for me to come. Every instinct I had said we were in trouble—but I didn't want to take it on. I figured that when I came back from Paris we would spend some time talking and I could find out why Ted was pulling away from me.

There were some nice moments alone and a dinner with a close friend of his that I thought went well. I didn't sense a relationship emergency. I felt I could go to Paris for a week without any major crises. Nonetheless, before I left I asked Ted if we were okay.

Ted was less than effusive but explained away his mood saying, "Sorry, I have a lot on my mind with work and everything."

He drove my daughter and me to the airport and kissed me good bye sweetly.

I tried to call him from Europe to share, as we normally would, what was happening on the trip. No answer. I called early, late, several times. I called his home, his office, his car. Left messages. Nothing. Days and days went by.

Finally I found him, and overwrought, I asked him, "Why haven't you called and kept contact?"

He said those awful, fateful words: "We will talk when you get back."

Naturally, compulsive soul that I seem to be, I pressed, "What do you mean by that?"

He resisted and said, "Let's wait till you get back." I was a mess. I pressed on until he finally told me, "This is over. It is never going to work."

I gasped. I had no idea he was even close to feeling this way.

"Why?" I asked.

"We are too different," he replied calmly.

My heart was in my throat. I couldn't believe this. To me, it came out of nowhere. There had been few complaints and no real fights. The only tough thing that has happened in our recent history was when he had slammed a door in my face when I walked into the office and unwittingly interrupted an important conference call. I was speechless, but he had been almost immediately contrite about it, telling me that I "didn't deserve that" and that he would never do anything like that again.

I said, "I know we are different but I thought we enjoyed those differences. I know I did."

He said, "Let's just talk when you get back."

I was devastated. I knew Ted. He hadn't said these words lightly and they weren't conditional. He wasn't going to rethink this.

Even though I knew the answer, I had to ask, "Are you sure? Isn't there something we can do? We haven't talked about any of this. I didn't know you felt this way."

He said, "I'm sorry. But it really is over for me."

I was crying hard by this time and after I said good bye and he said good bye I really lost it.

I was consumed by tears. My daughter got to see me sobbing, pretty uncontrollably, for the next three days. We went to Provence as planned and I continued to be sad and depressed there. What a waste of a perfectly enchanting setting. What a bore I was with my dear friend Nadi who was my host again and a fountain of French wisdom.

Nadine said, "I am so sorry. But we will try to stay busy. You will find a better man, I am sure."

I said, "I know, Nadi, I know."

But I didn't believe one word of it.

Being Humbled

Worse yet, I just couldn't snap back. I couldn't remember being that depressed. The only good thing about it was that my daughter got to see me destroyed and vulnerable. Since she had previously seen me as a bit too indomitable, she was thrilled to be able to be a comfort to her mom. So we got closer, although if I had a choice, I would have picked another way to do it.

I had not been dumped in a long time. I'm sure it's good to be humbled; I'm sure it makes one more empathetic; I am undoubtedly a better person for this experience. I learned that I could love deeply and I learned to not let communication lapse for any amount of time. While many of my friends liked Ted very much, some were not happy with the way he treated me at various dinner parties. Critics said that he was arrogant, a cold character, and not nearly affectionate enough with me. My friend's critiques of Ted didn't help. When someone gets in your bloodstream it takes a transfusion to get him out. I knew what I would eventually need was that new blood, but for a while, all I wanted to do was watch myself bleed.

▣ *Advice to Myself (And Others)* ▣

Talking About Sex Problems

One of the biggest issues in relationships can be the different ways of approaching sex. Some people have rather rigid ideas about how sex ought to be. Men and women get fixed opinions based on their own experience and perceptions of past lovers. The issue, of course, is not who is right or wrong, but whether all aspects of sexuality can be talked about without causing defensiveness.

In most of my experience, everything can be worked out—whether it is favorite positions, how to have an orgasm together, or how to touch each other. But it does take an open mind and the ability of each person to still feel desired and loved even if some changes in approach are required.

You can make some progress through communication. And there is a whole field of sexual counseling for couples that is based on the idea that passion can be increased if couples work on sex the same way they would work on other parts of their relationship. I believe that if the basic chemistry is present, sex could just get better and better.

Faking Orgasms

This is one of the oldest and most gendered issues in sexual relationships. No one likes to be lied to, and faking an orgasm is definitely a lie. Nonetheless, many—maybe most—women have faked an orgasm at least once in their life for a number of reasons. One reason women fake it is because many men cannot feel good about sex unless a woman has an orgasm and she is just not able to have one every time. Another common reason for pretending an orgasm is occurring is when there has been a lot of thrusting going on and she is tired, sore, or just plain out of orgasms. She turns in a credible performance. He is happy. She can go to sleep. Is this a reasonable thing to do? Maybe. But it's not a good long-term solution.

An intimate relationship is intimate because people tell each other the truth and can mutually use it to find solutions; also, lies tend to become more inconvenient or harder to maintain over time. It would be a lot better just to be able to say "I am tired and sore or just not able to have an orgasm tonight" than to feel some kind of performance was the only way to preserve a partner's sense of sexual adequacy or his belief that there was appropriate sexual passion in the relationship.

A particularly difficult situation is when a woman has never had an orgasm, is ashamed or afraid to say so, and has been faking every orgasm from the beginning of the relationship. I get letters all the time from women who have done this, who are tired of faking it year after year, and would like to know how to have a real orgasm but can't bear to reveal the truth. Sometimes revelation is necessary—even though it is emotionally difficult for both her and her partner—but they need to go to square one to learn how to make love so that she can have a climax.

It is also possible just to explore "new ways" of touching each other, using a vibrator, changing positions, or lasting longer. A partner who cannot bear to tell her mate that she has been faking orgasms for a long time can sometimes forgo that revelation just by experimenting with vibrators together and learning how to have an orgasm in a new way without having to critique older sexual patterns. A really observant man will note a huge difference in a woman's body before a real orgasm versus a fake one—the difference being a speeded-up heart rate, severe muscle tension, perhaps a reddish flush on her chest after orgasm and involuntary spasms that can be felt inside the vagina.

In the best of all possible worlds, no faking is necessary. In fact, total honesty about everything is the most intimate thing that can happen between two people. But if total honesty is going to prevail, punishments for being honest have to be taken off the table. Men and women need to communicate supportively and withhold judgments about sexual confessions so that honesty can flourish.

I know for myself, whatever other issues I had with my ex-lover Dennis, I could tell him anything and everything about what was, or wasn't, working in bed for me. He never felt judged; he was more like a scientist collecting data so that the biggest orgasms in the world could be manufactured by him. He was always on a quest for new ways to have an even better sex life. Ted wanted a "natural" experience, but I don't think sex is a natural act. We are creatures of our past, our values, beliefs, cultural scripts, and individual fears, preferences and needs. All of this has to be managed in a given sexual relationship.

Type A Personalities

I am eclectic in my taste in men but because I adored my loving but domineering father, one kind of man I find especially attractive is your typical type A character: accomplished, resilient, energetic, charming, ambitious, slightly to greatly narcissistic, smart, and slightly to moderately difficult. I find these guys attractive because they generally invent or control the world they live in and when you want someone to lead (some of the time), they are already there. The difficulty is they often feel they own the truth and are entitled to dominate decision making. They also don't like rethinking procedures or doubting their conclusions. A lot of them are willing to live at the surface of relationships rather than create deeper emotional investments. They are, I believe, high-risk partners, and personally I am working on getting over my attraction to them.

I would advise other women to think about the pitfalls of involvement with an alpha male. I know how devastatingly attractive they can be. What I would say is: Be careful what you wish for. Unless they are retired and on the down slope from their alpha past, they are unlikely to give sustained time, compassion, or emotion. When they do give it, they give it on their own schedule, for their own needs, not yours. For women who are private and pretty cool, that's a relief. But for women who want a soul mate—what type As seem to offer in the beginning may be pretty spare in a longer relationship. You are not the center of their world—or at least not for much of the time. When type As meet, it can be fireworks, but compromise is the last thing alphas usually want to have pried out of them. Be prepared for ongoing struggles—at least out of bed. In bed, it can actually be quite wonderful. All that power, energy, and will exploding together. That's often what makes it so hard to leave—even if you are not getting what you want in other areas of the relationship.

Instant Attraction Versus Slow Simmer

There is a lot to be said for thinking about slow starts and simmering emotions versus instant attraction and jumping in without checking the depth of the water. I have spent most of my life doing the latter—and I am really becoming a fan of the former. Slow has its advantages. You can really understand who the other person is before your hormones cloud your judgment. You can develop attractions that might not be apparent at once, that are truly present when you have experienced someone's personality for a while. And you can evaluate each other before you are already involved physically.

I know this is an elementary observation to more cautious women—but for many of us, this is a discipline that needs to be practiced. Slow, of course, is a relative term. But most of us might agree it means not acting on one's first attractions (or lack thereof), and getting to know a person better over time. That might mean four dates or fourteen, depending on your values, your experience, and your comfort with a specific individual.

Warning Signs and Dealing with Them

I need to cop to how many warning signs I ignored while there was still time to address them. I could kick myself for all the incidents that happened between Ted and me that I let pass by rather than address. Part of this was respecting his more private nature. But it was a bad idea. I let distance and dissatisfaction build up in the relationship and get so far ahead of us that catching up was impossible. I am not saying that this relationship could have been saved by communication. I am saying it was doomed when no communication occurred about serious issues. A good relationship shares as early as possible the disappointments, irritations, and incompatibilities that emerge, and tries to find a way to a better fit. Any delay in this process is dangerous and can be fatal to even a good relationship.

I felt unable to talk with Ted, or had to edit my approach, at least 25 percent of the time we were together. I would say that editing more than 15 to 20 percent of the time with a partner or lover is a big fat orange warning light. I would have liked to talk about our sex life at least half again as much as I did. I would have liked to have known what he really wanted me to do to please him or stay appealing to him. I don't think he gave me his real feelings and so there was nothing I could do to address the things that were bothering him. That is no way to conduct a serious relationship.

After this debacle I promised myself that open communication on both sides is a deal breaker: If we can't talk about our feelings as they are occurring, I don't want to get in any deeper. Ironically, way after Ted and I broke up our relationship, I asked him many of the tough questions I should have asked sooner and was more open about how I really felt, and we became better friends. But by then it was too late.

About Anger and Lovers

Anger is a huge issue—we carry around a lot of damage from earlier in our lives and many of us have plenty to be angry about. But expressing anger, or carrying it and nurturing it, is abusive to our peace of mind, our happiness, and our ability to love. Much of the research on anger has indicated that expressing it in small ways may help identify problems and lead to solutions, but major eruptions merely lead to more anger and more toxic reactions inside of us.

Anger is best traced down to its roots. What I do when I feel myself getting annoyed, aggressive, upset, or combative is to immediately ask myself where this anger is coming from—and is it from the present provocation or really from some old wound that I have not yet healed.

I know that almost without exception, whenever I act in anger, I do not act in my best interests. While expressing outrage may be satisfyingly Old Testament, it is a short-lived satisfaction. Anger feeds anger and the cycle increases rather than decreases unhappy feelings.

All this is especially true for romantic relationships. When fury hits there is usually no desire or ability for analysis. Combatants struggle to dominate the definition of what is at stake and who is wrong, or someone capitulates and nothing is solved. Healthy approaches include:

a. Feeling anger, but waiting to confront the issue
   until the worst of the anger has passed and
   conversation can be civilized and constructive.
b. Expressing anger, but never letting it get so out of hand
   that name-calling or contemptuous criticism occurs.
c. Expressing anger as a problem to be solved with guidelines
   for exploring the issue that are monitored and adhered to.

Fighting isn't bad if you are fighting fair, or getting outside help. The important thing to remember about anger and fighting is that it is about a goal: understanding the problem and finding a solution. Just "venting" is fine to a point, but anger is often fueled by venting, not relieved. Many relationship researchers have found that if a couple feels like they are caught in a continuous cycle of recrimination, never solving the issue, they are more likely to break up.

Getting Dumped

You know the old phrase, "No pain, no gain." It is true that we tend to learn more from pain than pleasure. I don't recommend getting dumped, but it doesn't matter what I recommend in this department—there are few of us who will avoid the experience. The question is: How are we going to let it affect us when it happens?

I know many women who have just decided to close up shop after a painful breakup. They avoid romantic love. They stay away from attractive possibilities and cultivate their garden, their families, or their work. I understand this feeling—the loss of love is so devastating that it makes us fearful and protective. Our hearts hurt for years. I know just writing about Ted's and my relationship had me in tears again. And yet, I think love is so wonderful when it happens, and the connection so exquisite, that I think it's worth the pain. I understand people who do not. But I still feel the way I do.

That said, it took me a while to recover from this loss and be able to look optimistically at love and feel that I could love another man. I also feel that if I never loved again, I would still feel like a very fortunate person because I have experienced profound love several times in my life. I have felt euphoric, I have felt absolute joy, and I have experienced being adored. I know firsthand that the loss of being loved and giving love is sickeningly painful—yet I would endure it again, for the possibility of experiencing true love again.

There is a leap of faith required. Being able to love requires honoring your heart and trusting your emotions. So I would say to you: Think many times about what you are missing when you turn away from love. Imagine love to be possible—if you decide to be vulnerable again. I do believe we can recover from pain, even if there is scar tissue. No, we don't emerge from a shattered relationship unscathed—but I still think the best medicine for a damaged heart is to open it up again to a special person.

eight

A SPECIAL FRIENDSHIP (WITH BENEFITS)

Same Time Next Year

Climbing Back into the Saddle

It took me a long time to get over Ted. It helped that eventually we salvaged a good friendship out of the romantic wreckage, but the pain of the end of that relationship would haunt me every now and then. When you have shared love with someone it takes a long time to stop craving him. But you have to move on, and I was determined to put those hopes and feelings behind me.

Pumping Up

When I finally reentered the dating world I found a profile that I liked and set a rendezvous in motion. I met Damon, a movie star–handsome guy in his early sixties who had the body of a thirty-five year old. He was a writer and the son of a noted novelist. Our conversation at the tiki bar, which was the site of our first rendezvous, was seamless and entertaining. I found myself fixated on his face. He had angular features, a lot of black hair with much of it going silver grey, and full lips. His body was quite notable, too, made lean and muscular by end-less biking. We had a few glasses of wine, rather than my usual latte on a first date. Our conversation eventually traveled to my work as a sex-ologist. After discussing all sorts of quirky aspects of human sexuality, which Damon found fascinating, he decided to share.

"I have a rather unique situation you may find interesting, given your career," Damon said.

"Oh, really? Do tell," I said.

"Because of my decades of bike riding I have developed a condi-tion that leaves me unable to have an erection without assistance," he said. He was watching my face closely for a reaction.

"Fascinating," I said in all earnestness. "And what type of assis-tance do you need?"

"I have a little pump," he said.

Hmmm. This is going to be interesting.

"I can pump up my penis to a sturdy erection anytime," he said, "and deflate anytime, as well."

"And can you have an orgasm?" I asked.

"Oh, yes, it works quite efficiently," he said with a sense of pride.

I thought that might be something I wanted to see.

Our evening ended with a warm hug and we went out a few more times. Once we necked quite passionately, but I never did get a chance to see his bionic penis in action. He was an amazingly attractive and intelligent man but our relationship never got traction. I am still cu-rious about what sex with him would have been like.

The Blind Date in Toronto (with the Irish-American Man Who Lived on the Other Side of the Planet)

I found a man's profile on the Net that looked cute and had some humorous pictures attached of him eating spaghetti with a much older woman who I hoped was his mother. We started exchanging e-mail

and I found him very witty, sometimes LOL funny, and bright. About
the third or fourth e-mail however, I got a jolt from my new friend
Mick.

> Dear Pepper:
>
> While it was true I am from Seattle and that I intend to return to the
> Northwest, it is also true that I am presently living in Qatar.

Qatar! As in halfway around the world.

I found it amusing, actually. A pen pal in Qatar. Let's see where
this goes.

And so began a series of long e-mails back and forth, about life,
love, the bizarre ex-pat community in the Middle East, religion, politics, and any number of interesting topics.

Mick was a good writer. In fact, he did copywriting for a living.
As I continued to send and receive entertaining e-mails from Mick, I
found myself feeling quite affectionate toward him.

Am I going to be like other people I have heard about who get
emotionally involved with long-distance pen pals over the Internet?
What's the sense in that?

And yet, I thought about a woman I had met who was corresponding with another woman across the country. Each letter brought them
closer and finally, while neither had had any homosexual experience,
they told each other they were in love. One of them bought a plane
ticket, their first live sight of each other was in the baggage area, and
they went from the airport to a motel. They were deeply, intensely in
love, left their respective boyfriend and husband, and are together
to this day. It was an amazing story, quite reckless and very romantic.
The idea of a relationship that triumphed over great distance and total
improbability attracted me quite a bit.

Making It Real

After about three months, four phone calls, and fifty-plus fascinating e-mails. Mick, the American-born Qatar–based temporary ex-pat writer-designer sent an e-mail under the subject heading "Real."

The message read:

Dear Pepper:
How about making this real and meeting?

Real? Real with someone living in Qatar? I hadn't seriously thought about meeting in person even if I had had great fantasies. Still, my sense of adventure piqued, I thought about it now.

Why not? I had really enjoyed talking to Mick and his e-mail correspondence was beautiful. He was funny and insightful. We seemed to share most values. I calculated the free mileage I had left after using so much of it for my romantic adventures. I wondered if I could fly to the Middle East for free. I could.

The worst-case scenario is that it would be an interesting rendezvous even if it turned out not to be a romantic one. Still, I would be in a really foreign world if I met him on his exotic but rather scary turf.

Mick and I talked on the phone and got serious about what would be a good place to meet up. We tried to have a plan B or C.

We decided we would go some place that was fun and just have a good time there and not expect anything physical unless we were both obviously enthusiastic about a romantic relationship.

I asked, "Mick, are you completely comfortable meeting as platonic friends and staying platonic friends?"

"Yes," he said. "I think spending time with you will be worthwhile as friends or more."

Ultimately I decided to put off meeting in the Middle East until later (if this turned out to be a real relationship). We tried something closer and safer, agreeing to meet in Toronto, where Mick said he had some business errands to take care of.

After getting the plane tickets, I had a sobering thought. I was doing something that ninety-nine times out of 100 is bound to end badly. I was not only going to fly to meet someone I had never seen except for a couple of photographs, but I was also signing up to stay with him for a weekend in a snowy little romantic resort hotel. Nutty, nutty, nutty.

Still, I figured I was in North America, and the flights were free courtesy my flight miles. I had always wanted to see Toronto and Lake Placid and friends told me I would have a great time shopping there with or without a date. If things went badly, I could get my own hotel room, order room service, and call Dom to share a laugh about my "worst-case scenario." Dom had e-mailed me a friendly bon voyage:

Dear Pepper:

Here is hoping you don't find yourself having a thirty-minute blind date in Toronto with an Irish-American man living in Qatar who turns out to be a Swedish sociopath wearing Viking horns over a 400-pound frame.

Call at the first sign of trouble.

Big hug,
Dom

The Blind Date

As I exited the airport security area to baggage claim where I had agreed to rendezvous with Mick, my heart was pounding. I was prepared, if Mick did not match his picture and ooze the charm he demonstrated on the phone, to book the next flight to New York City.

As I walked out of the security area I spotted Mick right away. He was holding up a sign saying "Lake Placid or Bust" and he looked even cuter than his picture. I told him so.

He smiled broadly and said, "At long last we meet, Pepper. You look adorable."

He sounded warm, solid, and charming. I felt lucky and relieved. I also watched his face very carefully to see if he really did like the way I looked. He seemed genuinely pleased with me.

We hugged in a way that was warm and comfortable. The conversation flowed smoothly and Mick seemed very much at ease. I grabbed my luggage from baggage claim, we rented a car, and effortlessly found the hotel in downtown Toronto. We had made a reservation for a room with two beds and my instincts told me that this was a man I could share a room with without fear of being pressured. After finding a restaurant for dinner we settled into an interesting conversation. During dessert he did the most charming thing: He brought out some well-designed "coupons" that he had made for me.

Mick said, "These are for you to use when you feel like it."

I looked at the coupons more closely. They all had my name on them and they had various drawings on them. One offered ten minutes of neck massage; another, five minutes of handholding. There was one for a passionate kiss, a very tempting one for fifteen minutes of snuggling, and a few other equally unthreatening items.

I was impressed with how gorgeous and professional the coupons were and how much trouble he had gone to in order to make them. The fact that he actually presented them to me was also a good sign.

It seemed very natural to stroll back to our room, take turns in the bathroom getting ready for bed, kiss him good night on the cheek, and tuck myself into my double bed while he did the same in his own. It felt right, at least on the first night, to sleep alone but close to a new potential lover. I slept soundly.

So Far, So (Very) Good

We spent the day braving the Toronto weather, doing some shopping. That night, after an excellent dinner and intimate conversation at the hotel, Mick and I slept in the same bed. I felt a bit shy but it felt right. He started to kiss and touch me. Mick was a lovely kisser and held me in a romantic and gentle way. Sex, however, was more cautious than passionate. There was very little foreplay and no oral sex. We cuddled that evening but my first thoughts the next morning were that I was a little disappointed. He was an attractive, interesting man—but the chemistry didn't seem to be there. It didn't matter. We were having fun together and I enjoyed his company. We went on to Lake Placid and had two great days, trying out dog sledding and even the Olympic bobsled. I had a few experiences I never would have picked by myself and I was happy that I had come. I liked Mick and I liked my new adventures.

Exploring the World (and Mick)

In fact, I enjoyed him enough that when he said he would like to continue to explore the relationship, I decided to keep seeing him. Dating between Seattle and Qatar had its comic aspects (for example, thinking about what activities to plan that could take place in hellish temperatures), and yet we managed to have several adventures with each other that I thought were worth the trouble. He invited me to Dubai and, thanks to my frequent flyer miles, I went. It was a fascinating adventure—Dubai is the new Disneyland for grown-ups: fantasy buildings everywhere and an emphasis on elaborate restaurants, expensive shops, and other indulgences. Our afternoons were spent in an almost unbearable sun doing adventurous activities: Jeep rides in the desert, riding camels, exploring the souks, viewing the oil fields. The days were great, the nights, not so hot. Sadly, our lovemaking remained tepid. I felt that there was something about him that I didn't quite trust, even though I found him enormously entertaining. One element of that gut feeling was that I noticed that Mick was a stickler for splitting every economic outlay to the penny. I felt fine about splitting costs. But his fastidiousness about who paid what got old almost immediately. For example, when we would check out of hotels, Mick spent a good five minutes going over the bill, circling phone calls and food items that were mine. It was the way he did it, not the principle, which annoyed me.

He even made sure we went dutch when we had lattes in the park. This would have been a serious problem if I had been more serious about him. But given my limited ambitions for the relationship, I just coded it as unattractive.

Innocent Questions About
an Uncooperative Penis

On our last night in Dubai together we had a sexual malfunction. Mick's penis did not cooperate during an afternoon attempt at intercourse. It did not bother me in the least but I thought it would be interesting to discuss what happened and find out what was going on. So at dinner that night, feeling relaxed and reasonably intimate, I brought the matter up.

I said, in what I thought was my best nonjudgmental, collaborative, and matter-of-fact earnest way, "You know, I noticed that you seemed a bit frustrated when you were not able to get hard. Anything going on that we should talk about or that I can help or change?"

Mick's face literally whitened and he was speechless. After what seemed like a full minute, he finally choked out a response.

"How could you say such a thing?"

It was my turn to be speechless.

"Well," I said somewhat sheepishly, "I thought it would be helpful to talk about our sex life so we could understand each other better, or I could please you more, or for that matter, know when to back off."

He glared at me. Then he just sank into depression and the rest of the meal was quiet. I thought about trying to persuade him to relate to me about this but it was clear he was completely shut down and would have considered more effort on my part to be painful. We climbed into bed that night without much additional conversation. I was pretty ticked off myself at this point about his behavior and I didn't want to talk until I cooled off. The next morning, however, he was willing to address the whole incident and his response to it.

He explained, "Pepper, sometimes, if I am feeling pressured, or insecure, or emotionally disconnected I can't function."

"That's completely understandable. Could you tell me how I made you feel pressured or in some way undermined our lovemaking? I honestly didn't notice anything about this particular time we made love."

He shrugged his shoulders. "I really can't name it. I was just feeling some anxiety."

This was frustrating to me. How could I fix something if some-one doesn't know where it's broken? He did apologize for becoming so angry and distant but he never did tell me what bothered him. I intuited that it might be something about who I was that was impos-sible to change—my past sexual experience or perhaps just a stage in our relationship—or the fact that neither of us was committed at this point and we weren't going to be committed. As a result, I felt like I had to back off a bit and let him operate within his own comfort level. I started waiting for him to initiate. I tried to be as warm and reas-suring as possible. But I think it was just a symptom of the end of a relationship. In any case, our inability to communicate and solve this problem made up my mind that this relationship had run its course. I didn't care whether he had an erection or not, but I didn't want to stick around when something like this was undiscussable and discus-sion itself is seen as an attack.

We repaired the relationship enough to have a few more adven-tures, but it was a downhill slide from there. I thoroughly enjoyed our trips but we never quite clicked and became a passionate item. It didn't bother me. It was what it was. We were two people who explored the world together who never quite reached that magi-cal place of connection. Over time, however, I stopped admiring his character and when that happens, the relationship has to be over. We both agreed the romance was over. I went into a period of high work mode and just stopped dating for a while. I needed a breather.

A Wonderful Reunion

As luck would have it, during this partnerless period, I found myself in Texas on an academic panel with my old friend Scott. I had first met Scott when we were both in graduate school and some friends introduced us at the annual meetings of the American Sociological Association. He was more of a mathematical sociologist and only tan-gentially interested in my area of study, but we discovered that we had both had a love for riding horses and that connection began a deeper fascination with each other that culminated in a brief affair. We both were dating other people at the time and he married the woman he was with, a quite beautiful and talented economist. Our friendship, however, stayed intact, and we kept in touch over the following decades. We hadn't seen each other often but when we did, we always spoke of our special bond. There was always a strong physical and emotional chemistry.

Even though I suffered no delusions that made me think I looked the same as I had when I was twenty-five, Scott seemed not to notice the changes. He continued to make me feel great with lavish compliments, and of course I never got tired of hearing his version of how witty or beautiful I was. Scott still had the knack of making me believe what he was saying.

As a result I never felt self-conscious with Scott, even if I was at my worst weight, which occasionally I was. Like millions of other women, I have ranged thirty pounds over my lifecycle. At the lowest weight I feel like I kick butt and at the highest, well, you have to love me for my mind. But I was feeling pudgy in Austin and a little of Scott's adoration would be just what my libido needed. I had some marks on my psyche from Ted's rejection and Mick's ambivalence. Having Scott next to me—looking at me as if he were the luckiest man in the world merely to be standing next to me—was just the perfect remedy for the blues.

Happily, the Texas meeting had a lot of downtime. Scott and I both had an evening off and we decided to get away from the larger group and spend time doing one of the two things we did so well together: talk. We hadn't had sex in ages and ages. He had been monogamous once he got married. I respected his commitment but I really enjoyed our mutual attraction. This night he was even more attentive than I remembered him to be. He kept staring at me, intimately, longingly, with lustful looks, and I was lapping it up. While our eyes might speak of attraction and desire, we said nothing and did nothing. We had been totally respectful of his emotional commitment and of my own. We had done nothing but flirt for decades.

A Special Arrangement

This evening was different, however. At dinner he wanted to confide in me and I promised he had my attention and loyalty. His story surprised me. Somewhere along the line, his wife of many years had decided that while she still loved him, she did not desire him anymore, and in fact was more attracted to women than men. She did not want to end her marriage with Scott but she did not want to have sex with him anymore. Strangely, he didn't want to end the relationship either. They had three adult children and young grandchildren and they both wanted to keep the family intact. He loved her as his best friend and they got along well.

Some people might say this is a sham marriage but I disagree. Marriage is about more than sex. It's about mutual values, goals, family, finances, security, and how you interact with other people and a community. I have known several women who are married to gay men and while it is not a bargain I would make, I have to say they were pretty happy. But when Scott mentioned that he was not having sex with anyone, I couldn't understand his celibacy.

"Scott," I said, "you are a guy who truly loves sex and, if I remember correctly, you have a sexual appetite second to no one. How can you manage not having sex at all?"

"Part of it is habit," he said in a very low voice. Even though our table was isolated, he didn't want to say any of this any louder than he had to.

"I have just been faithful and it was hard to be unfaithful even when our sex life got more and more absent. She and I got married too young. She never really felt comfortable about sex with me. When she started to avoid it I thought if I was very patient she would get to like it better. Neither one of us really understood the origins of the problem for a long time."

"So what were you doing during this time?" I was shocked to think that this sensual, lusty man had allowed sex to become rare and then disappear all together.

"I masturbated a lot. We would make love every now and then because she felt sorry for me. I found myself eyeing every good-looking woman in my classes and at parent's meetings. I have had the most active fantasy life you can imagine." He smiled and laughed very softly. "You have been in my mind a lot over the last twenty years."

I put my hand over his and squeezed it. I looked him in the eyes. "Scott, you should have told me. You should have called me."

"I know. But I was trying to protect my marriage. And yours. For a long time I thought we could fix this. I was unsure what was the best course. I have been so frustrated and so lonely but I didn't want to make some stupid mistake like getting sexually involved with some college student and blowing up my marriage and humiliating Deidre. We are too close for me to do that to her. And I didn't want to become one of those sordid scandals you read about in the *Chronicle of Higher Education* every so often."

Scott twisted his wedding ring around and around his finger as he talked about his greatest fear: that he would succumb to one of the female students who periodically would get a crush on him and come on strong. This surprised him even though it no longer shocked him. He saw himself as unremarkable looking and felt that these come-ons were all about his high status as a professor rather than physical attraction.

But Scott was a very good-looking man, sweet and solicitous of everyone, and female students were just about climbing into the windows of his home to get him into bed. They didn't think about consequences. They just thought about what a trophy he'd make. And he knew that. While this attention from lovely young women fed his fantasies, he retreated from actualizing them. He did not want his married and professional life to end in disgrace.

"So what do you want to do about this, Scott?" I asked. "Why, if you don't mind my asking, would you stay celibate when she has obviously discovered where her sexual pleasure lies and is taking it?"

"I know, I know." He looked down at the table. "I am still working my way through this, and, well, here I am talking to you. I want to be responsible. I don't want to break up what has been a lifelong happy family. My children wouldn't know how to deal with it. Deidre feels the same way. She has always kept her personal life focused around a particular woman and she acts with utmost discretion."

He looked up at me. I could see it in his eyes. I knew what he was going to suggest and I could feel my pulse pick up.

"I have always thought you were one of the most wonderful women on earth. I have never felt worthy of you. But you have flattered me with your company and I have thought about what it would be like to make love with you again."

I was there. "Scott. You need someone safe. Someone who cares for you and who you can have a sexual relationship with without causing a catastrophe down the road." I smiled broadly. "I think I can help you out with this problem.

"We could be lovers," I said happily, "I would never say anything to anyone. You can count on my loyalty—and friendship."

"You would do that for me?" he said, as if I had just offered him a kidney.

I continued, smiling, "This is not exactly a sacrifice."

He paid the bill hurriedly and we went back to my room. We barely got the door closed before he was all over me. He kissed me repeatedly—something I think most women love if the guy has any talent for it at all. In Scott's case, he did. Scott was telling me, by the way his mouth sensitively searched mine, that he cared about me, wanted me, and wanted me to want him.

As he slipped my shirt over my head he put his face deep into my neck and smelled my body as if it were a many-petaled rose. I smelled his hair and we took a few seconds to just inhale each other. We both loved breathing in each other's scent for a few extended minutes. Then he laid me down on the bed and touched me, very handily unhooking my bra in the process. He had all my clothes off before I could even get to his belt.

He took a good look at me as I lay on the bed. I had only a temporary twinge of modesty. This came and went in a few seconds because his obvious passion for me gave me confidence. If someone makes you feel beautiful, being nude feels natural and good. I started to slowly undress him, too. It felt very erotic to take his clothes off. However, Scott interceded and had me lie back down. He wanted me to just lie there so he could look at me while he undressed himself. I watched him carefully take off each piece of clothing—and it created a lot of sexual tension for both of us. It had been so many years since the last time we had made love—and the flirtations we'd had over the years had produced a profound sexual tension.

Good News

Scott had absolutely no problem getting hard and staying hard. I really appreciated that! When you are a young woman with a young man you can pretty much take that erection for granted, and as an older woman with an older man—you can pretty much expect creative challenges.

Not Scott, though. No problem from the beginning and no problems with the three times we made love in two hours. Several hours later I was about as satisfied as I could be. After a bunch of orgasms I felt lucky in life—and generous. I sometimes believe that if everyone had mutually satisfying sex every night, world peace would be more attainable. It's just hard for your average person to feel anything but mellow after great sex.

The wonderful thing about Scott was that he was the same ardent lover after his orgasms as he was before them. And he still felt like my dear friend and colleague. I didn't feel he had turned me into some mistress just by making love with me. On the other hand, I do believe the research that says our chemistry is different after orgasms and that all that dopamine and oxytocin we are producing can change the way we feel about each other. It was impossible to look into Scott's eyes and not feel strongly attached. A flash of sadness, quick as a shiver, ran through me. Scott might care deeply for me but he could never commit more than an infrequent evening.

Still, Scott and I had a real ability to be great friends and lovers.

Being Careful

I had to be careful not to fall in love and get all mopey and weepy over the limits of this relationship. I had to perform an act of will right then. It would have been easy, especially in my postorgasmic haze, to fall in love with Scott and get blue about what couldn't be. But I was determined to live in the present. There wasn't a chance in hell this would be anything except what it was—and so I was wistful, but chanted a "glass is half full" mantra.

Scott stayed the night. He held me tightly until the morning, which came all too soon. We had to wake up early for the morning sessions, scheduled to start at 8:00 am. I woke up at 6:00 am. When I turned to Scott I felt affectionate and eager for sex again. I could hardly believe my own hormones. Didn't they know they were supposed to be defunct? Either my body was an anomaly and needed to be gifted to science or there was more to postmenopausal sex drive than most research was mentioning. Personally, I think it's a "the more you get, the more you want" phenomena. When I am getting some, I want more. When I get more, I get insatiable.

I found myself wondering what things I could teach Scott. He had only been with a few women in his life. I mentioned my ambitions and asked him how he felt about toys. Scott declared that he was thrilled to be a student again, would try anything, and would attempt to excel. It was hard not to love this guy.

The Toys

So the next night, we went back to my room after the evening presentations. It was hard not to look at each other but we were trying very hard not to give any inadvertent clues about our relationship. This was harder than it sounded. Scott was like an excited kid. He couldn't wait to make love again and again and he was equally keen to try something new. He had been in a relationship where he had been rejected nightly and their sex life produced children but not much passion. He had no "attitude" about following my lead and he eagerly communicated what was on his mind.

"What's next?" he asked.

I did two things.

First I laid a few sex toys out on the bed and asked, "What intrigues you?"

He looked at my travel vibrator, a G-spot stimulator, ribbed condoms, multiple packets of lubricant, and a silk scarf. He laughed and said, "I could tell you if I could figure these things out!"

"When I went to sex shops not so long ago, I couldn't figure out about a third of the gadgets. But you know the old saying, 'Learn one, teach one.'"

Scott smiled.

"So, my dear," I said sweetly, "I might be just a few steps ahead you." I started him out slow. I took out the condoms, warming lubricant, and the silk scarf. I promised him that if he enjoyed these toys, someday we'd have the sex-toy equivalent of a wine tasting. While Scott lay on the bed, I gently created a blindfold out of the scarf and stroked his body with slick fingertips. The "blindfold" intensified his reaction to touch and I had him moaning right away. He was a happy professor.

It's strange. We humans love variation so much and yet we are creatures of habit. By offering something a little out of the ordinary, the erotic heat in the room went into tropical temperatures.

I told Scott to lie back and let me be his teacher for a while. I made sure he couldn't see out of the blindfold. Then I stroked his body first with fingertips, then with my hands and finally with my pocket vibrator. I varied where I touched him so he couldn't predict where I would touch him next. I asked him to tell me what felt particularly good so that I could repeat it. Some of the time he used words, other times he just made sounds. After about ten or fifteen minutes of this I took off his blindfold and asked him how it all felt. He looked dazed with pleasure and reached for me.

"Not yet. Now put the blindfold on me." He did.

He teased me as I had teased him. Teased enough, I told him I was ready for him. Good student that he was, he drew out our foreplay and refused to go further for quite a while. Sexual tension kept building and when we did have intercourse it was ferocious in a wonderful way.

My Needs

Scott and I put our calendars together the next day and we realized that even the best-case scenario allowed us to meet less than once every three or four months. We were both grateful for those times but chagrined at how our busy lives got in the way of seeing each other very much. Still, it became something for me to look forward to and it made me take my time getting involved with anyone else. I didn't confuse my relationship with Scott with a relationship with someone whom I might have as my own.

Ironically, my relationship with him allowed me to slow down—but not avoid—relationships with other men. I had decided to date people for a longer time before I had sex with them. The situation with Scott was perfect in some ways and not in others. Over the months, he took care of my sexual needs and I took care of his. We both gave and received. But we couldn't let our affair drift into full-blown, all-out love. It had to stay boxed.

After I returned home from one of my meetings with Scott, I spent a lot of time thinking about whether having Scott in my life would get in the way of finding a more complete relationship. I started thinking that maybe it was time to curtail or retire sex until I was with someone who loved me and wanted me as a daily partner.

This musing over the future wasn't sad. I had no regrets about the last five years. I had found love and emotional and sexual fulfillment for long periods of time. I had seen parts of the world I never would have known and I loved the sheer exotic quality of the places I had been able to travel to and enjoy with a lover. Even though there were many disappointments and frustrating revelations, I found my life enjoyable and remarkable. If life was supposed to be more about the journey and less about the destination, I was having a wonderful trip. Still, I wondered, was I getting in my own way? And was Scott, sweetheart that he was, still emblematic of ways I lived my life that kept commitment at bay?

▣ Advice to Myself (And Others) ▣

Same Time Next Year

There was a great film called *Same Time, Next Year* made some decades ago. The premise was that this couple, who were married to other people, would get together for a tryst once a year. Over the years they talked about the crises and joys of their regular lives and they grew old together in a sporadic but intimate long-distance relationship. The film was pretty racy when it was introduced, and in some ways it's no less revolutionary now.

The subversive ideas in the film were: Married people who were cheating on their spouses weren't awful people; long-distance lovers could have a profound relationship even with very limited time together; extramarital sexuality could happen over a long period of time and not damage either the participants or their spouses; marriages could survive nonmonogamy and affairs could continue and not have to become a "relationship;" and finally—people could want sex and even love outside of their marriage and still not be "bad" people.

The idea of having a parallel life to marital fidelity is not one that many people espouse. This way of looking at love and sex is hardly unique to America. But there are parts of the world that play this scenario in their own way. Many Europeans have much more tolerance than Americans for sexual affairs. In some Mediterranean countries there is a tradition of keeping the family intact but dealing with disappointments and the loss of sexual attraction by having liaisons outside the marriage. At the funeral of the ex–Prime Minister of France, pictures of the Minister's mistress standing next to his wife appeared in newspapers around the world. Americans may have been shocked and surprised, but the French weren't. This was a compromise for the former minister that many French people understood and even admired. One has a responsibility to support the mother of your children, and remain part of the family—but there is also an understanding that there is a lifelong ability to fall in love and lust with someone new without breaking up your marriage.

Being the second woman in someone's life (or having a man who has a minor role in yours) has the possibility, maybe even the probability for heartbreak. Still, *Same Time, Next Year* didn't lie. Sometimes these infrequent but emotionally connected lovers have something that makes their life infinitely better and that may be all this particular pairing should be. Maybe it is bittersweet, but it could still be worth it.

Even more controversial is the idea that maybe an extramarital affair can help a marriage. Research on the topic shows that when marriages are troubled they last *longer* when one partner is having an affair than when both spouses are monogamous. Why? Because the person who is unsatisfied in the marriage is not feeling so deprived. It's also true that the unfaithful partner could want to stay in the marriage for all kinds of reasons and so chooses a controlled sexual affair rather than some sexual fling that might be more likely to blow the relationship up. People have an abundance of motives for nonmonogamy—they want validation, or affection, or adventure, or whatever—but they don't want to end the relationship they are in. Even horrible marriages might have compelling reasons for staying together. I don't think there are good statistics on affairs or parallel sexual lives. The research on it is hard to do: Most of the people I know who have been nonmonogamous would never admit it on any kind of questionnaire. The national figure (depending on which study you look at) is somewhere between 10 and 20 percent of the married population has had nonmarital sex in the past year, maybe a quarter to a third of women and men during their lifetime. Who knows what the real statistics are? Again, the research seems to indicate that even for people who are nonmonogamous, the likelihood is that it happens rarely and with few people. But again, who really knows? I have known a number of single women who have in their back pocket that married lover or "friend with benefits" who filters in and out of their life over a lifetime. People are not always what they seem to be—and that goes double for their sex lives.

All that said, sex almost always stirs strong emotions in women and some of these affairs have had painful endings for one or both partners. If you find yourself in this kind of situation and it is hurtful and depressing, get out. Listen to you heart—and if it's breaking, you have to do whatever you can to save it and become whole again.

Friends with Benefits

"Friends with benefits" refers to a far less engrossing kind of sexual connection. This terminology originated in my kids' generation—but the behavior is far older than that. Sometimes sexual partners are more friends than lovers and they both think that's about right. When the mood hits, one of them calls the other up and says "How would you like to watch *V for Vendetta* tonight, eat pizza, and have sex?" And the other person says, "That sounds great, except why don't we skip the movie and the pizza?"

It's playful, and when it's nonabusive, both partners are in the same emotional space: I like you, I respect you, I want you, but I don't want to be a couple. I don't want to date. I just like you and want sex every so often. They skip the rituals of romanticism. There are zero expectations of getting more committed and serious.

This particular organization of human affairs is not to be confused with one that resembles it closely in behavior but not in meaning or impact. That is the situation where a man just drops over at the woman's place, has sex with her, and leaves, and she feels used, disrespected, and unhappy. It is not the kind of situation where she is looking for more and settling for crumbs. That is not friendship and I'm not even sure the sex is a benefit under these circumstances.

If you have never had this kind of relationship it's hard to believe it could be satisfying. And it probably isn't, in the sense of that deep need for love and connection that exists in most of us. But there are times in people's lives where a friendship like this is useful and not hurtful. If you think you could handle it, you wouldn't be alone. But here's what you'd best consider:

> Are you really hoping for this relationship to change and turn into the love of your life?

Will you feel used and abused if the person
you are seeing doesn't love you?

Will you get caught up in this casual relationship and let it
inhibit your ability to be in a real committed relationship?

Could you get hurt or vindictive if this
doesn't turn into a real relationship?

Do you think you can change his mind?

Will you feel guilt and self-loathing because it is what it is?

Think hard about these questions—because if you answered yes or
even maybe to any of these questions, don't even think about having a
sexual relationship like this. It won't pay off.

From Vanilla Sex to Cookie Dough Dulce de Leche Chocolate Chip Sex

While I am a big fan of sex toys, there is something about the first sex
you have with a highly desirable partner that begs for a certain purity
of position and approach. No fancy technology (other than a great
lubricant and a high quality condom)—just bodies, sweet screams, and
sexual bliss. You know, we sex experts often make snide remarks about
"vanilla sex," but vanilla is really a flavor that goes with everything. So
wrist restraints or things that buzz and whirl would seem kind of pa-
thetic during the first nights of a sexual relationship. Those early days
should require desire and not much else. Well, maybe lots of good
old-fashioned intercourse, oral sex, and a lot of eye contact.

On the other hand, as you get to know someone, there is trust that a
certain amount of affection, love, or desire has been established. At that
point, sex toys are an erotic and often humorous addition to a couple's
sexual life. It is a well-known research finding that men appreciate sexual variety with their partner, and sex toys are a great way of showing

how uninhibited and playful you are as a lover as well as helping satisfying your guy's appreciation for the kinky.

Here are my stock toys that I think almost anyone can introduce without raising more than one eyebrow.

Massage Oils: I like the new scented and flavored ones (but be careful to distinguish between lubricant and massage oils—they look similar but feel different). I also like plain oil from places like The Body Shop where you can get essential fragrance oils to scent them the way you like.

Lubricants: Intercourse and touching feel much different depending on the viscosity or temperature of a lubricant. Try a whole bunch of them. Almost all brands have a warming version. Some people love them, others don't, but you won't know unless you try. I like lubricants with silicone but other people feel they are too slippery. The percentage of silicone is negligible and there is no research I have seen that says it is at all dangerous. Flavored lubricants can be fun but you have to be careful—most flavored lubricants have sugar in them, which gives rise to yeast infections, and how sexy is that? But there are supposed to be some that don't have sugar and if you can find those, the scents and taste can be a turn-on. It's personal taste (as it were) but I like FDS (a new nonsilicone brand), Elbow Grease (made for gay guys—and who would know better than them!), K-Y Silk E (for just a touch of help), Hydra Smooth (kind of creamy), and the new Elexa line for women from Trojan (full disclosure: I am on their advisory committee—but I really do like the product). I suggest trying these and more to see what you like. What I like to avoid is sticky, fast-disappearing, and goopy.

A blindfold: Being blindfolded increases all your other senses. You can take turns as the passive "captive." One person touches the other in an unexpected ordering of body parts and perhaps with unexpected textures such as silk, a feather, a lubricated finger, a warm cloth.

A mirror (and a dimmer): Men love to watch; women get hung up on how their thighs look. To please both of you, put up a mirror and install a dimmer on the kilowatts so that the light is flattering and you can enjoy watching (since there are no dark shadows that make you look ghastly and no way to concentrate on cellulite).

Vibrating things: Almost all women who have tried them love vibrators, and variations like the G-spot stimulators and the Rabbit are precious to millions of women. They are great when your partner takes the controls and "pleasures" you to an almost unbearably erotic point. But men can also get stimulated by vibrators, and there are rings that fit over the penis during intercourse that feel good to both partners. Some variations on this theme can be found online by Googling "sexual toys," and companies like lovers.com, goodvibes.com, and evesgarden.com are woman-owned and cater to women's sensibilites.

Cuffs: A simple restraint (to be used only with someone you know very well and trust totally) can lead the way to erotic sensations and great fantasies. There is something to being "helpless" that can be sexually stimulating to both men and women. Use the Velcro kind (unless you are into bondage a whole lot more than I am and want real metal handcuffs). The regulation police kind can hurt if you are struggling against them (that's the point, I guess). Anyhow, the sex shops can sell you velvet versions that get a different kind of point across.

For Vanilla-Only Lovers

After reading the previous list of toys you may be wondering where you fit if you only want sex to include you, your lover, and a bed. Well, you fit securely in the majority. Less than a third of all people have used any kind of sex toy, ever. There is nothing superior about either camp. I think sex is wonderful just using our bodies and nothing else—and I think it is fun to be playful and experimental, but not necessary. Everyone evolves their own sexual style and the joys of simplicity are as valid and sexy as the persons who create a whole fantasy world for themselves and their lovers. You don't even have to be consistent—I know that I am a different kind of lover depending on whom

I am with. With Dennis and Scott, sex was affectionate, playful, and experimental. With Ted it was straightforward, intense, focused, and loving. They were all satisfying and right for who we were together. I firmly believe that there is the right time, place, and situation for almost everything.

A Lover for the Adventure of It!

Friends of mine thought I was totally nuts to consider beginning a relationship with someone who lived a mere 12,000 miles away. But I am so much the optimist I don't want to think that anything is impossible. At a bare minimum, I wanted this rendezvous for the sheer improbable adventure of it! I believe in the now-hackneyed phrase "it's the journey, not the destination." Even if I would like to have a destination, reaching it is not what validates trying to get there. I think being in foreign places with someone you care for, engaged in exploration, discovery, and, occasionally, awe, creates more depth and breadth as a person.

And then there's the sex part. Sometimes the rush of adrenaline when you are doing something like going on a plane to meet your lover where just about everyone else is in robe-like burkas or *thobes* seems like a catalyst for hormones. It's not just the realized act of sex that creates sexual energy in a woman; it's the feeling that you are utilizing all your senses and challenging your heart and mind. This sense of being a sexual force doesn't even have to happen during a romantic relationship—I had had this feeling when my twenty-one-year-old daughter and I participated in a three-day roundup of 400 horses with Montana Horses! near Bozeman, Montana. It was one of the most exciting—and risky—things I have ever taken on. I needed to be focused, brave, and strong. While I was exhausted at the end of the ten-hour days, I also felt super alive, turned on, physically competent, and thrilled because I had met challenges that scared me. It's not the same as direct sexual adventure—but there is a parallel. Physical adventure produces—for lack of a better word—a virility in both men and women.

Generosity Versus Stinginess

In previous books and papers (for example, *Love Between Equals: How Peer Marriage Really Works*), I have written at length on egalitarian couples, and I think it's good to promote equality in all areas of couple life. Sometimes that means doing the same thing at the same time—sometimes it means taking turns. But it is one thing to share and another to count pennies. Friends or lovers who are stingy are setting up a situation that wouldn't work in a business partnership, much less a marriage. You can decline to pool all your funds. My research has shown that keeping some separate money reduces conflict and creates a better balance of power. But generosity is also required in relationships, and trust is essential. Dividing expenses fastidiously and evenly feels wrong. It is an overall equality that is the aim, not an accountant's mentality. I think a relationship with someone stingy—with either resources or their heart—is doomed. Love really needs a gracious and giving attitude to survive.

The Planet Is Your Dating Pool

The world is a lot smaller now that Internet dating is common. A big question for women and men is "Do you want a serious relationship with someone who lives faraway?" The plus: someone just right for you might be in another state—or a faraway place. The minuses: you get far less information on him; your dating is always recreational or on foreign turf; and time is so precious you rarely just hang out together. I obviously think it's worth pursuing your feelings over even great distances, but there is no doubt it puts a heavy burden on the relationship. It takes a much longer time to get a good understanding of who the other person really is, and it may never be a complete picture.

If you are going to date someone who lives far away from you, you need to do as much due diligence as possible, and understand that it will be hard to get an accurate picture of each other for a while.

Meanwhile your heart may feel like it belongs to this person without having enough information to truly warrant that kind of attachment. Be honest with yourself and your lover about what your long-term hopes are for the relationship. You may not like the truth you hear, but you need to know it.

Talking About Penis Problems

I don't have an easy prescription for talking about malfunctioning or uninterested penises. When a man isn't hard, it could be due to medications he's taking, psychological inhibitions, lack of desire, stress, fatigue, biological problems, distraction or guilt, alcohol or recreational drug use, or a hundred other reasons. What is difficult is that except for the most secure men, many men find a lack of erection so distressing that they can't bear to talk about it.

If there is a problem, it is best to talk about it out of bed since usually any in-bed discussion is going to end even the tiniest smidgeon of sexual energy. But as my incident with Mick showed, sometimes, no matter how kindly, gently, or supportively you broach the issue, a man can be insulted and defensive. A secure man, however, will think a temporary or even occasional lack of a hard erection is no big deal.

He will accept an unpredictable pattern of his erections, and concentrate without rancor or worry on what he *can* do. A sexually confident man knows he can be a wonderful lover even without an erection. He knows he can satisfy a woman one way or another, and he's more likely to be able to accept conversations about why he's not erect. If a man is generally defensive, it's likely that communication about sexuality is also going to tough.

One last point: The first thought many of us have is that erectile difficulties mean he is just not interested or attracted. Don't jump to that conclusion.

You need to know the things that can be fixed, and if there is the will to fix them. But if chemistry is weak or uneven, if your partner lets you know that in one way or another you are just not quite sexy enough for him, it might be best to let the relationship go, even if the guy is willing to stay in it. Sex won't stay hot forever with anyone, except in rare super-lucky situations. But you do want someone who is naturally turned on by being with you. True, sexual issues between people who are in love and committed to each other can probably (although not always) be fixed. But sexual issues between uncommitted partners that remain the unremarked-upon "elephant in the room" are destructive enough to make me recommend a new relationship.

With Romance, Trust Your Gut Feelings

I have almost never been wrong when my instinct was telling me to pay attention to something. "Instinct" is a poor word for what I think is really going on. Our mind is an unbelievable computer that we don't fully understand yet. I think instinct is that marvelous computer of ours whirling at warp speed, giving us flashes of information we don't know how to process. We don't know why we feel a certain way but it's all those little bits of observation and knowledge that inform our feelings and tell us to stay or run, doubt or believe.

If I feel there is something "not right" I hold on to that hypothesis, and watch for confirming or disconfirming evidence—I don't dismiss it. And neither should you. I get so many questions written to me where an inner voice has already given the person asking the question the answer. They just have to listen to themselves and they won't need me.

nine

DANCING WITH A
BALINESE COWBOY

Trying Things One Might Not Try at Home

A Deadline

I had six months to finish this book. Dom was lobbying me to complete it in Bali.

"Think of it, Pepper," he said over the phone. "It will be a peaceful, inspiring place to finish your book. The airlines are having a sale. It will be almost free!"

I wasn't so sure.

Bali was a place I'd gone with Ken, the venereologist I had been with for five years, at the height of our tumultuous love affair. Bali was a place Dennis and I had visited with some uneven results.

"It might be full of memories for me that are anything but restful."

"Pepper, you can do hotel reviews for your next book on perfect places for passion. We can also stay in some charming and inexpensive bungalows. The massages are really, really cheap."

Ah. There was the winning argument. Cheap massages. Before I knew it, I was online booking a plane to Bali.

The Foodie

Online again, I found a guy who seemed to be quite the Renaissance man. His profile picture was blurry, a bad sign. But I liked his wry sense of humor and his personal essay was well written. I sent him a message and he responded pretty quickly with a warm note. Kyle expressed interest in getting to know more about me. I still did not have my picture on the Internet so I e-mailed him one. It turned out that we were in overlapping social circles. I knew his brother slightly and he was a good friend with a very good friend of mine. When we chatted on the phone the conversation flowed easily because of our common network. We decided to skip coffee and go directly to a lunch.

I met Kyle at a French bistro. He was waiting for me at a table and looked quite nice. He was wearing a Hawaiian shirt, had thick dark hair, was about five-foot-ten, and his laid back approach put me immediately at ease. He was a "foodie"—food was very important to him. No mystery about that: He had worked as a chef most of his adult life.

We talked animatedly, especially about politics, and we shared our mutual dismay about recent political policies and events. Afterward we took a walk around the Pike Place Market and we ended the date with a hug. We agreed to get together again.

Time Flies

Three weeks passed and I didn't hear from Kyle. But that didn't bother me. I had gotten used to dates that seemed promising but turned into nothing. I didn't fully understand such experiences but I accepted them. He slipped out of my memory quickly. When Kyle did call I was surprised but pleased to hear his voice. I didn't question his long pause between lunch and this call. It didn't really matter and I didn't feel he owed me an explanation.

"How would you like to dine at my house? We can shop for the ingredients together and share a significant bottle of wine I have on hand. Interested?"

"Being cooked for? Hard decision, but I accept," I said with a laugh.

It sounded intimate, too.

Two days later, we went to a specialty market and he picked out produce and protein the way a decorator would pick out fabrics. We discussed menus but I just echoed his choices. They all sounded great to me. I loved the way he looked at food. He looked for what was perfect and he knew what was at its peak. Grocery shopping had been transformed into a tour de force.

We went back to his house near the university. He shared it with his teenage son, who was at his mother's house that day. The dinner took about six hours to create. Kyle would prepare a course. I acted as sous chef. We created each course, talked for a while, ate for a while, and then went back to the kitchen for the next phase of cuisine creation. Kyle had talent and, even more attractive to me, he was in the grip of an authentic passion. The day and evening were absolutely perfect. We kissed good night and it was sweet but not sexy. We had several other dates that also went well, and they also ended with some kisses but not kisses that promised more. I accepted what Kyle offered, not feeling the need to categorize our times together. It felt nice to enjoy the present with Kyle and not worry about the future.

"The Old Pepper" Versus "The New Pepper"

Months went by and my book deadline and trip to Bali approached quicker than I expected. My dates with Kyle were casual and affectionate. They were not sexual.

The old Pepper would have been angry that this relationship had not gotten sexual. Why was I not upset this time? Did I not really find him attractive? Or did he not find me attractive? Or was it actually inevitable, that getting older means dating is just going to be less impulsive and sexually charged?

I didn't sense that was the case, although I was puzzled by my new-found ability to just enjoy getting to know this man without needing the affirmation of his sexual response. It really took the pressure off.

The slow way I was getting to know Kyle had me thinking more and more about my approach to relationships since my twenty-three-year marriage.

Kyle and I had been seeing each other about once a week for four months. I liked this guy. And the more we were together, the fonder I got of his dry, intelligent quips about people and politics. But in all that time he had not pushed for more than a few kisses.

There may not have beeen enough sexual chemistry to make this relationship more than platonic. But that was okay.

The Couch or the Bed

One night Kyle picked me up at my place and we had a lively evening with friends at a dinner party. While we weren't a couple, we collaborated at carrying conversation the way couples often do. When he drove me home I asked him if he'd like to stay over. It was late, we'd had some wine, and it wasn't smart for him to drive the forty minutes it would take him to get home.

I could see that Kyle wasn't sure if he was sleeping on the couch, in the guest room, or with me. I indicated with me was the best choice. We went upstairs to my bedroom, undressed rather shyly, neither of us entirely clear about what was going to happen. Since neither of us could read the other's intensions, we left on our t-shirts and got under the covers. He turned, kissed me gently. I responded more passionately. Then he was all over me.

He actually surprised the hell out of me. Up to this point, he had been very tentative with me sexually and I expected him to be a gentle and reserved lover. This was not who he turned out to be. He was very male, very directive, and intense in a way that I found exciting. He was an iron man with the ability to keep me awake and aroused for most of the night. He was great fun, not yet knowledgeable to what my specific sexual needs might be. But that kind of tinkering can come later. Kyle had a very sexual side to his personality and I was glad I hadn't missed this.

The next day Kyle left after a nice breakfast and lovemaking well into the afternoon. It had been a long time since this had happened at my home. The morning was more intimate than the evening and I felt more comfortable with him.

As I walked him to his car, I said, "I am so glad you stayed over. Thank you for a great evening and morning. The bad news though is that I have a series of trips starting almost immediately and I won't be able to see you again until they are over—which is almost a month."

Kyle had an easy temperament. He smiled and said, "No worries, I had a great time, too. Have a wonderful time on your trips and we can keep in touch with e-mail."

We kissed good bye and I walked back into my house smiling.

An Inner Journey

I thought of Kyle as I packed my bags to fly off to Bali. Looking at the bigger picture, what would I have to do with my life to make something work with anyone who is local, available, and wanted a real relationship and not a drop-in lover?

I realized that the time in Bali would not only be spent thinking about the past, it would also need to include some hard thinking about the future. I had had a spectacular time in my fifties and I was now looking at a new decade. I needed to think about whether it should be more of the same—or different in some important way. The facts were that out of the past five years I had only had one in-town "real" relationship with a man. How much of that was happenstance because of work and travel—and how much of that was me running away from commitment and monogamy?

Kyle was becoming a symbol for me. He was making me think about who I wanted to be and where I wanted to spend my time. I was torn. I loved the way I lived but I also felt I wanted a real and abiding love in my life.

I promised myself that this trip to Bali would be spent trying to figure out who I really was and what I really wanted.

Returning to Bali

"Bali is now coming into view," the flight attendant announced. I felt relieved. Dom had e-mailed me from Bali the day before, assuring me there was nothing to worry about. I knew the odds of a terrorist attack was as great on my trips to New York City as any place on Bali, but the region had had a lot or recent publicity. Java had had a tsunami, all of Asia was worried about bird flu, and volcanoes were rumbling. Dom knew I wouldn't back out but he wrote to reassure me:

> Dear Pepper:
>
> I have been in touch with the spirits on the island who assure me that the volcano, tsunamis, and earthquakes on Java would not disrupt your important retreat on neighboring Bali. Trust me, I have not only fixed everything by doing the appropriate offerings to the gods, I have also done my research. Much of Bali is protected from such natural disasters—and anyhow—do you want to be a sissy or an adventuress? This is your moment of truth!
>
> See you at the airport.
>
> > Ciao,
> >
> > Dom

As I exited security control, I saw Dom in the crowd. He was easy to spot, as he was about twice as tall as everyone else there. I was relieved.

"Welcome to your Bali," Dom gave me a big hug.

"It's great to be here," I said, and I meant it. "You look well." He did. He was relaxed and happy.

"This is what a week on Bali does," he said, "and I'm already brimming over with travel stories."

Dom helped me roll my luggage to our hotel's driver. The Indonesian driver smiled broadly and held the door as we got in a meticulously clean car covered with white linen on the seats and headrests. Thus welcomed, we headed south to the Conrad Bali Resort where my good friend Lisa, as a publicity person for Hilton, had secured us two rooms at a super discount.

As we drove, Dom offered, "Balinese lesson number one: The only phrase you really need to know is *matur suksma*, which means 'thank you'."

Unwinding in Nusa Dua

The Conrad Resort was quite impressive, built on the beach facing the Indian Ocean and with a great entryway that was simple and beautiful. A friendly and attractive public relations director, Ruth, met us in the lobby and offered us cold face towels and a glass of banana juice. I loved this custom. The tropics are synonymous with fruit drinks, and I don't feel like I'm there until I am sipping something with the equivalent of an umbrella in it.

Ruth had a charming Australian accent. She wore her blond hair back tight in a ponytail that set off her lovely eyes and smile.

Ruth asked, "And what is your program here in Bali?"

"Sad to say I'm finishing up a book so I'm actually working."

"And what is the book about?" I noticed that Ruth was not wearing a wedding band.

"Dating after fifty and exploring one's sexuality."

"My dear," she said with a slight chuckle, "we simply will have to chat about that over some drinks."

I appreciated her verve. Ruth's face was alive and expressive and the mischievous twinkle in her eyes suggested past or present adventures that I'd love to hear about. While Dom explored the primitive art in the lobby, I focused on Ruth.

I was suddenly interested in her age and asked, "May I ask how old you are?"

She didn't hesitate and said, "Sixty-five."

I would have taken her for ten years younger. She must be doing something right.

Her face, while softly lined, radiated the youthfulness of someone who loved her life and took joy and strength from people. She was another role model.

I wondered what it's like for a single, older, Western women here on Bali. I knew I should take Ruth up on her offer for a drink.

Dom and I checked into our rooms, which were side by side, allowing us to bend over our outside patio railings and share collective "aaahs" at the tastefully appointed rooms.

Ruth gave us a tour of the expansive grounds, filled with pools, intertwining lagoons, and a long beach that offered different vistas of the ocean. I remarked that the lagoon suites which had stairs leading from the private patios into the pools were quite romantic, and I could imagine lovers taking midnight swims au natural.

"Oh, yes," she answered, "I suppose we might have some naughty things happening at midnight."

I adore it when people use the word "naughty." Dom strolled off to check out the spa while Ruth deposited me in a giant Balinese gazebo-like structure that was really a huge square outdoor bed with a thatched roof.

"This lovely place for resting outdoors is called a *bah-lay*," explained the thoughtful Ruth, carefully enunciating the Balinese term. "And *bales* are delightful for relaxing in all day." I removed my sandals and climbed onto what felt like a king-size bed filled with oversize cushions.

"I'll have Komang bring you your welcome drink while you rest," Ruth said, "and I'll check in with you later."

Ruth walked back to the main lobby while I luxuriated in my bale, staring out at the Indian Ocean. Moments later, a young, well-built Balinese man in a sarong was offering me a large drink.

I tried out my one Balinese phrase, "*Ma-tur suk-see-ma.*" The waiter smiled broadly and laughed a bit.

I am sure my accent was humorous.

"You speak Balinese?" he said with a wide grin, showing his perfectly filed teeth.

"Well, just *thank you*."

He smiled and then said in a sort of English shorthand, "Please enjoy."

Alone in Bali in my huge cushioned *bale,* I relaxed sipping my refreshing fruity concoction, well aware that a personal trainer had once said that I should never drink calories, only eat them. She was so right, but at this point though I felt the need to be expansive and enjoy the damn fruit drink. (This, of course, is the kind of devil-may-care attitude that rewards you with a tummy and thighs.) I breathed in the fresh air, and felt the fragrant breeze. I looked at the surf curve around the beach. My head started to clear and I realized there was emotional as well as physical space here for me. I felt released from the anxieties and obligations of everyday life, and perhaps most important, from my cell phone. I thought fate had given me this break to assess the meaning of the choices I had made about my life up to this time.

Dom had been right to get me here.

The Bungalows

Since one of my purposes here was to evaluate romantic destinations as well as finish my book, Dom and I had made the decision to try out five or six places on different parts of the island. After two days of writing and relaxing, we moved from the Conrad in Nusa Dua to Seminyak, a busy beachside village west of Kuta, filled with places to eat and shop.

Tomo, the serenely composed manager of the Sura Villa, met us in his open-air lobby. After the required welcome drink, he led us to our two-story, thatched-roof bungalow, which was at the end of the walled grounds. Dom took the bedroom and bathroom on top and I took the the ground floor. My romantic bathtub, big enough for two, fired my imagination. I thought about what it would be like to be in it by candlelight at night. Someone had already thought about that: The tub came complete with two candles perched on its ledge. This charmed me.

Once we unpacked Dom and I sat on our wooden porch overlooking the pool, the koi pond next to us and the greenery surrounding us.

"I have a bold idea," Dom said with a grin. "How do you feel about writing for a while, then having a late lunch, followed by a four-hand massage?"

"Did you say four-hand massage?"

"I did, indeed."

"How long do I have to write before I deserve that?"

"Just an hour or so, my dear,"

"Oooh-kay. No problem," I responded. "But just to whet my appetite, can you tell me what this massage is like? Is it like a sports massage or just a classical massage or what? Do men or women do it? Does it get, dare I say, 'naughty'?"

"You don't need to worry," Dom said. "I have experienced this massage myself at a number of places. The masseurs down the road at *Jari Menari*, which means Dancing Fingers, are very professional guys. Or perhaps for an adventure we'll go to Antique Spa, which gives great massage treatments out in the countryside. I will orchestrate the afternoon. Just get to work."

Thus motivated, I did.

Scanning the Beach

After lunch at the beachfront Gado Gado bistro Dom and I took seats on two beach lounge chairs in front of the restaurant, paying a vendor a few rupias for the rental. I had my straw beach bag filled with my travel guide to Bali, small laptop, cell phone, and passport.

"I'm going to take a stroll up the beach. Care to join me?" Dom asked.

"No, I'll just rest a bit and enjoy this idyllic setting," I said, "I am getting in the right mood for my four-handed massage."

Dom strolled away and I scrutinized the beach, spotting assorted tourists and various men who I thought might be Kuta cowboys interacting with women of various ages.

That didn't hold my interest for as long as I thought it might. I was thinking instead about my book, the chapters of my life, and the risks I might be willing to take in my writing. This book had turned out to be intensely personal and had exposed more of myself than I felt comfortable with. I wanted to be honest and give people complete information about what my life had been like and what advice was prompted by my own life as well as my research. But I was feeling overexposed and I winced when I thought about what my students would think and say to me.

Sharing everything with other middle-aged women didn't bother me at all. Sharing everything with the twenty-one year olds I would be grading made me want to move to Terre del Fuego.

My eyes drifted back to the beach again, noting the handful of single women strolling the beach, as well as the ever-present hand holding couples, and gracefully moving vendors. A single fifty-ish Western woman passed by, slowly strolling near the water's edge.

I wondered if she was a woman alone on an adventure or was she just taking time away from a husband or lover?

Time seemed to pass quite quickly and after a few more unconfirmed Kuta cowboy sightings, I heard a familiar voice saying, "Are you ready for your four hands?"

Dom had returned from his walk to take me to my much-anticipated massage. "The men at Antique Spa are waiting," said Dom as he guided me up the beach to a taxi.

Why was I suddenly feeling a bit nervous?

The Mother of All Massages

In the cab ride to the spa Dom asked, "Are you ready for a truly amazing experience?"

"Well, if I must, I must," I snickered playfully. "Only in the service of research, of course."

"Would that be travel research or sex research?" Dom joked.

"I will tell you after the massage," I quipped back.

As we traveled ten minutes into the countryside near Seminyak, I started feeling a bit disoriented. The rural landscape didn't seem like a likely place for a massage.

After seeing a sign for horse stables, I asked, "Dom, what kind of spa is going to be out here?"

"You'll see," said Dom.

We turned down an unmarked lane with rice paddies on either side and came up to a low grey stone fence with a sign "Antique Spa." The spa looked quite modest from the front, looking more like a small home than a commercial business. I wondered if we were going to get a bargain. Dom assured me he had been here before and that the façade was deceptive. As we drove up, people appeared in front of the building and we were greeted at the open-air spa lobby by the smiling, handsome manager. I was loath to let the cab go, but Dom was relaxed and so I figured I should stop imagining a debacle and just trust Dom's past experience. The cab left us and the manager asked us to be seated at a table to review our spa options. Dom and I were both served the customary welcome drink and we sipped some kind of refreshing juice while we reviewed the various massages. Dom recommended a two-hour, four-hand session with a "body shampoo and rose bath."

I turned to Dom and said, "Two hours! I am not sure I can lie still for that long. Passivity, even for pleasure, is not natural to me."

Dom turned to me and quietly said, "I am sure you will have no trouble enjoying two expert masseurs touching your body for two hours."

"I hope so."

"And to show my solidarity, while you have four hands, I will take on a two-handed massage."

We told the manager our choices and he asked, "Please pick your massage oil from the choices of Wellness, Relaxation, or Aphrodisiac."

"Relaxation," said Dom.

I pondered choosing Wellness.

"Aphrodisiac," I said.

Dom and I were ushered through the main door and he was right about the interior. It was quite lovely inside. I was facing a beautifully designed hallway and high reed ceilings. This was reassuring. Two truly attractive young Balinese men, probably in their twenties, one with long wavy dark hair, the other with a crew cut, appeared in front of me to show me the way to my room.

Dom smiled and said, "Remember, if it gets too pleasurable, you can always stop them."

"I know that. But I hope I don't need to exercise my superpowers," I retorted.

I followed the two young men past a half a dozen private treatment rooms. They brought me into my room, which was open air. The room had a stone floor and stone walls and was not much wider than the massage table in the middle. The massage table itself was centered under a long aluminum tube that hung down from the ceiling. At the end of the room there was a sunken tub next to a tiny stream with fish. The sun peered in over a small fence that provided privacy. The man with dark wavy hair handed me a sarong.

I looked around the room for a moment and thought, *Okay. There is no dressing room to change into my sarong. So what do I do?*

The men smiled shyly and left the room.

This was a bit unusual.

I felt slightly worried about what was going to happen next but I decided to just be present. Be brave. Be open. Go with it! So I calmed down. I looked around again. The room itself was reassuring, tastefully designed, and the equipment all looked quite professionally set up.

If Dom brought me here I knew that I am perfectly safe. I changed into my sarong, hung my clothes on some hooks, and looked at the little stream and listened to the water rush by. The young men came back in and closed the door. Then one man locked it. I didn't feel scared but I was watchful.

I liked the fact that at least one end of this room was open and all the rooms along the hall opened to the same stream. I was not too far from other human beings.

The young men indicated that I should sit down on a wooden chair next to the tub where a very big wooden bowl sat on the floor.

The men smiled. I smiled.

These guys knew little to zero English. I could barely say *"thank you"* in Indonesian.

I sat on the chair. One of the men started rubbing my shoulders. It felt somewhat awkward. The other one smiled sweetly, and gently placed my feet in the wooden bowl, which was filled with warm water and topped with rose petals. He carefully washed my feet.

Then one man spoke to me in broken English, "Please. Table."

The massage table was high enough so that I had to clumsily climb up it. Not an attractive thing to do in a sarong. I laid face down on the table, putting my head in the conventional headrest that cradled it, and I could see the strategically placed flowers in a small vase on the floor. I loved the attention to detail, and the perfume of the flowers was really strong and sensual.

The men covered me with a sheet as they gently took the sarong away. Then the sheet was pulled down to cover my lower torso, with my back, the side of my hips, and legs exposed.

Okay, basically I was nude except for a big bunched-up piece of sheet between my legs, alone in a room with two young Indonesian men. I stopped staring at the flower on the floor beneath the massage table and closed my eyes. What the hell. Let's see what happens.

The young men were practiced masseurs and their strong hands were all over my body. I was feeling pretty good. One man kneaded my shoulders while the other stroked my legs. They had obviously been trained to work together on a body as there was a certain practiced synchronicity to their sensual strokes. Warm oil was everywhere. The feeling was both stimulating and intense. One man was working on my left side, running his hands up my thigh to my back bone, while the other man took the right side. The synchronized sensual movement of the men's fingers was unlike anything I had ever experienced before. And it was heavenly.

Turning Over

After what seemed like a very long and enjoyable time, the men stopped massaging me.

The masseur with wavy hair bent over and whispered in somewhat broken English, "Please, you turn over."

He held up the sheet and after I rolled over, covered me again.

Then, unlike any other massage I've ever had, he took the small, folded sheet off my chest and pulled it down to cover my pubic area, leaving my legs and my breasts completely exposed. The two masseurs then proceeded, using the warm scented oil, to do long strokes up and down my body, each one taking one side. The massage went from my legs to my stomach to my breasts to my shoulders.

My breasts? This is very unusual. Dom had told me that this was a spa that catered to a mixed group of clients, including gay men. Maybe that explains it.

As the men continued to massage my torso, which felt quite wonderful, I thought, maybe these masseurs are gay and think that breasts are no big deal so they are going to massage me like a guy.

The men weren't making love to my breasts. Actually, I felt as though my breasts just seemed to be in the way of their strokes. So I just relaxed into it and let them do what they liked. It was surprisingly unerotic, but extremely pleasant, and I became more of a participant-observer than swept away by sexual desire. If I were a little gutsier than I am, I would have observed it all eyes wide open. But to keep from being embarrassed, or even more engaged, I kept my eyes closed most of the time. I could feel them move around me and address new parts of my body, however, so I was very present. One masseur focused on my torso while the other paid attention to my thighs. Four hands worked their magic. Occasionally the guy doing my thighs would get into the inner thigh area just below my crotch and I flinched when he came close to my pubic area. He backed off gently as though he got the message, and knew precisely what I did and did not want rubbed. After more than what seemed a half hour of sensual, expert massaging, the men stopped.

Wavy Hair leaned down to me and quietly said, "The massage over."

I sat up, holding the sheet over my breasts. The second man smiled at me and left the room.

Wavy Hair softly said, "Please. Off table. You stay."

"Sure," I said.

I got off the table, using the sheet as a sarong, and stood by the wall watching my young masseur ready the room for my body shampoo. I looked up at the ceiling and I noticed that the metal bar over the bed was actually a sprinkler. It was shaped like a long pipe, about three feet long, with holes on the lower side for water to stream out along the length of the table. So much for my bathtub theory. The masseur turned on the water and tested it to get the temperature right. The water sprinkled over the table, which now had a waterproof covering over it, and disappeared into the floor drain. Then the masseur took an extension hose off the wall and let me feel the water to make sure it wasn't too hot. I indicated it was fine. This produced quite a dazzling smile from him and he motioned for me to get back on the table. This was somewhat daunting. There was no lady-like way to climb up on that table. But I'd gone too far to get coy now and I was continuing in my definite "what the hell" mood.

Still, I had to stiffen my resolve. The next step had to be to get naked. It was clear my sheet-sarong was inappropriate for a shower bath. Whatever. I placed my sheet on the chair. I was quite aware that I was perfectly nude and that I had to crawl back up on that table. I sucked up my courage and, rather awkwardly, climbed back on the table, and then lay on my tummy facing down. I did not think it was my most attractive angle.

Well, now. I was completely nude alone with a young man who had just had his hands all over me. I couldn't remember his name, and I didn't know what he was going to do next. Things were going just fine.

I turned my head and looked up from the table at the masseur who smiled politely. What was he thinking? Was this guy gay? Was he straight and expecting something during this next phase? I waited.

I lay facedown while the sprinkler drenched me with copious amounts of warm water from above. It felt really good and very sexy. At the same time Wavy Hair picked up a handheld hose that rhythmically pulsed water and used it to cover my body, head to feet. Some of that rhythm was producing erotic results in my body. Then he stopped the upper shower.

Now what happens?

I felt his hand, covered in some type of cloth mitt, soaping up my back.

Oh God, oh God . . . this felt so good. I edited my automatic response, which would have been to moan. I wasn't ready to help create a full-fledged sexual event.

Then he started soaping up my legs. When his fingers occasionally reached into the upper inner thigh region, I didn't flinch.

This felt fabulous. I was not sure how to label this. Was this on the edge of sex or was this a type of sex? Who cares!

Wavy Hair leaned over to my ear and quietly said, "Please turn over."

I complied. He soaped me up again with the same ministrations to my upper body. Occasionally I opened my eyes and smiled at him.

This was one of the most amazing, sexy, and satisfying experiences I have ever had. And my job was just to allow it to happen and enjoy it. Lucky, lucky me.

He began soaping my upper thighs. His touch coupled with the warm soapy water was extraordinarily sensual. I was aware that each long stroke up my thigh came inches closer to my genital area.

As this point something changed. This massage crossed from sensual to sexual for me.

My whole body was tingling and turned on. This massage might not have survived a legal definition of sex, but if I had been married I would have coded it under infidelity.

The masseur stopped soaping me up and rinsed me off with warm water.

He softly said, "Your body shampoo, over."

Then he motioned for me to stand up. I did and he toweled me dry, carefully and professionally. He handed me my sarong, bowed with a smile, and finally our eyes met with—what? Recognition of having had an experience together? An acknowledgement that some extra service had been given? There was something there but I couldn't label it. He left me alone in my room.

As I dressed, I thought about my experience. I had just paid to be fondled and I'd enjoyed it tremendously. It had definitely been massage heavy, or sex light, or something further on a certain continuum than I had ever been before. The overall impact on my psyche, however, was bigger than anything that had been done to my body. I felt like I owned my sexuality just a little bit more than I did when I walked in. I had let myself enjoy an erotic massage that was far more commonly enjoyed by men than women. I had felt in complete control of what I wanted. While the masseur had touched me in places no masseur ever had, he hadn't crossed any boundaries without tacit, if not explicit, permission. I could have, at any time, told the masseur to cut it out and I was absolutely sure he would have obeyed my instructions. But I communicated nonverbally that what he was doing felt good.

As I put on my t-shirt and shorts, I felt well taken care of and very, very satisfied.

I met with Dom in the spa lobby, paid my bill, generously tipped the two masseurs and walked toward the waiting cab.

When I was in the taxi heading back to the villa with Dom he asked, "How was it?"

I was dying to tell him about it.

I said, "Just what kind of massage was that supposed to be?"

Dom looked disturbingly clueless. "What do you mean?"

"Well, Dom, don't tell me you haven't had one of their massages with 'benefits.'"

Dom, looking kind of shocked, asked, "What do you mean? It's just a regular massage place."

"Oh, really," I said. "Well, I got a rather irregular massage and I assumed that's why you sent me there."

Dom started to look genuinely upset.

I interjected, "But don't worry. I liked it. And maybe they're used to gay men but they massaged my chest which is a first for me."

Dom stared at me looking perplexed, "I am very surprised. I've had many massages there and they have always been totally professional massages. And nothing else."

He thought for a moment. Then he said, "Should I talk to the owner?"

"Absolutely not," I said vehemently. "I was totally in charge of the massage. I didn't feel unsafe. Anyhow, it was another life experience. I am learning how to take pleasure here as I want to and as it's offered."

"You sure?" asked Dom with a note of concern.

"I think there is some lesson here, not that I think it's part of a greater design. But you know I am taking each situation as it comes, and learning how to handle it."

"You are being very Zen about all of this," Dom said with a laugh, finally lightening up.

"Who needs Kuta cowboys?" I kidded him. "I have my own version of pleasure on my terms."

A Real Kuta Cowboy

When Dom and I returned to the Sura Villa we strolled by the open-air lobby and a young man saw us, jumped up, smiled, and walked toward us. He was small, had long dark hair, light brown skin, developed forearms, a broad, powerful face, and a sweet smile; he was wearing a blue shirt, sandals, and jeans. He appeared to be in his mid-twenties. I took a quick look at his very nice, smooth body and I assumed, given that he now was focusing intensely on Dom, that he must know him.

"Hello, Jon," Dom said with a wry smile. "Good to see you again."

"Hello, Mr. Dom," he said.

Hmm, I thought, *Mister?*

Dom looked at me slightly perplexed.

"Jon, this is my friend, Dr. Pepper."

Jon smiled broadly and said, "Hello. Very nice to meet you."

"Nice to meet you, too."

"And what brings you to the Sura?" Dom asked. He sounded warm but a little confused.

"I was near. I wanted to ask if you have a program."

A program, I thought, *what kind of program does this young man have in mind?*

Dom looked at me with a reassuring smile and then turned to Jon.

"Yes, Jon, we do have a program. We are busy with work and meeting friends for dinner, right, Pepper?"

"Right." I had the feeling that something unspoken was going on between Dom and Jon but I had no clue what it was.

"But thanks for stopping by," Dom said.

Jon didn't seem to understand everything we were saying but kept smiling at Dom, then at me.

"Well, we have to get ready for dinner," Dom added. "Have a good evening, Jon."

I looked at the young man who now seemed a bit sad and said, "Good bye." Jon strolled out of the lobby as Dom and I strolled to our bungalow.

Once inside our living room Dom started laughing.

"Well, my dear," Dom said, "That was your first official Kuta cowboy."

"What? I thought he was for you," I responded.

"Quite the opposite. There was a miscommunication, " Dom explained. "Jon is a Kuta cowboy and a friend of a waiter I know. We met last week and I told them about your book project. Trust me, I didn't invite Jon over—I think my waiter buddy sent him here by mistake."

"That was it? That was the famed Kuta cowboy?"

"Yes. That was the real thing, according to my source."

What a letdown. There had been a seductive young man with a good sense of humor at the Conrad check-in desk whom I found very attractive. I had seen so many elegant and graceful Balinese men. I thought the Kuta cowboys would be like that. Somehow I didn't realize how much fantasy I had imposed on this whole Kuta cowboy thing.

Thinking about this real Kuta cowboy at my doorstep, I realized now that I had seen several guys of his style—scruffily dressed and not particularly charismatic—on the beach. Maybe these guys were enticing to some women but I did not find them seductive in the least.

"My dear Dom. Maybe it's all the buildup, but I guess I thought the Kuta cowboys were going to be devastatingly attractive, able to single-handedly romance a Western woman out of her shorts with a single conversation. I guess I need a lot more soul and brain power before my libido starts to function."

"Of that I am sure."

"But maybe," I said, "these young guys with their great bodies and sweet demeanors, at times down and out and available, are exactly what some women want for a vacation romance. And there is absolutely nothing wrong with that. Well, each to her own."

Dom and I strolled to his favorite place for a sunset drink called La Luciola. It was a charming beachfront bar and bistro with a stunning view of the Indian Ocean. Our elegant waiter Putu, dressed in a long-sleeve white dinner jacket and dark sarong, served us creamy fruit drinks and heated cashews as we watched the sun set. I wistfully let go of any fantasies about Kuta cowboys understanding that I wouldn't be dancing with one of them on Bali.

Desa Kala Patra

Our villa had taken on a magical look as darkness fell, and strategically placed lights showed off the lush vegetation surrounding the bungalows and pool. Dom and I had made dinner plans with a friend of a friend named Suzi and her friend, another ex-pat named Jamie, a writer from New York City. Suzi picked Dom and me up in her Jeep. She was a sharp and attractive forty-ish woman with a tanned, trim body, delicate features, wavy blond hair and intelligent eyes. It was a bit demanding to talk to her. Suzi was a postmodern conversationalist who liked to blurt out all kinds of information jumping from topic to topic. In a ten-minute car ride Suzi shared that she was a former Seattleite who had worked as a gallery owner on Bali for more than a decade. She had dated a prince from a royal family on Bali and lived in the Royal Palace for a while. That turned out to be a lot less glamorous than it sounded. She said there was no modern plumbing in the palace so she spent years bathing in cold water scooped out of a large wooden bowl in her room. This woman was a genuine adventuress and I admired her spunk.

When Dom, Suzi, and I got to the Casa Bonnita restaurant we were greeted by Jamie, a light-haired, English-looking American writer with a kind smile. He motioned to a table and soon the four of us were engaged in all kinds of interesting conversation about my book, Dom's design work, Jamie's writing projects, and Suzi's overview of Balinese philosophy.

"*Desa Kala Patra* is something you need to know to understand the Hindu Balinese," Suzi said to us as we sipped our fruit drinks—a combination of banana, strawberries, and watermelon. "*Desa* is place. *Kala* is time. *Patra* is situation."

"Very intriguing." I said. "What does it mean to the Balinese?"

Suzi explained, "When a Balinese person faces anything new it requires a clear understanding of the place, the time, and the situation. Perhaps a woman goes to live in another village with her new husband and senses new laws and customs. She must think how to respond, situation by situation, in a way that is both respectful and pragmatic."

I turned to Suzi and said, "I like that mindset. I think what happens to all of us is we get a vision of how life should be with rules that we created to serve us at one time. And when new times present themselves we inappropriately rely on old answers. We often don't know how to create a new self for new situations when it's called for."

Suzi listened in earnest.

I said, "I do find that Bali has its own mood and I am trying to see what changes it might ask of me."

The dinner conversations moved on as dishes of fish, chicken, and spicy rice were served but I kept thinking how *Desa Kala Patra* might apply to my life. I thought about my four-handed massage and how right it was for this time, place, and situation. Of course, it occurred to me that part of the art of love is to know how to take advantage of the time, place, and situation you are in.

Beauty and a Kind of Romance

The days were passing by too quickly. Dom and I woke up and shared a lovely breakfast hand-delivered by the Sura staff. On writing breaks, we spent the next few days strolling the beach and the village, discovering new restaurants, indulging in more spa treatments, and discussing my writing. On our fourth morning at the Sura, Dom and

I enjoyed Balinese banana pancakes before heading south to a hotel called Amanusa, one of three Aman resorts I booked on Bali to experience and research the ultimate in romantic getaways.

As Dom and I walked into the dramatic entrance of Amanusa, I marveled at how beautiful it was without being pretentious. In that mood, Dom and I were greeted and escorted to our separate villas. Mine was spectacular, spacious and elegant. A vase full of tuber-roses infused the air and an artful presentation of tropical fruits added to the aromatic delight of the moment. I mused that the huge bed artistically draped with mosquito netting would be a particularly ideal erotic cocoon.

I had three hours before I was to rendezvous with Dom in the bar, so I decided to skinny dip in my own private pool. Afterward I ordered a latte from room service, worked on the book, and relaxed on my *bale* looking out toward the ocean. This would have been perfect with a lover—but surprisingly, it was perfect without one, too.

After an over-the-top dinner served at the side of their huge, glamorously lit pool, Dom and I retired, he to see some friends, I to a thoroughly relaxing in-room massage by a professional and gifted Balinese masseur. Afterward, I lit the thoughtfully provided candles, and placed them strategically around the sides of the sunken tub in the bathroom. Ah, happiness.

The next morning Dom and I had breakfast in a *bale* on the almost deserted beach. Over a meal of eggs, pastries, juices, and coffee, we debriefed as we watched the waves curl into the white sand. We were both silent, not a natural state of being for either of us. I couldn't help but note the change.

"It's hard to explain," I said, "I am literally at a loss for words."

"Me, too," said Dom.

It was so beautiful and peaceful, and I felt so absolutely relaxed and taken care of, that I felt tears welling up. I looked at Dom, and I saw his eyes were glistening a bit, too. Life can be so gracious and protective from time to time, and we both were fully appreciating the moment. How long had it been since I felt this appreciative of life's offerings?

North to Ubud

With ginger chicken sandwiches tucked into lunch boxes, Dom and I enjoyed the drive to our next home in Ubud, up in the hills of Bali. As our car climbed in elevation, the topography and plants changed into thick jungle vegetation. I looked forward to the peace and green tapestry of the jungle. Our car passed shops and vendors, then made a turn into a back road and followed it down a narrow drive to the subtle beauty and grace of the Amandari Hotel. As I got out of the car, two absolutely exquisite prepubescent girls approached in bright gold, pink, and red dress sarongs. One of them giggled sweetly and threw some flower petals over me. Then they tried to throw petals over Dom but his six foot–plus frame was a challenge and petals hit him in the face. He grinned.

I was led to my room by one of the ever-smiling Balinese porters and I was totally charmed when I entered the exterior gate and found that we had to cross lily pads and a koi pond on stone steps to get to my front door. Entering the room, I looked across its large open bedroom to the glass doors facing the view and, past the private pool, I could see hundreds of shades of green, the disorder of heavy vegetation punctuated by the fastidious rice paddies that climbed up and down hills. I was just about overcome with the composition. The spacious villa was an elegant adaptation of local housing with high ceilings made of reeds and local woods, and beautiful hand-crafted furniture. I would have loved to have just stayed there but I was summoned to lunch.

A Place for Women

Dom and I enjoyed lunch with Liv, a charming woman of Indian-Swedish ancestry who was the manager of the Amandari. Liv had a wealth of knowledge about Balinese culture. I peppered her with questions, including questions about male and female relations in Bali.

"Do you find many women traveling alone here? Is it a place where single women are comfortable?"

"This is very safe place for women travelers and one that offers many rewards." Liv smiled and didn't specify exactly what those rewards might be. But I was feeling that all of Bali was just one continuous sensuous prompt—massages, gentle men, caring women, beautiful places to stay, exquisite fabrics, and awe-inspiring views. Every day my senses were satisfied.

That night at dinner in a *bale* overlooking the jungle, Dom and I talked about why Bali enticed our senses.

"I find myself getting calmer and calmer," I said as I ate my coconut rice dish. "I am not a whit less sexual, but I feel so nourished by this environment that I'm feeling at peace each day."

"That's wonderful to hear," Dom said. "I know getting to Bali wasn't easy but I'm really glad you did."

"I am, too. I can see things a lot clearer now." I thought about my charming foodie, Kyle, back in Seattle. I had been in a very different time, space, and location for months, unavailable for intimacy with him or any other man. I needed to ask the question: Did I want to create a life where I could also build a committed relationship with someone? But an answer didn't seem pressing. I felt life held gifts of friendship and sensuality and a partner would come in time—without struggle. Or not.

A Chance Encounter

The next day, while Dom enjoyed the spa, I wrote for a few hours, enjoyed a short jungle trek with an athletic hotel guide named Darma, then cleaned off in the outdoor shower, a feature of Balinese villas that I had come to love. I decided I had made enough headway in my chapter to treat myself to a visit to the town of Ubud and see how it had evolved since my visit almost three decades earlier. I took a short taxi ride to the center of the town, now filled with bungalows, hotels, cafés, galleries, boutiques, and vendors of all types. After strolling into a number of jewelry stores and basket shops, picking up a few gifts here and there, I passed a little café that had an espresso machine near the counter. Latte addict that I am, I could not resist, and ducked in. No sooner had I said "with extra foam" than a woman sitting near me at the counter started a conversation about the peculiarities of how Americans like their coffee drinks. She asked me where I was from and how I was enjoying Bali. I took the seat next to her and we introduced ourselves and started chatting away. Among other topics, I told her about my book project. I liked her open, friendly style and I always got a kick out of an Australian accent.

Angelica was about my age and had a career somewhat like mine: public health. She had moved from Sydney to Bali about six years ago, to "take a break from ex-husbands and adult children." She lived near Ubud and worked with a social service agency for the villagers. We bonded during our conversation about why people don't follow prescription instructions or avoid obvious sexual health risks.

She smiled mysteriously and said, "Life is too short to avoid *all* risks." Naturally, I followed up on that lead.

Angelica had strong opinions on everything and was willing to let me know her deepest feelings and most private habits. She was a party girl in the body of a fifty-ish woman, with sparkling, warm eyes. I was impressed with her verve and guts. Here was a woman living out her fifties as I thought they should be lived, grabbing life and following her instincts. On the other hand, she was way more of a free spirit than I and I was somewhat intimidated by her ability to pull up stakes and move. She had started her family with a truck driver who was always away from home. It was an unsatisfying situation, so once the last child went off to college she felt free to pursue her own happiness. On her fiftieth birthday she packed her suitcases, left her husband, and moved to Bali.

Here is where the story got extremely interesting to me. Shortly after she arrived, she met a charming Balinese man almost twenty years her junior, who I realized was her own Kuta cowboy. They began to date and soon he was living with her. A few months later they were married. I was more than curious. What happens when a foreign lady tried to domesticate a Kuta cowboy? I asked her how it all began and if she thought she was taking a big risk—or not.

"I met him on the beach near Kuta, and looking back it was all so crazy. But I was lonely and trying to start a new life. I knew what I was getting into with him."

Angelica paused for a moment in thought, as she pondered her young husband. "He can be very naughty."

There was that word again. I smiled.

Angelica wove a complex story of desire, impulsiveness, and transformation. It involved her gigolo/lover/husband, an adopted daughter from her new husband's ex-girlfriend—and settling in (and settling for) the distinctly non-Australian morality of her new island home. Angelica had found herself in the wild, wild East, Kuta cowboy–style.

Not that she could really afford this guy. Angelica made very little money but her lifestyle looked good to this particular class of gigolo. A lot of these men have so very little worldly goods that a woman with a roof over her head and the ability to produce three regular meals a day is going to have the patina of a Microsoft millionaire.

Angelica was well aware of what the exchanges were in the relationship. But the bargain didn't last and after a year of emotional clashes her husband disappeared to another part of the island. Still, she had no second thoughts about her choices. "Yes, he was very naughty," she confided. "I lost a lot of money. But I did get my residency permit and can stay here forever. I have a life here now with my lovely adopted Balinese daughter and I don't regret a thing."

To sum it up, she was his meal ticket and they exchanged green cards. It made economic and erotic sense to her. They had had an adventure and a relationship for only a short while—but she was happy with her life now, and that was all that really mattered to her.

East to Candidasa

Dom and I were off to lower, dryer country—and to the black sand seaside of Candidasa. Reluctantly leaving Ubud, but excited about seeing a new venue, we talked about a woman's romantic choices as our car passed majestic hills lined with rice paddies. Naturally we discussed Angelica and the Kuta cowboy option for women. After two hours we came to the Amankila turnoff. I had been told that the hotel had a spectacular relationship to the water and so I was prepared to be wowed. Standing in the outdoor entryway there was sparkling blue water as far as the eye could see. Tiered lap pools went down, one after another to just above the perfect beach. Mountains tapered down to the sea on both the extreme left and the extreme right view. This had to be one of the most romantic destinations I'd ever seen.

As Dom and I checked into registration, I said, "With this view, I'd be happy in a thatched roof over a gardener's shed."

Dom and I were led by two broadly smiling porters off to the right of the open-air lobby, past a restaurant, to a little walkway that ran parallel to the sea on our left. We went down a long stairway to just above sea-level where a pool that was cantilevered over the beach. It turned out to be just for us! Delighted and a bit stunned, we were escorted to our villas, which were on two different levels, but almost next door to one another.

The villa was my dream writing place with an outdoor room that had a desk facing the sea. Time. Place. Situation. Things had fallen together in just the right way. The blue pool, the aquamarine sea, and the vistas of ocean coves were my muses. I slipped on a bathing suit and swam a few laps in my bit of heaven before I returned to work.

Last Night

That night Dom and I strolled down the stairs to a private cove, just past the palm trees facing the water. We were directed by our hotel guide, another Putu, to a table on the beach. We smelled our dinner cooking on a grill next to a small bonfire.

The surf was our background music while we had fish, salads, and grilled vegetables. We ate slowly, thoughtfully, and savored the moment. When the ginger crème brûlée came, we accepted it as if it were the final offering from a generous deity.

We sat there looking at the sea in silence for long periods of time. After a while Dom asked, "So how do you feel about this trip and your book?"

"The trip has been fabulous, of course. But it struck me that, when it came to love, a reader might think, 'Poor Pepper, all those rejections, all those emotional starts and stops and disappointments and failed expectations. She is on a search for something elusive and she will never find it.' But Dom, you know that's not how I've experienced my life. It could sound too sad and I am among the happiest people on earth. What do I do about this?"

Dom thought for a moment and said, "Why do you think readers might think 'poor Pepper'?"

"Well, because I don't go off with a prince or a Pulitzer Prize–winner or the chef at the end. I think most people don't believe in the journey, they believe in the outcome."

"I think readers will appreciate the process."

"I want to make sure that I'm clear. My belief is that there are many ways to be happy, sensuous, and emotionally fulfilled. But it is the mix of being open to love and, dare I say it, following the philosophy of *Desa Kala Patra*, that holds at least a large part of the answer to staying in one's prime until grave sickness or death intercede. It is the adaptation to new situations; it is the inclusion of new relationships, new crushes and sexual animation that sustains sensuality and vitality for women, especially for women after fifty. It's about living your life to the fullest. I don't want that message to be lost."

"It won't be," Dom said. He looked out at the sea for a moment and then turned his warm gaze on me. "Good memoirs are about authors taking risks, aren't they?"

"Yes, I think they are."

"I propose a toast," I said, holding up my latte, "to risk taking, the sweet moments in life, and to the many ways we can love and be loved."

▦ Advice to Myself (And Others) ▦

Staying Lush

I think about my sexuality the way I think about water. We are water creatures. We respond to it visually, we pay a lot to be near it, and we need to drink it, spray it on us, bath in it. If we don't drink water, we shrivel. Hydrated, we plump up, and our lines of stress, anxiety, loss, and pain fade a bit away. I think being sexual has a parallel impact on us. There is a lushness about a body that is enjoying sex, interacting with someone we are interested in, basking in the aftermath of an orgasm or pleasing sexual encounter.

I am sure there are many ways to stay lush. I know exercise does it for some people. The euphoria of climbing a mountain, running a race, or Rollerblading down the street brings a flush to an athlete's face and an endorphin high. I know women who swear by the sensual mindset of yoga. But personally, for me, there is no moment I feel more womanly or grateful to be alive than when I am in love or in lust. Granted, they are often two widely different feelings but they are powerful and healing separately, as well as the best gift in life when they come together.

I can recognize a woman who is maintaining her lushness. Her eyes smile, her expression is relaxed and happy and whether she is thin, heavy, or in between, she has a positive relationship with her body. I understand that there are times when our body isn't what we'd like it to be, when sex feels unwelcome, and other needs and crises take us far away from romance and sexuality. But there is also a time to come back. *Desa. Kala. Patra.* There surely should be a time to be lush again.

Find Your Own Answer to Body Hunger

One aid to staying lush, or reclaiming your sensuality, is to hire someone to touch your body. Four hands would be nice—but not necessary.

A good massage is a balm for the soul and recognition of our need for touch and physical pleasure. We do get body hunger and if we lose touch, that's a real cause for alarm. Submitting to someone's hands and allowing ourselves to experience a sensual connection can help us find the way back to our core sexuality. The vast majority of all massages are sensual, not sexual, and for most people, that inviolable line separating the two allows us to relax inhibitions, permit pleasure, and let our senses remind us about the truth of our body: that it was designed for pleasure and for sexual expression.

For those who seek more erotic bodywork, that option also exists. As with all massages, you want to make sure you are in the hands of someone you trust, and having a referral from a friend is always the best approach. I have to admit, though, there was a special thrill in letting that inviolable line be crossed during my spa visit. It was another kind of adventure, and an experiment that could have been awful—but wasn't. An erotic massage is not to everyone's taste, values, or comfort—but you know, just typing about *four hands* makes me smile.

Kuta Cowboys and Other Gigolos

The Kuta cowboy experience is not to my taste, but I can understand it. In Bali I met several women who had "dated" Kuta cowboys and even a woman who had married one. They were not pay-for-hire prostitute-client relationships. These relationships were between an attentive, seductive guy with few material resources who used what he did have: flattery, admiration, affection, and sexual attention in exchange for dinners and some gifts. I am aware of the dicey politics of such relationships—the trade of sexuality for economic support is a complex issue and it often brings up both class and race inequities. These deeper issues of inequality are beyond the purpose and scope of this book. All I will say is that given that these barters exist in the world, there are times, places, and situations when they work for women as well for men. I don't have any expertise in this arena, but it seems to me that the women I know who have had these vacation affairs on Bali have enjoyed them without angst, the men profited financially, and everyone involved had a pretty clear vision of what the relationship was—and wasn't.

About Being a "Savior" (and the Saved)

As Angelica spoke of her Kuta cowboy I thought to myself that there is a particular kind of person whose sexual energy is fed by being someone's savior. I know a woman, a prominent attorney who has had four husbands, each one more dependent and inept than the last. Not one earned a living, each one interfered with the things she liked to do best, and all of them were expensive spendthrifts. Yet she loved each, and when the relationships disintegrated from the sheer pressure of inequality between the spouses, she would pick another spouse who fit, more or less, the description of the last incumbent of the position.

I think about all those selfish souls on earth looking for one of these caretaker types. They know that the woman (or man) in question understands their needy nature. They know they can betray their lover and still be taken back as long as their protestations of reform are passionate enough. They often get what they can and run—or they stay as long as they are being kept well. Their dependent behavior makes their lover feel twice as good—and twice as necessary, although their refusal to take care of themselves can finally become more than even the good savior–type can bear. Still, if the sex is good enough, the body attractive enough, the person charming enough, and their background sympathetic enough, these unbalanced liaisons can go on for quite a while. Sometimes the Sugar Momma (or Daddy) is just so lonely, or so in need of emotional and physical attention, that she or he really doesn't care what the price is. Bali seems to have perfected this exchange and older (and some younger) women come to the island looking for a Kuta cowboy, knowing all the risks, and, seemingly, embracing them.

But what about the erotica of the situation? I thought about it in a new way. Many of these Balinese guys were fabulous looking. And when you think about it, could be engaged for a trivial expense. And obviously for Angelica and some other women, it wasn't just for sex. It wasn't the same as hiring a prostitute. Her man delighted her. She loved him. She married him. There was something good going on there that kept him in her affections rather than keeping her infuriated. She was never blind to the economics of the situation, and I think she felt she got her money's worth. When you think of it, what is better: to be alone or with someone who does not emotionally or sexually excite you, or to be with a young, vibrant, attentive man who makes you feel sexually alive? It is clear that in some cases, the relationship of the Kuta cowboy and the interested woman is the right exchange for both of them.

Getting Out of the Country (Prioritizing and Planning Your Getaway)

Sometimes you just have to break with the ordinary to get a crack at the extraordinary. All of life takes place in a stage setting and the ones we travel to or construct have an impact on what happens. I believe that some adventures work best in exotic or unfamiliar places or places of great scenic scope and grandeur and beauty. I travel a lot. Too much, I'm sure. But I know that many people travel very little and it's not so much the cost but rather just getting stuck in routines that become inflexible.

Traveling as a couple, almost any romantic getaway adds a bit of pizzazz and allows for more invention. Granted, the travails of travel may be revelatory about things that aren't so wonderful about your travel companion, but I am of the "all information is worth having" school of dating and mating.

Traveling alone can be stressful, especially as a single woman in a developing country. But for the bold, such adventures can offer many rewards. You don't even have to be that bold. A place like Bali is incredibly exotic but still offers a woman safety, sensuality, and fanciful lodging at prices that are affordable. If you don't want a totally solo trip, traveling with an adventurous girlfriend gives you the comfort of a girls' getaway, with the backup to have a few flings. If you did this while you were at college or in your twenties, you will find it still works in your fifties and beyond.

Finding Your Own *Desa Kala Patra*

Today, we are all also exposed to the world's diverse and enriching religious philosophies, and multiple perspectives on spirituality. I think women in particular have become searchers, looking for new takes on religion and meaning. Books having a feminist perspective on gods and goddesses have become extremely important to many women who find that the older Judeo-Christian texts either ignore women or have only a few rare and exceptional inspirational and celebratory stories about them. Many women have searched elsewhere and found strength from previously unfamiliar world religions and the cultures that birthed and grew them.

Bali's unique blend of Hinduism and Buddhism creates a mood of gratitude and celebration that permeates the island. There is an acceptance and flow in the culture that embraces visitors and encourages one to easily adopt their new "place, time, and situation." One can be truly integrated into the island's rhythms and rituals very quickly. Bali is one of those places that not only allows you to put your everyday thoughts on pause, but also encourages you to create a new way of being for a while. I think that's a very good thing.

ten

THE PINEAPPLE

About Risks and Rewards

Reflecting

It was the last day on Bali. I hadn't slept much at all but I woke up early, before the sunrise. I went down to the pool and sat on the *bale* and stared at the calm sea that had crashed against the mountains most of the night and seemingly had worn itself out.

My reverie drifted from the peaceful scene before me to more anxious thoughts about returning home. I began to make mental lists of things I had to do when familiar steps intruded into my consciousness.

"Good morning," Dom said. "I'm sorry to say that we are being picked up for the airport in two hours."

"So soon?" I had conflicting feelings. It was time to go home. I missed my life there. But I didn't want to leave paradise and the easy, happy feelings I had nurtured here.

"I'm afraid so," Dom said with a wistful look.

"Well, I'm going back to finish the chapter and I'll meet you in the lobby, okay?

"Perfect," said Dom. "Pepper, this has been one mind-blowing trip. I am so glad we made this happen."

"Me, too," I said as I gave Dom a hug.

Risks and Rewards

Back at my desk facing the ocean I thought about how my life has just gotten fuller and bigger and more interesting. My thesis is simple: Live large. Be all of who you are and can be. And if that involves some pain and some loss, so be it.

The men in my life have given me far more than they have taken. I have no doubt about that whatsoever. The adventures I have had have increased my self-knowledge—imperfect though that will always be. They have enriched my life, my work, and my capacity to love.

Consider this: I have studied sex since my early twenties. I have had lovers since I was sixteen. I am considered a sex expert, nationally and perhaps internationally, and yet I still learned things in my fifties with Dennis that I did not know before. I reached new sexual peaks after fifty-five that I would hate to have missed. I understand more about what I want, and who I should be in a relationship, because of Ted. I have had the deepest of friendship and intimacy with Scott. All of this at ages women have been told to be afraid of, ages that have been ignored or lampooned by books and movies, ages that the common wisdom has pronounced as sexless and loveless.

As a result, some women feel unwanted and noncompetitive for male attention. They back away from the pain of dating in part because they no longer believe the rewards will be there for them. They cut short their emotional romantic and sexual life because there is no known path to sexual fulfillment and romantic adventures after fifty, and certainly nothing that tells us about our sixties and seventies and eighties. But I fervently believe that this doesn't have to be true. It is only true if our imagination, energy, and courage fail us. It is only true if we believe we are not worthy. It is only true if we allow the loss of love to condemn us to never seeking love again. It is only true if we have only one model of what sex and romance should be, and we give up all other kinds of relationships if they don't fit that one template.

Being open to love, to being aroused, to being passionate, can be a central ingredient in every woman's personality. It is in mine. Exploring love is really just that: an adventure that could end up discovering a wonderful destination, or just be an adventure in and of itself. I am always left with something. Love is not always entirely lost. Affairs can turn into profound friendships. I am changed, challenged, enlightened, or touched. I grow as a person. Certainly there are some experiences I would have bypassed if I could have. But the failures or mismatches are the price for entry into the adventure. And the price for not taking risks is equally high.

Hope

What happened in Bali is that I discovered that the search for love could get in the way of fully appreciating the blessing of just being alive and the gifts of nature and friendship. And that I have to be careful not to let that happen. Over the last ten days I had been filled with bliss—not just happiness. The beauty and peace of the environments I've been in created space for my soul to feel whole and grateful. I became good company for myself. I liked being alone. For me—one of the most gregarious human beings on the planet—this is quite an accomplishment.

I will go back home from Bali without expectations. I have no idea what is going to happen with Kyle. Maybe we will create a serious relationship. Maybe what we had was the best we could do together. I enjoyed those moments but I am not hurt if the relationship becomes a friendship rather than a love affair. Life will be what it will be and love comes in its own time.

The Pineapple

I have learned not to take rejections too personally. They are just a difference of style, taste, or personality. I try eating pineapple every now and then, but in my heart, I know that I will never really enjoy eating it. It is not pineapple's failing that I don't like it. And somewhere out there is a person who thinks a perfectly ripe pineapple is the best fruit on earth. I try to think of love that way.

The power of our culture's ambivalent feelings about sex is that discomfort with sexuality can make people angry that *anyone* seeks it and enjoys it in untraditional ways. The sexually adventurous woman of any age, but especially those who are older, is extremely threatening to male and female traditionalists. I mention this because I recognize that there are a lot of people who do not like sex at all, who particularly don't like sexually free women, and who would very much like single women past their childbearing and child raising years to be sexually neutered rather than active, vibrant sexual beings. This book is a plea to say don't let that happen. We need to filter out the anti-pleasure, anti-sex messages that condemn our desire to lead full passionate lives. Otherwise external judgments can become internal judgments.

But some women who have nothing but support for their sexual life also refrain. Why? Simply, to protect their hearts. I understand this fear. It's not unfounded. But we lose so much when we work so hard not to get hurt. I want us all to be brave enough to get what we want, and to want more than we think we might deserve.

Inspiration and a Prescription

This book shares the way I have lived my life since my divorce. It may also illustrate the way many women have lived their own prime years— and not felt able to talk about their experiences. It is my hope that my experiences will inspire a rethinking of what is possible in maturity and provide support to the many women who write me, afraid of dating, afraid of being undesirable if they don't have a perfect body or face, afraid of being too old, afraid of getting too hurt, or afraid of looking foolish. Believe me, the fears are worse than the reality and the risks are worth the rewards. It takes some courage but not so much that you can't enjoy the journey. All it takes to begin are baby steps. "Baby steps" means that we don't have to get everything done right away and we can start out slow and simple and increase the risk or the level of difficulty gradually over time. But sometimes change takes a leap of faith, a starting date and the discipline to follow through. Baby Boom–generation women know about change. Many of us have had to reinvent ourselves many times; in fact we have had to reimagine ourselves so we were capable of change.

This book asks women to retrieve something they may have put away or perhaps never had: a sense of sexual adventure—the search for passion—or the continuation of romance. I don't think that's so hard to do for the generation of women who found they had to retool after a divorce or learn a new skill after a long hiatus from work. We are women who know change and have faced challenges and had the gumption, grit, and spirit to go for rewards and freedoms denied to generations of women before us. All we have to do now is to extend the time we get love, sex, romance, and passion so that it is no longer a fanciful thing to imagine. The prime of life has lengthened and it would be wasteful not to live it to the fullest. We who have claimed equality are surely up to this particular challenge—if we choose to do it. And if you agree that we are truly in our prime—then why should we not fully enjoy the sensual years? What's holding us back? Just ourselves—and we can change that. Now.

acknowledgments

No one has had a better support system that I have had. My life, as the *Prime* reader understands, requires juggling many different tasks, deadlines, professional challenges, personal and business trips, and a truly complicated social life. It takes the whole damn village (plus a few suburbs and rural areas) for me to live this satisfying but intricately orchestrated life I have constructed, and I am delighted to have this moment to thank some of the people who have made it possible.

First, to my dear friend and collaborator Dominic Cappello, with me every step of the way on this book, other books, and life's journey. To the "Clitoritti," lifelong friends, some in the formal meeting group I have been in for thirty years, others just as close to me but in other cities or in other friendship networks. Several of these women are also colleagues and coauthors on other projects, and their intellectual contribution to my life, in addition to our friendship, has helped my work and helped satisfy my endless need to know more about love, relationships, and sexuality. Thanks to Jane Adams, Patti Adler, Ginny Anderson, Cynthia Bayley, Elizabeth Bayley, Laurie Beckleman, Donna Britt, Martha Brokenbragh, Sharon Brown, Colleen Cameron, Anne Chauveau, Nadine Chauveau, Lisa Cohen, Stephanie Coontz, Jan Condit, Gail Sage DaMazo, Paula Derrow, Diane Du Mauro, Cynthia Epstein, Vicki Fabre, Linda Farris (deceased but always in my heart), Helen Fisher, Nicky Fitzgerald, Lila Gault, Kathy Gerson, Gloria Gonzales, Debra Haffner, Allison Harris, Michelle Hassan, Julia Heiman, Barbara Heynes, Toby Hiller-Ziegler, Bethany Hornthall, Vivian Horner, Sue Hovis, Judy Howard, Donna James, Tracey Johannson, Laurie McDonald Jonnson, Nancy Klopper, Roseann Lapan, Maria Larinoff, Karen Lawson, Janet

Lever, Margaret Levi, Sandra Lieblum, Kiman Lucas, Lynn Lyndsey, Nancy Mee, Susan Mercerieu, Sharon Nelson, Marie Peters, Kate Pflaumer, Tina Regan, June Reinisch, Simone Reitano, Barbara Risman, Virginia Rutter, Carol Schapira, Angela Schwartz, Andrea Selig, Lisa Skolnik, Celia Schwartz, Amy Solomon, Julie Speidel, Sue Sprecher, Lana Staheli, Debra Szekely, Margo Wellington, Rosanna Bowles Wollner, and Linda Young.

A special thank you to Ruth Krauss, my gynecologist–keeper of stories, repairer of passing problems, on call 24/7 as friend and physician. And to Julie Blacklow, a friend beyond imagination: my confidant, my ranch manager, my eyes, ears, and collaborator at the ranch and in life; the person I turn to in crisis and on road trips. Julie is the friend of one's dreams—a platonic life partner few are lucky enough to experience. Several women literally make my life possible. Julie is the first of them; the second is Linda Cobb, a jack-of-all-trades who backs me up in dozens of ways, too numerous to list here but all critical. Thanks also to Sara Zinn, my student assistant at the University of Washington who with graciousness, good will, and tenacity helps me deal with academic and personal obligations and solve sudden crises. Sara is the latest in a long line of gifted and diligent UW students who have run my office over the years and continually impressed me as the next generation of amazing women (and occasionally a great guy like Josh Misner, Sara's immediate predecessor). So many of them have gone on to be doctors, lawyers, environmental activists, academics, and corporate whizzes. I know Sara will, too. Thanks to my graduate students, teaching assistants, present and past, who make all the difference between a passable class and an excellent one, and my UW colleagues who allow me to be an idiosyncratic scholar and support my professional work as a public sociologist (and now, a *really* public sociologist). I know many of them will be embarrassed as hell to read this book about my life. I apologize ahead of time—but you kinda knew, didn't you?

I also want to thank two people who helped make Bali the experience of a lifetime: the elegant and openhearted Christine Tabora, and my travel collaborator and longtime friend, Peter Greenberg. They were my introduction to Aman Resorts, the most romantic group of places to stay on this planet. Thank you to Monty Brown and the exceptional staffs of Amanusa, Amandari, and Amankila, including Liv Gussing, Tracy Atherton, Chrissie Lincoln, Craig Peter Diss, and Hamish Lindsay. Ruth Zuckerman's kindness at the Conrad Resort on Bali, along with Henry Gunter Manik and Prami Pratiwi at the Four Seasons Resort on Bali at Jimboran Bay, and V. Bihesti Tomo and Mr. Gatot at the Sura Villa is much appreciated. Much thanks for all the help of Lisa Jasie, friend and public relations person extraordinaire. Thanks, too, to the producers and executive producer of *The Today Show* for so many chances to talk to a national audience about my work and my perspective.

And to some of the men in my life who have supported me in a number of ways—not all in the way you are thinking. I am so lucky to have many platonic (and not so platonic) men in my life, men who have helped me with my professional life, and men who been confidants and advisors—this is a mixed list! Thanks to JJ McKay, Rick Schenkman, Peter Adler, Joe Atkins, Chris Bayley, Karl Beckly, Philip Blumstein (sadly missed), François Chauveau, Dan Chirot, Mark Clark, Ray DaMazo, David Deetz, John Duff, Charlie Ebel, Roger Ebert, Mick Fleming, Ralph Fascitelli, John Gagnon, Barry Glassner, Paul Goldberger, Jonathon Goodson, John Gottman, George Hamilton, Gil Herdt, Bob Hernreich, Charlie Hirshman, King Holmes, Bruce Jackson, Gerry Jordan, Bob Kolodrey, Dave Kerley, Jim Hornthall, Fred Kaesburg, John Kucher, Michael Levin, Barry Lieberman, Karl Lutz, Jim Miller, Joe Miller, Chip Ragen, Mimmo Rosati, Gary Schwartz, Herb Schwartz, Michael Schwartz, Aaron Schwartz, Art Skolnik, Howard Skolnik, Graham Spanier, John Strait, Jeff Swanson, Don Tuzin, Tom Vaughn, and others not to be named.

Of course, I want to thank the amazing people at perfectmatch.com who have been my introduction to online dating, and have provided a second professional home for me after my University of Washington colleagues. In particular, my admiration and gratitude to founders Duane and Cindy Dahl, solid supporters and providers of new and exciting opportunities year after year. Who knew I'd be doing singles events at ballparks, whirlpool showrooms, and Hollywood openings?

Finally, a warm note of thanks for my agent Fred Morris and to the people at HarperCollins: uber-boss Joe Tessitore, and editor/publisher Mary Ellen O'Neill. Thank you both for your belief in me and in this book. A truly grateful thank you to the talented Victor Mingovits of Mucca Design who designed the great cover of this book.

I know there are people I have forgotten to mention or for various reasons could not mention. I apologize in advance and promise to take you out to dinner, do a mea culpa over a great bottle of wine, and make it up to you in suitable ways.